THE
INESCAPABLE
LOVE
OF
GOD

Thomas Talbott
Willamette University
Salem, Oregon 97301

For my parents

ISBN: 1-58112-831-2

Published by
Universal Publishers/uPUBLISH.com
1999, revised printing 9/2002
USA

www.upublish.com/books/talbott.htm

"Heaven will solve our problems, but not, I think, by showing us subtle reconciliations between all our apparently contradictory notions. The notions will all be knocked from under our feet. We shall see that there never was any problem.

"And more than once, that impression which I can't describe except by saying it's like the sound of a chuckle in the darkness. The sense that some shattering and disarming simplicity is the real answer."

C. S. Lewis, *A Grief Observed*

Preface

This set of reflections is neither a textbook nor a piece of scholarly research. It neither summarizes a specific field of study for students nor advances scholarship in some area of research. It is instead (what I would call) a *real* book, by which I mean that in it I have tried to reach the most demanding audience of all: that of educated non-specialists. The book is in part an intellectual auto-biography, in part the elaboration of an argument, and in part an attempt at persuasive writing. In these pages, I have sought to share with others, particularly those who call themselves "Christians," some of my own deepest convictions about the nature of God and the world. I have sought to work out, with some degree of consistency, the idea that the universe really is an expression of love, as some of the mystics from many traditions have always insisted. My principal aim has been to elaborate an overall picture and to illustrate a way of putting things together; hence, I have been less concerned than I might have been in other contexts with the details of specific arguments. In a few cases, indeed, I have taken more detailed arguments, which I have published elsewhere, and have rewritten them in an effort to prevent the details from obscuring the larger picture.

I do not expect, of course, that everyone who reads this book will find my convictions, or my arguments for them, compelling. I ask of my readers, however, only what I would also ask of my students: that you consider my arguments carefully, and then work out your own convictions with as much consistency as possible.

Legion are the teachers, authors, and friends who have influenced my intellectual development. At every stage of my education, it seems, I encountered some very special teachers: Mr. Larry Strickland and Mr. Arthur C. Wade in high school, Dr. David Newhall in college, and Professor Noel Fleming in graduate school, to name just a few. In the area of the philosophy of religion, I am especially grateful for what I have learned from Alvin Plantinga and William Rowe. But I am perhaps most indebted of all to those who over the years have paid me the compliment of challenging, either in print or in private correspondence, my views on the nature of human destiny: Jerry Walls, Jonathon Kvanvig, William Craig, Larry Lacy, William Hasker, Victor Reppert, John Piper, and Neal Punt. Though I may not always have appeared to appreciate such criticism as I have received, I have benefitted greatly from all of it. And finally, I express my gratitude to my sister, Cathy Thienes, whose eagle eye caught scores of copy errors, and to those who commented on the manuscript at one stage or another: John Thienes, Michael Morbey, Steve Talbott, and the most demanding critic of all, my mother.

Unless otherwise noted, all quotations from the Bible in this work are from the New Revised Standard Version copyrighted in 1989 by the National Council of Churches of Christ in the United States of America. I have also incorporated into the work, some-times in rewritten form, parts of the following articles, which were published previously:

"The Love of God and the Heresy of Exclusivism," *Christian Scholar's Review* XXVII:1, (Fall, 1997)

"Three Pictures of God in Western Theology," *Faith and Philosophy* (January, 1995).

"Punishment, Forgiveness, and Divine Justice," *Religious Studies* (September, 1993).

"Craig on the Possibility of Eternal Damnation," *Religious Studies* 26 (1992).

"Destruction and Redemption: A Reply to Larry Lacy," *Christian Scholar's Review* XXII, (September, 1992).

"The New Testament and Universal Reconciliation," *Christian Scholar's Review* XXI, (June, 1992).

"The Doctrine of Everlasting Punishment," *Faith and Philosophy* (January, 1990).

"C. S. Lewis and the Problem of Evil," *Christian Scholar's Review* XVII, (September, 1987).

"Vessels of Wrath and the Unpardonable Sin," *The Reformed Journal*, (September, 1983).

TABLE OF CONTENTS

PREFACE

PART I: SOME AUTOBIOGRAPHICAL REFLECTIONS

PART II: UNIVERSAL RECONCILIATION AND THE NEW TESTAMENT

PART I:
SOME AUTOBIOGRAPHICAL REFLECTIONS

I. AN ENCOUNTER WITH WESTERN THEOLOGY

> "To say that God's goodness may be different in kind from man's goodness, what is it but saying, with a slight change of phraseology, that God may possibly not be good?"
>
> John Stuart Mill

My purpose in this essay is to impart, or begin to impart, a vision of God. "Oh taste and see," says the Psalmist, "that the Lord is good; happy are those who take refuge in him" (Psalm 34:8). That is the vision I have in mind. Against the many religious doctrines that appeal to and cultivate our fear, I shall urge upon my reader this simple proposition: Contrary to what we might fear, the Creator and Father of our souls—the Lord of hosts and King of kings—is good.

Towards the end of communicating that vision, however, I shall not begin where some might think I should begin: with some kind of an argument for the existence of some kind of a God. For though I have reflected upon such arguments for the better part of my life, and though I now find some of them far more compelling than I once did, the vision I have in mind is larger than any specific argument; it includes more than any series of arguments could establish beyond question. Indeed, the full vision includes more than I could possibly write down within the confines of a single book. It includes an interpretation of the world as a whole—that is, a way of putting things together, of understanding our religious traditions, and of making sense of our experience. Above all, it includes a particular conception of a worthy or a fitting object of worship. I have therefore chosen, as a kind of thesis for the essay, a statement that some may regard as especially vague because, as they see it, the word "good" is itself especially vague. I could no doubt do a lot, even at the outset, to sharpen that thesis—by pointing, for example, to the New Testament idea that God is good, because God is love and love is good; love is the one quality that makes any life, whether human or divine, worth living forever. But I can think of no better place to begin than with something a little vague—a mere hint of what I hope eventually to communicate with greater precision.

Neither can I think of any better place to begin than right in the middle of my own religious and philosophical concerns, however provincial some may find them to be. For like many others, I have felt a need to come to terms with my own heritage, particularly my religious heritage; and though some of that heritage now seems to me limited and defective, I have nonetheless tried to penetrate to the very best within it. I have an abiding faith, moreover, that beneath the particular forms of the religion I acquired in my youth—and, for that matter, beneath the particular forms of many religions and many mythologies—there lies something of enduring and even permanent value.[1] But as we embark upon a quest for that which has enduring value—a quest for religious truth or spiritual enlightenment, if you will—we must all proceed today from where we are today, and where we are today is, at least in part, a function of where we have been in the past. Accordingly, I shall begin not with an argument, but with a story, a bit of autobiography: an account of how my own religious views evolved during the early years of my formal education when I, like many of my classmates, began for

---

[1] I do not mean to imply, however, that all religions are equal. I see no reason to begin with the assumption that my religion is better than, or embodies more of the truth than, someone else's religion does, or that someone else's embodies more of the truth than mine does. Nor do I have any inclination to say of two contradictory doctrines, whether they be expressed within a single religion or between different religions, that they are in some mysterious way both true. We know the status of contradictions; they are quite false. And we also know the status of apparent contradictions; they are either meaningless or false. But once you penetrate beneath the surface of any one of the great religions, you will find, I believe, something of enduring value and a great deal that is true.

the first time to raise serious questions about serious matters and to search for satisfying answers to them.

God and Evil

After a relatively sheltered childhood, I attended a conservative Christian high school of a kind that may no longer exist. I say "may no longer exist" because, at my high school, a good Christian was identified as someone who does not smoke, drink, dance (roller skating was "iffy"), play cards, or attend Hollywood movies. But I thoroughly enjoyed high school. I made a lot of friends, and we argued about everything—about whether, for example, the Rapture (i.e., God's sudden removal of Christians from the earth) would occur at the beginning or in the middle of the Great Tribulation, about whether someone who accepts the theory of evolution could still be saved, about whether it really was a sin to attend Hollywood movies (I ran with a group of rebels who let it be known that we sometimes did go to the movies). It was here also that I first learned to challenge authority. One of our Bible teachers had taught that in the last days the stars will quite literally fall upon the earth; and when a friend of mine pointed out that a single star would consume the earth long before striking it, he was severely reprimanded. But my friends and I, being something of a rebellious lot, would have none of that. It was also here that I encountered the writings of C. S. Lewis, who first awakened me to the larger world of ideas and inspired me to take a philosophy course during my first year in college. But nothing I experienced in high school had quite prepared me for what awaited me when, after graduation, I enrolled at Portland State University.

As fate (or providence) would have it, my first philosophy course was one in which we examined traditional arguments for and against the existence of God. The instructor, I quickly decided, was simply the most brilliant person I had ever known, an honest man who seemed prepared to follow any argument wherever it led, though more often than not an argument seemed to lead in the wrong direction. Our class critique of the arguments for the existence of God was not a problem for me; in fact, I found it almost exhilarating (even liberating) to join with others in a vigorous critique of bad arguments, or what I then regarded as bad arguments, for the existence of God. But one of the anti-theistic arguments was different, because it attacked my religious beliefs in a powerful way and at the most fundamental level possible. That was the so-called argument from evil, which begins with a worry that almost every religious person thinks about at one time or another, namely this: How can we square the idea of a loving God with the mess that the world seems to be in or with the profound misery and suffering found almost everywhere in the world? How can we possibly affirm the love of God in the face of, for example, heart wrenching pictures of starving children in India or Somalia or Rhodesia, or in the face of suffering children in a place like war-torn Bosnia? Many good and sensitive souls, such as my first philosophy professor, have reflected upon such questions and have concluded, perhaps even reluctantly, that they pose an insoluble problem for traditional theism; as these persons see it, the horrendous quantity of suffering in the world is inconsistent with, or at least is strong evidence against, the existence of God, as traditionally conceived. For if God were truly omnipotent, he would have the power, it seems, to prevent every instance of human suffering; and if he were perfectly loving, he would want to exercise that power. So if he were both omnipotent and perfectly loving, there would be no suffering at all in the world. But there clearly is suffering. Therefore, a God who is both omnipotent and perfectly loving does not exist.

People sometimes speak of a defining moment in their lives, a momentous occasion when they undergo some experience, or perhaps make a decision of some kind, that has a profound effect upon the rest of their lives. Well, I am here talking about a defining moment in my own life. On that day when the teacher I admired more than any other presented the argument from evil as a decisive objection to traditional theism, the entire course of my life was changed. For I interpreted this quite rightly as a fundamental assault upon the very convictions that gave meaning to my life; in effect, I was being asked to believe that the idea of a loving God—an idea I had taken for granted throughout my childhood—is overly sentimental, too good to be true, just one more example of wishful thinking to be discarded as we mature into adults. During my undergraduate days, I encountered a good many other anti-theistic arguments; for the most part, these were just silly, mere prejudices that anyone who has had a good course in critical thinking should be able to expose. But there is nothing silly about the argument from evil, and it galled me that my instructor, who was always three steps ahead of me, was able to counter my own moves so easily. It galled me even more that he seemed to have such a low opinion of C. S. Lewis, whose book, *The Problem of Pain*, I had read with great excitement during my high school days, though I doubt that I had understood very much of it. I never for a moment doubted that my instructor's arguments were defective in a variety of ways, but neither did I doubt that I would have to find better answers than I had at the time, answers that would at least have the virtue of satisfying me.

A Demonic Picture of God

By cast of mind I tend to be rather conservative. So when I first encountered the argument from evil as an undergraduate, my instinct was to turn to the great theologians of the past upon whose shoulders I was quite prepared to stand. Little did I anticipate, however, the shock and the crisis of faith in store for me when I did just that. For though it came as a complete surprise to me, I found the writings of Christian theologians to be far more disturbing— and a far greater threat to my faith, as I understood it—than those of any atheistic thinker whom I had encountered. The problem was that I kept bumping up against this awkward fact: I seemed unable to find a single mainline Christian theologian who truly believed, any more than my atheistic professor did, in a *loving* God. They all claimed to believe in a *just* and a *holy* God, but this God seemed not to care enough about created persons even to *will* or to *desire* the good for all of them. And anything less than a perfectly loving God, I was already persuaded, would be far worse than no God at all. So in the end, the shock of discovering what the mainline theologians actually taught—and asked me to believe—precipitated a very real crisis of faith.

Part of the problem may have been the "authorities" to whom I then turned and the filter through which I then viewed the tradition. One of the first things I read, even before turning to the great theologians of the past, was a book that a friend of mine had recommended: Gordon Clark's *Religion, Reason, and Revelation*. Clark is what some might call a "hyper-Calvinist" or "double predestinarian"; he believed that even before the foundation of the world God had already foreordained that some would be saved and others lost forever. It is all predetermined. According to Clark, God causes us to sin and then punishes us for it; in the case of the reprobate, those whom he chooses to reject, God will punish them throughout eternity for sins that he himself caused them to commit. And his punishment, furthermore, will be just, since whatever God does is just solely and only because he does it. Here are a couple of examples of what I read:

> God is the sole ultimate cause of everything. . . . The men and angels predestined to eternal life and those foreordained to everlasting death are particularly and unchangeably *designed* [my emphasis]; and their number is so certain and definite that it cannot be either increased or diminished. Election and reprobation are equally ultimate. God determined that Christ should die; he determined as well that Judas should betray him. There was never the remotest possibility that something different could have happened.[2]

> God is neither responsible nor sinful, even though he is the only ultimate cause of everything. He is not sinful because in the first place whatever God does is just and right. It is just and right simply in virtue of the fact that he does it. Justice or righteousness is not a standard external to God to which God is obligated to submit. Righteousness is

---

[2]Gordon Clark, *Religion, Reason, and Revelation* (Philadelphia: Presbyterian and Reformed Publishing Co., 1961), p. 238. The potential here for modal confusion will be obvious to any professional philosopher, and in fact Clark provides several textbook examples of fallacious modal reasoning. But when I first read this book as an undergraduate, I had, of course, never even heard of modal logic.

what God does. Since God caused Judas to betray Christ, this causal act is righteous and not sinful. By definition God cannot sin. At this point it must be particularly pointed out that God's causing a man to sin is not sin. There is no law, superior to God, which forbids him to decree sinful acts.[3]

I was utterly dumfounded when I read such passages as these and searched in vain for at least an echo of the love of God as I had learned of it at my mother's knee. If this was an example of sophisticated Christian thinking, I wanted nothing to do with it. I assumed initially that Clark's was simply an aberrant way of thinking, an idiosyncratic view at odds with the tradition. But then, the more closely I looked at the tradition, the more I seemed to find the worst of Clark almost everywhere. Wherever I turned—whether it be to such Protestant Reformers as Martin Luther and John Calvin or to such philosophical theologians as St. Augustine, Jonathan Edwards, and even St. Thomas Aquinas—I seemed to find the same narrow predestinarian theology, the same exclusivism, the same attempt to restrict God's mercy to a chosen few. Augustine, whose name I had been taught to revere long before I became acquainted with his thought, extends his conception of God's limited mercy even to children, arguing that God will reject, and eternally separate himself from, even some who die in infancy; after all, he says, they are all drawn from a corrupt mass anyway.[4] The more I read, the more bewildered I became and the more convinced I became that

---

[3]*Ibid.*, pp. 239-240. One can agree with Clark that "righteousness is not a standard external to God to which God is obligated to submit." But there are two very different ways in which this might be true. According to Clark, God could will anything whatsoever, even that we torture babies for our own pleasure, and thereby make it righteous; hence, according to Clark, no loving nature stands behind (and explains) what God wills. But if, alternatively, God's nature (or essence) is perfect love and his righteousness expresses his own nature, then it is logically impossible for him to will in an unloving way. This does not mean that God's will is bound to an external standard; it means only that his will is bound to his own nature.

[4]Augustine, *Enchiridion*, XXIV and XXV.

Clark's view was no aberration at all; that he had simply made explicit, and with greater consistency, a demonic picture of God that pervades Western theology. And the deeper I delved into the mainline theologians in search of a theology of love, the more I seemed to find, lurking beneath the surface, a theology of arbitrary power.

It was, then, the writings of Christian thinkers and Christian theologians, not the argument from evil *per se*, that precipitated my own crisis of faith. I turned to the great theologians of the past in the confidence that they would help me to formulate a convincing theodicy—that is, a convincing reply to the argument from evil— but what I found in them disturbed me far more than did the arguments of my atheistic professor (with whom I had a very cordial relationship). I knew instinctively that I could never worship a God who is less kind, less merciful, less *loving* than my own parents, but that is just what I seemed to encounter in the mainstream of Western theology: a God who, though gracious (after a fashion) to some (the elect), refuses to will the good for others (the non-elect).[5] And I could not imagine my parents *refusing* to will the good for anyone.

Even more disturbing to me at the time was the curious fact that those who seemed to have the greatest respect for, and the most intimate knowledge of, the Bible—those who actually knew Greek for example!—were precisely those whose theology I found most appalling. I'll probably never forget the time, after a long and heated argument with the pastor of a Calvinistic church, that I read carefully Romans 9 for the first time. I was not only shocked; I fell into a deep depression as well. This was as bad as Gordon Clark! Of course it never occurred to me at the time that I was simply reading Clark into the text, or that my naive view of revelation needed considerable modification. What did occur to me was that the message of the text seemed clear: According to Paul, God loved Jacob but hated Esau; and not only that, God has divided the entire

---

[5]But as we shall see in Part III, God's refusal to extend his love to a single person would undermine his love for all others; hence, it is necessarily true that God does not restrict his love to a limited elect.

human race into vessels of mercy, or objects of his love, and vessels of wrath, or objects of his hatred. Concerning such teaching, moreover, the Apostle seemed to ask exactly the right questions (first about justice and then about finding fault), but his answers seemed utterly absurd in the first case and not a real answer at all in the second. In the end, I decided I could no longer be a Christian in any orthodox sense. If Paul really taught, as Augustine and many of the Protestant Reformers insist he did, that God restricts his mercy to a chosen few, then Paul was, if not an outright fraud, just another confused and small-minded religious zealot. I believed that then, and I continue to believe it today.

As I have already suggested, my parents were at least partly responsible for some of my early struggles and for my stubborn refusal to accept, regardless of what the Bible might appear to teach, a tyrannical picture of God. In church I had been taught that the Bible is the final authority on everything (including the theory of evolution!), but in my home I was *experiencing* the true meaning of love. I was the second born in a large family of six children, and in our family it was unthinkable that our parents might favor one of us over another. There were no favorites, period; we were all equal objects of our parents' love and equally precious to them. So it is perhaps not surprising that I should have found myself unable to worship a God who, unlike my parents, was quite prepared to play favorites. In fact, what I have here called "a crisis of faith" and at the time regarded as such was not a crisis of *faith* at all. For it was precisely an unshakable faith in the love of God—a faith that my mother in particular had instilled within me—that made my doubts about Christianity and the Bible possible; and had I known more about the Bible at the time, or had I possessed a less naive view of revelation, I might have been spared these doubts as well. Indeed, I now occasionally look back at these early struggles with something akin to amusement. At the time it all seemed so serious and so threatening, but the truth is I had nothing to worry about. For as I shall try to demonstrate in subsequent chapters, the picture of God I found so morally repugnant is also riddled with logical impossibilities; the exegesis upon which it rests is remarkably weak, far weaker than I at one time feared; and the great theological tradition that embraced it must be weighed against another that, although not so successful when judged by the standards of this world, steadfastly affirms the unlimited and inescapable love of God.

2. RELIGION WITHOUT FEAR

"There is no fear in love, but perfect love casts out fear."

I John 4:18

After graduating from college, I spent three years at Fuller Theological Seminary, during which time I became increasingly weary of the standard theological fare. I would have no one take this to imply, however, a criticism of Fuller Seminary itself. I am truly grateful not only for what I learned there, but also for this remarkable fact: Though I had many profound disagreements with some of my professors, I always felt absolutely free during my seminary days to be myself and to follow my own muse. And I can think of no greater compliment to pay any institution of higher learning. Still, I found it disconcerting that so many of my professors viewed the world through an Augustinian lens and so few of them seemed even to appreciate the difficulties with which I was then struggling.

Here is an example of what I mean. One of my professors was far more enlightened than I in his consistent opposition to racial and gender discrimination, and yet this man was quite prepared to worship a God who, on the basis of little more than divine whim, divides the world into the elect and the non-elect; he was quite prepared, in other words, to worship the worst discriminator of all. His response to the obvious moral objections was simply to dismiss them as instances of fallible human reasoning. Again, this professor's understanding of revelation was far more flexible and sophisticated than my own; he was quite capable, for example, of either setting aside or reinterpreting Bible texts that seem to place women in a subordinate position to men. But he rejected as unbiblical any suggestion that *all* men and women are equal objects of God's redemptive love. At first I found such a combination of views utterly mystifying; but over time, I simply lost interest in them and became bored. If God himself discriminates against specific individuals (the non-elect) in the more important matter of *salvation*, why get excited about the lesser forms of discrimination, or even the racial bigotry, to which human beings are prone?

The Idea of Universal Reconciliation

It was also during my seminary days, however, that I first encountered a vision of God that seemed to resonate with my own instincts and convictions. For it was at this time, thanks to my brother, Stephen, that I first encountered the Scottish writer, George MacDonald (1824-1905). I could not overemphasize the importance of that encounter: It was as if I had finally discovered a voice of sanity in what then seemed to me an asylum of theological babble. For though MacDonald rarely addressed theological questions in the abstract way I had come to expect, and though his understanding of Christian piety seemed almost quaint at times, he also articulated with great power and compassion, and with greater clarity than most, a stunning vision of Omnipotent Love. Here, at last, was a religious writer who seemed to appeal not to fear or guilt or mean-spiritedness, but to the very best within me. Here was someone who never—and I mean *never*—asked me to believe something that seemed unreasonable; who insisted, to the contrary, that I not accept anything—not even anything he might say—that seemed to me, for whatever reason, unworthy of human belief. Whereas the mainline theologians I had read—Augustine, Aquinas, Calvin, Jonathan Edwards, and the like—all asked me to believe things about God that violated my own sense of justice, Mac-Donald's sermons were sprinkled with such exhortations as these:

> Let no one persuade you that there is in Him a little dark-
> ness, because of something He has said which His creature
> interprets into darkness. . . . Neither let your cowardly con-
> science receive any word as light because another calls it
> light, while it looks to you dark. Say either the thing is not
> what it seems, or God never said or did it. But, of all evils,
> to misinterpret what God does, and then say the thing as

interpreted must be right because God does it, is of the devil.[1]

Here, it seemed to me, was the perfect antidote to those, such as Gordon Clark, who attribute heinous acts to God and then insist that such acts are just solely and only because God does them. MacDonald's sermons were also filled with such gems as these:

> . . . How terribly, then, have the theologians misrepresented God! Nearly all of them represent Him as a great King on a grand throne, thinking how grand He is, and making it the business of His and the end of His universe to keep up His glory, wielding the bolts of Jupiter against them that take His name in vain. They would not allow this, but follow out what they say, and it comes much to this.

> . . . Brothers, have you found our king? There He is kissing little children and saying they are like God. . . . The simplest peasant who loves his children and his sheep were—no, not a truer, for the other is false, but—a true type of our God beside that monstrosity of a monarch.[2]

> . . . the notion that a creature born imperfect, nay, born with impulses to evil not of his own generating, and which he could not help having, a creature to whom the true face of God was never presented, and by whom it never could have been seen, should be thus condemned [to everlasting torment] is as loathsome a lie against God as could find place in a heart too undeveloped to understand what justice is, and too low to look up into the face of Jesus. It never in truth found place in any heart, though in many a pettifogging brain.[3]

---

[1] George MacDonald, "Light," reprinted in condensed form in Rolland Hein, "The Creation in Christ" (Wheaton: Harold Shaw Publishers, 1976), p. 42.

[2] George MacDonald, "The Child in the Midst," reprinted in Rolland Hein (ed.), *op. cit.*, p. 34.

[3] George MacDonald, "Justice," reprinted in Rolland Hein (ed), *op. cit.*, p. 71-72.

I cite these passages not because they represent MacDonald at his best—which they do not—but because they illustrate the side of him that first caught my attention. During a summer vacation, my brother, who was an undergraduate at Wheaton College at the time, showed me a photocopied reproduction of MacDonald's *Unspoken Sermons* in an unedited form; and at that time I read two of the sermons. One was entitled "Justice" and included, among other things, MacDonald's reasons for rejecting a retributivist theory of punishment; the other was entitled "The Consuming Fire" and included some of the grounds for MacDonald's hope that God will eventually reconcile all created persons to himself. I cannot say that either sermon bowled me over from the start. For one thing, I was a proponent of the retributivist theory myself at the time; and though I had encountered the idea of universal reconciliation be-fore—in the theologian Karl Barth, for example—my knee jerk re-action had been that such an idea would be difficult to square not only with the Bible, but with the reality of human freedom as well. But two things about these sermons caused me to return to them again and again and also to devour MacDonald's other sermons as they were republished and made available: First, the *spirit* of what MacDonald had to say seemed utterly different from, and far more uplifting than, anything I had encountered in the mainline theolo-gians; and second, MacDonald's way of putting things together— the way he interpreted specific passages in the Bible, for example— seemed utterly fresh and imaginative. It was almost as if the paradigm from which he operated was entirely different from the one I had come to expect; from his perspective, everything seemed to have a different slant. Part of the difference was that Mac-Donald somehow managed to see *everything*, even divine judgment and wrath, as an expression of God's perfecting love, a love that is both all-pervasive and, in the end, inescapable. But in addition to that—and this is more subtle and therefore more difficult to ex-press—MacDonald seemed to have the kind of far-reaching vision that enabled him somehow to find deeper meanings in a biblical text. By this I do not mean that he would distort a text for his own purpose or wrench it from its own context. Quite the contrary; when compared to some of the mainline theologians, he was, I still believe, amazingly accurate in matters of detail. But the spirit or the tender heart he brought to a text—the hope and the trans-forming love—somehow enabled him to elevate a text without in any way distorting it.

Be all of that as it may, MacDonald's vision of divine love—the idea that it is both all-pervasive and inescapable—struck me, the more I thought about it over the years, as so glorious and so powerfully transforming that I began to wonder why the institutional church had so often backed away from it. Certainly individual Christian thinkers, particularly those of a more mystical bent, have embraced this idea and have done so enthusiastically in every age. But the church as a whole never did, and I found myself wondering why.

Given the profound understanding of divine love within the early church—that is, before the time of Augustine—and the powerful support in Alexandria for the idea of universal reconciliation, one might almost have expected orthodox theology to reject the idea of eternal damnation altogether. According to St. Clement of Alexandria (c 150-c 215), for example, God's omnipotent love is always and everywhere active, in the next life no less than in this one, in hell no less than in heaven;[4] and according to Origen (c 185-c 254), probably the greatest theologian before Augustine, God will in the end reconcile even Satan, the Prince of Darkness, to himself. Nor was Origen the only early Christian thinker to make such a remarkable claim. For though he later repudiated it, St. Jerome (c 342-420) had this to say in his *Commentary on Ephesians*: "The Apostate Angel will return to his first estate and man will return to Paradise from which he was banished."[5] What is important about such a view is not, in my judgment, the specific claim about Satan, which depends upon a particular understanding of what Satan is supposed to be; it is rather the vision that lies behind the specific claim, a vision of the extent and the power of God's redemptive love, a vision of a future age (or perhaps an end beyond the ages) in

---

[4]See C. A. Patrides, "The Salvation of Satan," *Journal of the History of Ideas*, 28 (October-December, 1967), p. 467.

[5]Jerome, *Commentary on Ephesians* (16).

which the very same "all things" created in Christ will also be reconciled in him (see Colossians 1:15-20). One of the most powerful
early voices in support of such a view was St. Gregory of Nyssa (c
330-c 395), who taught that, like the refiner's furnace, the fires of
hell will eventually purge sinners of all that is false within them, so
that "after long ages, they may be restored to God in their purity."[6]
Others expressing similar sentiments included Didymus of Alexandria (c 313-398), the blind and gentle teacher of "Gregory of
Nazianzus, Jerome, and Rufinus,"[7] and Theodore, the bishop of
Mopsuestia, who died in 428.

All of these early universalists were, as C. A. Patrides has
observed, "men of exceptional kindness and all-embracing love";[8]
indeed, Augustine refers to them somewhat condescendingly as
"certain tender hearts" even as he censures their views.[9] In the
Enchiridion, he diagnoses their "error" this way:

> It is quite in vain, then, that some—*indeed very many* (my
> emphasis)—yield to merely human feelings and deplore
> the notion of the eternal punishment of the damned and
> their interminable and perpetual misery. They do not
> believe that such things will be. Not that they would go
> counter to divine Scripture—but, yielding to their own
> human feelings, they soften what seems harsh and give a
> milder emphasis to statements they believe are meant more
> to terrify than to express the literal truth.[10]

As this passage illustrates, the idea of universal reconciliation
was very much a live option within the early church. For it was not
merely some, but "very many," who opposed the idea of eternal
punishment, and these "very many" were not pagans, but Christians, those with no desire to "go counter to divine Scripture . . .."

---

[6]Gregory of Nyssa, *Address on Religious Instruction*, 35.

[7]Patrides, *op. cit.*, pp. 469-470.

[8]*Ibid.*, p. 469.

[9]*City of God*, Bk. XXI, Ch. XVII.

[10]*Enchiridion*, Ch. XXIX.

Augustine even agreed with them on the all-important point that, in the end, "the will of the Omnipotent is always undefeated."[11] But Augustine also denied that God so much as wills, or desires, the salvation of all,[12] and those who think otherwise are guilty, he suggested, of "yielding to their own human feelings." Like many of his successors, then, Augustine too agreed with my atheistic philosophy professor whom I mentioned in the previous chapter; for according to Augustine, no less than this professor, the idea of an *all-loving* God, one whose mercy extends to all, is overly sentimental, too good to be true, just one more example of wishful thinking to be discarded as we mature into adults. Such an idea, Augustine argued, is incompatible not only with the observable facts, but with the biblical theme of divine judgment and divine wrath as well. And it was, of course, Augustine's view that finally prevailed in the West.

Heresy and Imperial Politics

Now as I reflected on these matters, I became more and more interested in the way in which the early church had managed to resolve some of its theological controversies. Why, for example, had Origen been condemned?   But it was not until several years later, after completing my graduate work in philosophy and adjusting to a rather heavy teaching load, that I found the leisure to pursue the matter further. When I began to dabble again in church history, however, I found that my whole attitude towards organized religion had changed; as a result, I began reading with a much more cynical eye than I ever had before.

During my undergraduate days, I had supposed, rather naively, that those with the strongest arguments—exegetical, historical, and theological—typically had prevailed in the early church councils. But as almost any historian could have told me, the truth is very different from that: Those who prevailed were those with the civil authorities on their side and the power of the sword at their right hand. The success of the early Christians in making converts had,

---

[11]*Ibid.*, Ch. XXVI.

[12]*Ibid.*, Ch. XXVII. See also Chapter 9 below.

it seems, an inevitable concomitant: Those who valued political power and influence and were prepared to settle disputes with a sword inevitably gravitated to the new faith as soon as it acquired the support of the masses and became otherwise respectable. It seems probable, for instance, that Constantine converted to Christianity (in the early 4th century) for the very purpose of shoring up the support of Christians and of bringing stability to the crumbling empire he had inherited;[13] in any event, as Leonard Verduin points out:

> When Constantine came into the Church he did not check his imperial equipment at the door. No indeed, he came in with all the accouterments that pertain in the secular regime. He was not just a Roman who had learned to bow to the Christ; he had been *pontifex maximus* hitherto, the High Priest of the Roman State Religion, and he entered the Church with the understanding that he would be *pontifex maximus* there too. And just as his sword had flashed in defense of the old religion so would it now flash in defense of the new.[14]

It was Constantine, of course, who called the First General Council of the church at Nicea in 325; it was Constantine who first tried to achieve theological unity in the church as a whole by persecuting other Christians; and it was Constantine who set the precedent for imperial interference in theological discussions. During the next few centuries, as an orthodox theology came to be crystallized, it was as much a product of imperial politics as it was of theological debate or biblical exegesis. That is, to be sure, no more reason to reject, than it is to accept, a given creedal statement, but it is, I believe, a ground for caution and for not identifying the Christian faith too quickly with what we *now* call orthodox Christian doctrine.

---

[13]Leonard Verduin, *The Reformers and Their Stepchildren* (Grand Rapids: Eerdmans Publishing Co., 1964), p. 31.

[14]*Ibid.*, p. 42.

The way in which the church came to condemn the doctrine of universal reconciliation is a case in point. Origen, the name most closely associated with that doctrine, was first condemned by a local council in Alexandria in about 400. But Origen was condemned for a variety of reasons—including, for example, his belief in the pre-existence of the soul—and the idea of universal reconciliation, which he shared with several others who were made saints, seems not to have been condemned until the late date of 543. At this time, the despotic emperor, Justinian I, who fancied himself a theologian and defender of orthodoxy as well as a military conqueror, condemned Origen in ten anathemata, one of which read: "If anyone says or thinks that the punishment of demons and impious men is only temporary and will have an end, and that a restoration will take place, let him be anathema."[15] This was not, however, the emperor's first attempt at thought control. In 529, only two years after he had become emperor, he closed the school of philosophy in Athens, a school that had remained open for 900 years; he then made heathen worship a crime punishable by death.[16] But as John W. Barker points out: "Among all the targets of Justinian's persecutions, it was those classified as heretics who suffered the most."[17] And in the end, it was Justinian who determined who the heretics were. Writes Joseph Cullen Ayer:

> According to Justinian's scheme of Church government, the Emperor was the head of the Church in the sense that he had the right and duty of regulating by his laws the

---

[15]Justinian, "Anathematisms Against Origen," in Joseph Cullen Ayer, *A Source Book for Ancient Church History: From the Apostolic Age to the Close of the Conciliar Period* (New York: Charles Scribner's Sons, 1949), p. 543.

[16]See Philip Schaff, *History of the Christian Church*, Vol. III (New York: Charles Scribner's Sons, 1886), p. 68.

[17]John W. Barker, *Justinian and the Later Roman Empire* (Madison: The University of Wisconsin Press, 1966), p. 100.

minutest detail of worship and discipline, and also of dictating the theological opinions to be held in the Church.[18]

Accordingly, after issuing his ten anathemata against Origen, Justinian convened a local council in Constantinople, which expanded his ten anathemata to fifteen; then, when he convened the Fifth General Council of the Church ten years later in 553, the fifteen anathemata were published along with the acts of this council.[19] Ironically, the supposed leader of the church, Pope Vigilius, opposed Justinian on many theological issues; and though the Pope could have participated in the Fifth General Council, being in Constantinople at the time, his disagreements with Justinian were such that he refused to do so. But less than a year later, he succumbed to imperial pressure and agreed to adhere to the Council's rulings.[20] And so, in the words of historian, Williston Walker, Justinian had succeeded "more fully than any other of the Eastern Emperors . . . in making himself master of the church."[21]

Now I have no doubt that, more often than not, a moral drawn from history lies in the eye of the beholder. But the more I read about the imperial church—the power plays, the petty jealousies, the various political intrigues—the less inclined I was to place any confidence at all in its pronouncements. In this, I suppose, my reaction was typically Protestant. Unlike some of my Catholic friends, I had inherited a bias against official church pronouncements anyway; and as I saw it, the imperial church's obsession with power and control inevitably bred, first, an obsessive fear of heresy, then, the persecution of heretics, and finally, a tendency to regard every deviation from the most rigid orthodoxy as heretical. Whereas the early church had sought to achieve unity through positive

---

[18]Ayer, *op. cit.*, p. 553.

[19]There seems to be some doubt as to whether the condemnations were actually *repeated* at the Fifth General Council. See Philip Schaff, *op. cit.*, p. 771.

[20]*Ibid.*

[21]Williston Walker, *A History of the Christian Church* (New York: Charles Scribner's Sons, 1959), p. 141.

confessions of faith ("I believe in God the Father Almighty . . ."), the imperial church sought to achieve it through the condemnation of error ("Let them be anathema") and the persecution of those thought to be in error. And neither the moral character of the one thought to be in error nor the circumstances surrounding the fall into "error" seemed to matter one whit to an emperor such as Justinian, as his condemnation of Theodore of Mopsuestia illustrates. For though Theodore—"the ablest exegete and theologian of the Antiochian school"[22]—had been dead for more than a century, though he had died in full communion with the church, and though Pope Vigilius had argued that no one can lawfully "judge anew anything concerning the persons of the dead,"[23] such was Justinian's arrogance that he insisted upon condemning, not merely the bishop's writings, but also the good bishop himself. And so, the Fifth General Council declared: "We, therefore, anathematize . . . the impious Theodore of Mopsuestia with his execrable writings . . ."[24]

So it went with Justinian, the Great. It is hardly surprising that a church under the control of such an emperor, who is famous for his anathemata and his persecutions, should have rejected the doctrine of universal reconciliation. For insofar as fear of eternal damnation and the power of excommunication, backed by the coercive power of the state, had become the Emperor's primary means of social control, he could hardly tolerate a doctrine that would seem to undermine that power altogether. Justinian thus illustrates an important historical truth. Many religious doctrines serve, among other things, a sociological function, and over the centuries the traditional understanding of hell has served one function especially well: It has enabled religious and political leaders to cultivate fear and to employ fear as a means of social control. That more than anything else explains, I believe, why the imperial church came to

---

[22]*Ibid.*, p. 133.

[23]Vigilius, *Constitutum*, May 14, 553, reprinted in part in Ayer, *op. cit.* pp. 547-551.

[24]Ayer, *op. cit.*, p. 551.

regard the idea of universal reconciliation as a threat not only to social stability, but to its own power and authority as well.

But herein also lies an irony, for there is more than one kind of power and one kind of authority. The power of the Cross is not the power of the sword; it is the transforming power of love. And the Christian message in its purity is not a message of fear; it is a message of hope and of love, the very love that casts out fear. Accordingly, by its willingness to embrace the power of the sword and to employ fear as a means of social control—by its willingness to embrace the weapons of this world, in other words—the imperial church managed only to undermine its own moral and spiritual authority. That, at least, is how I eventually came to view the matter. In addition, for reasons I shall try to illustrate in the following chapter, I came to view the bloody history of persecution and brutality within the Christian church as an inevitable consequence of the Church's loss of moral and spiritual authority.

3. A LEGACY OF FEAR AND PERSECUTION

"But there are not a few who would be indignant at
having their belief in God questioned, who yet seem
greatly to fear imagining Him better than He is."

George MacDonald

In his anti-Christian tract, "Why I Am Not a Christian," Bertrand Russell cites the history of persecution within the Christian church as one of his main reasons for rejecting the Christian faith. He writes:

the more intense has been the religion of any period and
the more profound has been the dogmatic belief, the greater has been the cruelty and the worse has been the state of
affairs. In the so-called ages of faith, when men really did
believe the Christian religion in all its completeness, there
was the Inquisition, with its tortures; there were millions
of unfortunate women burned as witches; and there was
every kind of cruelty practiced upon all sorts of people in
the name of religion.[1]

When I first read these words as an undergraduate, I dismissed them with the thought that anyone can claim the name of Christ and any self-righteous despot can commit atrocities in the name of Christ. What I then failed to reckon with, however, was the disturbing fact that some of the greatest theologians in the Western tradition, men still widely revered as heroes of the faith, not only advocated persecution in specific cases, but provided a theological "justification" for it as well. I am now inclined, therefore, to take Russell's criticism much more seriously than I once did; for as I now see the matter, the legacy of persecution within the Christian Church is a symptom not merely of moral failure within the church, but of theological error as well.

---

[1]Bertrand Russell, *Why I Am Not a Christian and Other Essays on Religion and Related Subjects*, (New York: Simon and Schuster, 1957), pp. 20-21.

I would therefore ask: Does not Jesus himself sanction the very kind of argument that Russell employs? When Jesus warned that not all who use his name—not even all who perform mighty works in his name—are true disciples (see Matthew 7:22-23), he explained exactly how to identify the *true* disciples: "A sound tree cannot bear evil fruit, nor can a bad tree bear good fruit. . . . Thus you will know them by their fruits" (Matthew 7: 18 & 20—RSV). Part of the suggestion here seems to be that a sound doctrine, soundly interpreted, will not bear evil fruit in the lives of those who sincerely embrace it; it will, to the contrary, bear good fruit. And in the gospel accounts, at any rate, Jesus is quite explicit concerning what he means by "good fruit." His true disciples, he tells us, are the peacemakers, those who bring reconciliation: the ones who turn the other cheek and walk the second mile and love their enemies and bear the burdens of others (see Matthew 5:9 & 38-48). Similarly for Paul: The "fruit of the Spirit," he says, includes (among other things) "love, joy, peace, patience, [and] kindness" (Galatians 5:22), whereas "the works of the flesh" include "enmities, strife, jealousy, anger, quarrels, dissension, [and] factions . . ." (Galatians 5:20). So if a sound doctrine, soundly interpreted, does not produce evil fruit in the lives of those who sincerely embrace it, then we are entitled, I believe, to regard acts of persecution within the Christian Church as a symptom of unsound doctrine or theological error.

That there are complexities (and difficulties) in evaluating such matters I doubt not at all. But the fact is that specific theological ideas seem to lie behind the disgraceful history of persecution, murder, and even protracted torture within the Christian church. Nor need it be any mystery what these ideas are, since a number of Christian theologians, beginning with St. Augustine, have explained them with great clarity—have explained exactly why, in their opinion, the use of the sword to terrorize pagans and heretics is theologically justified. Not every idea to which some persecutor appeals is, of course, automatically suspect. But when a religious doctrine appears consistently (and over a long period of time) to have destructive effects in the lives of those who accept it, then we have a *prima facie* reason, surely, to question its soundness. For as Jesus said, "A sound tree cannot [consistently and over a long period of time] bear evil fruit."

Theology and the Politics of Terror

I first heard the name of Miguel Servetus (1511-1553), whom the Calvinists in Geneva burned over green wood so that it took three hours for him to be pronounced dead, in an undergraduate history class. Here was a man whom the Christian authorities of a Christian city executed even though he had committed no crime in their city; he was executed solely for his anti-Trinitarian views and because he disagreed with Calvin on some fine points of theology. Nor is there any doubt that Calvin himself engineered the arrest, conviction, and execution of this "heretic."[2] Nor was Servetus the only "heretic" whom Calvin wanted put to death. Previously he had sought, unsuccessfully, the death of Jerome Bolsec, because of a disagreement over a matter as abstract as the doctrine of predestination;[3] and later he had Sebastian Castellio charged with heresy, principally because the latter had criticized the burning of Servetus.

Calvin's precise role in the Servetus affair is not my present concern, however. For two points, at least, are undeniable: First, as a letter to his friend, Guillaume Farel, illustrates, Calvin had desired the death of Servetus for many years. After the sharp tongued and exasperating Spaniard sent Calvin a copy of the *Institutes* in

---

[2]Calvin may have preferred, it is true, a less brutal form of execution. For in a letter to Guillaume Farel, he wrote: "I hope the judgment will be capital in any event, but I desire cruelty of punishment withheld" [Quoted in Williston Walker, *John Calvin* (New York: Schocken Books, 1969), p. 333].

[3]For an exhaustive (even monumental) treatment of the Bolsec controversy on predestination and of the lengths to which Calvin went in his efforts to get Bolsec condemned to death, see Philip Holtrop, *The Bolsec Controversy on Predestination, from 1551 to 1555: The Statements of Jerome Bolsec, and the Responses of John Calvin, Theodore Beza, and Other Reformed Theologians* (Lewiston, N.Y.: Edwin Mellon Press, 1993).

which he had marked its supposed errors, Calvin penned these por-
tentous words:

> Servetus lately wrote to me and coupled with his letter a
> long volume of his delirious fancies, with the Thrasonic
> boast that I should see something astonishing and unheard
> of. He would like to come here if it is agreeable to me.
> But I do not wish to pledge my word for his safety. For, if
> he comes, I will never let him depart alive, if I have any
> authority.[4]

These words, written several years before the actual arrest of Servetus, already reveal Calvin's willingness to have his adversary put
to death. And second, as Leonard Verduin points out, Calvin pas-
sionately defended the execution afterwards with "every possible
and impossible argument."[5] He sincerely believed, in other words,
that Servetus deserved to die.

But why did Calvin believe this? Why did he regard heresy as
a crime for which death is an appropriate punishment? It is no
answer, in the present context, merely to point out that Calvin was
himself the product of an intolerant age. For though that may be
true enough, it does not explain the theological roots of the intolerance; to the contrary, it merely underscores Russell's point about
some of the pernicious effects that the Christian religion, as organized in its churches, has had. Are we not talking, after all, about a
Christian age, one in which, as Russell himself puts it, people
"really did believe the Christian religion in all its completeness"?
Why is it that the so-called Christian ages have produced so much
intolerance, so much murder and mayhem?

So far as I know, St. Augustine was the first Christian theologian to advocate the use of terror against those whom he regarded
as heretical. In *De Correctione Donatistarum*, Augustine asks:
"Where [in Scripture] is what they [the Donatists] are accustomed

---

[4]Quoted in T. H. L. Parker, *John Calvin: A Biography* (Philadelphia:
Westminster Press, 1975), p. 118.

[5]Leonard Verduin, *The Reformers and Their Stepchildren* (Grand
Rapids: Eerdmans Publishing Co., 1964), p. 51.

to cry: `To believe or not to believe is a matter that is free'?"[6]
Against the contention of the Donatists that religious assent must be
free, Augustine cites several examples, including the conversion of
St. Paul, in which he claims that Christ himself employed physical
affliction as a means of coercion. He then goes on to argue:

> But we have shown that Paul was compelled by Christ;
> therefore the Church, in trying to compel the Donatists, is
> following the example of her Lord . . .. Wherefore, if the
> power [of the sword] which the Church has received by
> divine appointment in its due season, through the religious
> character and faith of Kings, be the instrument by which
> those who are found in the highways and hedges—that is,
> in heresies and schisms—are compelled to come in, then
> let them not find fault because they are compelled . . ..[7]

Here Augustine makes the remarkable claim that in coercing the
Donatists through physical affliction the Church was merely following "the example of her Lord." But that does not yet explain
why he considered the use of such coercive measures justified.
Why should anyone, even the Lord himself, be justified in coercing
people into the Church against their will? Augustine's answer
emerges clearly in his response to those Donatists who had resisted
unto death, in some cases by setting themselves afire. He asks:
"What then is the function of brotherly love? Does it, because it
fears the short-lived fires of the furnace for a few, therefore abandon all to the eternal fires of hell?"[8] In another place he again asks:
"Why, therefore, should not the Church use force in compelling her

---

[6]Augustine, *De Correctione Donatistarum* 22, as translated in Ayer, *op.
cit.*, p. 451. All other quotations from this document are taken from the
translation in Philip Schaff (ed.), *A Select Library of the Nicene and
Post-Nicene Fathers* (Buffalo: The Christian Literature Co., 1887), pp.
633-651.

[7]*Ibid.*, 23 & 24. Those who believe that Augustine's exegesis of the
Bible was more accurate than that of many of his predecessors would do
well to examine carefully the fantastic exegetical arguments he offers in
support of these claims.

[8]*Ibid.*, 14.

lost sons to return, if the lost sons compelled others to their destruction [i.e., to eternal death]?"[9] In other words, the use of the sword in coercing heretics back into the State Church is justified, Augustine believed, because the alternative would be to consign many more—those under the influence of the heretics, as well as the heretics themselves—to eternal damnation. As Augustine saw it, therefore, we must distinguish between two classes of people. For the righteous "who thirsteth for God," "there is no need of the terror of hell, to say nothing of temporal punishments or imperial laws . . ."; but for those who have fallen into heresy, "many must first be recalled to their Lord by the stripes of temporal scourging, like evil slaves, and in some degree like good-for-nothing fugitives."[10]

It is worth noting at this point that the Donatists, whose persecution Augustine advocated, agreed with him on almost all theological matters except the nature of a true church. They believed, first of all, in the separation of church and state and, secondly, in the separation of a true church from the surrounding culture. Because they regarded the State Church as fallen and impure, in part because it had appropriated the power of the sword to further its own ends, they refused to submit to its authority. I have no doubt, moreover, that they were a narrow and self-righteous lot, as purists and schismatics often are. But Augustine's defense of the use of terror against them remains one of the most appalling aspects of his thinking, and it is important to see that this defense was not an isolated quirk in his thinking. Indeed, within the context of his own assumptions, his argument is perfectly reasonable. If you suppose, as Augustine did, that heresy leads to eternal damnation and that, like a deadly germ, the heretic tends to infect others with heresy, then you have every reason to terrorize and even to murder heretics. Such brutality may be a tragic necessity on this view, but it remains a necessity nonetheless.

---

[9]*Ibid.*, 23.

[10]*Ibid.*, 21.

Though Augustine may have been the first Christian theologian to argue against freedom of conscience in religious matters, he was by no means the last. His arguments were repeated throughout the Middle Ages and then were picked up by the Protestant Reformers. Like Augustine, Calvin too regarded heresy as a sin worse than murder: "The mockers who would suffer all false doctrines . . . are not only traitors to God but enemies of the human race. They would bring poor souls to perdition and ruin, and are worse than murderers."[11] Similarly, Calvin's close friend and associate, Theodore Beza, once wrote: "The contention that heretics should not be punished is as monstrous as the contention that patricides and matricides should not be put to death; for heretics are a thousandfold worse criminals than these."[12] And the Reformers were, of course, quite prepared to act upon their convictions; in 1526, for example, the Christian authorities in Zurick "ordered Anabaptists drowned, in hideous parody of their belief . . .."[13] Here is how Urbanus Rhegius, an associate of Martin Luther, justified the persecution of Anabaptists (whom he also called "Donatists," using that term as a form of abuse):

> When heresy breaks forth . . . then the magistrate must punish not with less but with greater vigor than is employed against other evil-doers, robbers, murderers, thieves, and the like. . . . The Donatists murder men's souls, make them go to eternal death; and then they complain when men punish them with temporal death. . . . All who know history will know what has been done in this

---

[11]Quoted in Georgia Harkness, *John Calvin: The Man and his Ethics* (New York: Henry Holt and Company, 1931), p. 111. If, according to Calvin, those heretics who cause others to land in hell are worse than murderers, one wonders why he did not also regard, as worse than a murder, a "God" who would predestine some to hell.

[12]Quoted in Stefan Zweig, *op. cit.*, p. 168.

[13]Williston Walker, *A History of the Christian Church* (New York: Charles Scribner's Sons, 1959), p. 127.

matter by such men as Constantine, Marianus, Theodosius, Charlemagne, and others.[14]

Indeed! All who know history do know what such men as these have done in the name of Christ! Certainly none of them championed freedom of conscience, which they regarded as a threat to their own political power. So, whether they truly believed it or not, they all welcomed the theological assumption that, given the horrors of eternal damnation, heresy is a sin worse than murder. As the above quotations illustrate, moreover, religious persecution in the Western Church typically has had its roots in an obsessive fear of eternal damnation. It is no doubt possible to believe in eternal damnation without believing that God would be so unjust as to damn someone eternally for an honest mistake in abstract theology. But fear is often irrational, and, as a matter of historical fact, the Christian church has consistently employed the fear of eternal damnation as a weapon against "theological error." It has consistently cultivated in its constituency the fear that those who die in unbelief, or with certain mistaken beliefs, are precisely those whom God will damn eternally in hell. Such fear, which springs ultimately from a lack of confidence (or faith) in the character of God, has had disastrous consequences in the life of the church. Having no confidence in the love of God, those in the grips of such fear have too often wielded the sword in a sincere effort to protect their loved ones from the tragic consequences, as they see it, of error in religious matters.

Moral Progress and the Christian Faith

The more I have reflected upon the history of persecution within the Christian church, the more it has seemed to me that Bertrand Russell's indictment of religion, at least as a cultural phenomenon, has considerable merit. Like the harlot described in Revelation 17, the Christian church has at times become "drunk with the blood of the saints and the blood of the martyrs of Jesus" (17:6—RSV). For

---

[14]Quoted by Leonard Verduin, *op. cit.*, p. 50.

what else were many of the "heretics" so-called, except saints and martyrs?

But having said that, I think it also important to point out that Russell himself falls into confusion when he writes: "the more intense has been the religion of any period and the more profound has been the dogmatic belief, the greater has been the cruelty and the worse has been the state of affairs." There are two difficulties here: First, Russell ignores completely those intense forms of religious fervor that inspire love and charity rather than fear and suspicion; and second, he attributes all of the evils of religion, as he sees them, to dogmatic belief in general rather than to *specific* dogmatic beliefs. He fails to distinguish carefully enough, in other words, between different dogmatic beliefs. A dogmatic belief in the love of God, or in the sacredness of human life, or in freedom of conscience in religious matters not only does not lead to religious persecution; it probably provides the most effective opposition to it. So it is not dogmatic belief in general, but specific dogmatic beliefs, that we should indict at this point; in particular, we should indict that *conjunction* of dogmatic beliefs implying that heresy is a crime worse than murder. Had it not been for an obsessive fear of heresy, grounded in the traditional understanding of hell, most of the atrocities committed in the name of the Christian religion would never have occurred.

Russell goes on to expand his indictment of Christianity as follows:

> You find as you look around the world that every single bit of progress in humane feeling, every improvement in the criminal law, every step toward the diminution of war, every step toward better treatment of the colored races, or every mitigation of slavery, every moral progress that there has been in the world, has been consistently opposed by the organized churches of the world. I say quite deliberately that the Christian religion, as organized in its churches, has been and still is the principal enemy of moral progress in the world.[15]

---

[15]Russell, *op. cit.*, pp. 20-21.

By way of a reply, I would here ask: Has not the Christian faith also *inspired* much of the moral progress of which Russell speaks? Has it not provided the very standard by which many of us would measure moral progress in the world? Consider three beliefs at the very heart of the Christian religion: the belief that (a) God *is* love; that (b) through the death and resurrection of Jesus Christ, God is reconciling the world to himself; and (c) that in response to God's love for us, we must learn to love our neighbors—our enemies as well as our friends—even as we love ourselves. However foolish one might otherwise think them to be, such beliefs not only inspire moral progress of the kind that Russell speaks; they provide a much more rigorous standard for measuring such progress than most people would likely accept. I have no doubt that Russell's critical remarks about "the Christian religion, as organized in its churches," are true enough; religious establishments are no different from any other establishment, more concerned with their own power and self-preservation than with anything else. But is not the Christian faith, as displayed in the life of someone such as Mother Teresa, just the sort of thing that inspires moral progress? And did not individual reformers, under the inspiration of their Christian faith, vigorously oppose, for example, plantation slavery in the United States? It seems to me, at any rate, that the Christian faith has inspired much of the moral progress that, paradoxically, "the Christian religion, as organized in its churches," has opposed so vigorously.

Take the one issue of armed warfare. Virtually all of the early Christian converts, and in particular the early church fathers, were pacifists; they were prepared to bear the same cross that Jesus bore and, like Jesus, saw themselves as suffering servants. They no doubt acknowledged an obligation to the truth (as they saw it), to speak the truth in love for example, but they would never have acknowledged an obligation (or even a right) to wield the sword in an effort to make Christian converts, or to stifle dissent, or to settle theological disputes. Within a few centuries, however, the young and vibrant faith of the early Christians had congealed into an organized religion with its own orthodoxy and political intrigues; within a few centuries, Christians were killing other Christians, not to mention pagans, in defense of an orthodoxy they evidently had little confidence in. But here, I would suggest, a reasonable interpretation is this: Between the time at which Christians were almost universally pacifists and the time at which those who called themselves "Christians" began persecuting pagans and heretics, the organized Christian church had simply lost its prophetic vision; having twisted the Christian gospel into a message of fear, one that the early suffering servants would not even have recognized, it then felt compelled to defend its message of fear with the weapons of fear. So in that sense, perhaps the Christian church did become an obstacle not only to moral progress in the world, but to genuine Christian faith as well.

I am now inclined, then, to draw a relatively sharp distinction between the Christian faith, on the one hand, and the organized Christian church, on the other, and I am quite prepared to see the latter as, more often than not, an enemy of the former. Not that the organized Christian church is any worse than other human institutions; on the whole, it is just no better. Nor should we expect it to be any better. We humans tend to make a mess of all our institutions, and our religious institutions are no different from any others in this regard. That those who call themselves "Christians" have made a mess of the Christian religion is no more surprising, I would suggest, than that the scribes and the Pharisees (during New Testament times) made a mess of the Jewish religion, or that Islamic Fundamentalists (in our own day) have made a mess of the Islamic religion. Accordingly, though I still believe in religious inspiration, in divine revelation, and in the prophetic word, and though I still regard the Christian faith as one of the principal sources—if not *the* principal source—of moral and spiritual enlightenment in the world, I also believe this: Over time our religious organizations inevitably twist and distort the very prophetic word they were instituted to preserve. They inevitably twist a message of love and hope into a message of fear.

The Destructive Power of Fear

Having conceded that Russell's indictment of the Christian church has some merit, I would also, in an effort to strike a balance, caution against an overly moralistic attitude towards history. Here I mean to caution myself as much as anyone else. We who have enjoyed religious liberty all of our lives no doubt find it easy—too easy, I should think—to regard those Christian authorities who misused their power in the past as unmitigated villains. But we also need to bear in mind, at this point, the complexity of historical events. Whether it be the Spanish Inquisitioners who murdered heretics on a regular basis, the Calvinists who murdered Servetus and countless Anabaptists, or the Puritans in Salem, Massachusetts, who murdered young women charged with witchcraft, the real villains in such episodes are not those who, in their own historical circumstances, may have acted as well as they could; the real villains are the fear that inspired such acts of terror in the first place and the religious ideas, such as the doctrine of eternal damnation, that kindled the fear. When Western Christendom not only backed away from, but actually condemned, the idea of universal reconciliation, it also, so I shall argue in subsequent chapters, backed away from the only *consistent* theology of love; and it has struggled ever since with the only possible alternative: a theology that cultivates, even as it expresses, our fear.

Fear need not, of course, always express itself in the form of physical brutality against others. So far as I know, Jonathan Edwards never advocated the persecution of either heretics or unbelievers, but he nonetheless remains one of the great apostles of fear. In "Sinners in the Hands of an Angry God," perhaps the most famous sermon ever delivered in America, Edwards evoked such fear in the congregation he addressed that some, unable to endure it, actually passed out in church. Here is but a sample of what he said:

> The God that holds you over the pit of hell, much as one holds a spider, or some loathsome insect over the fire, abhors you, and is dreadfully provoked: his wrath towards

you burns like fire; he looks upon you as worthy of nothing else, but to be cast into the fire; he is of purer eyes than to bear to have you in his sight; you are ten thousand times more abominable in his eyes, than the most hateful venomous serpent is in ours.[16]

Clearly, Edwards needed no sword to sow the seeds of terror. Why he believed that God would look upon a human being, created in the divine image, as "worthy of nothing else" but everlasting torment, or why he supposed that human beings, however sinful, are "more abominable" in the eyes of God than a disobedient child is in the eyes of a loving parent, he does not say. But reflect, for a moment, upon the likely effect of his sermon on the mind of a child. Imagine growing up in a church (or Christian school), as I and many of my friends did, in which ministers, Sunday school teachers, and camp counselors (good people all, but in the grips of their own message of fear) try repeatedly—with less eloquence than Edwards displayed, but with no less fervor—to frighten children into the faith. My point here is not that my early teachers were all failures; far from it. Most of them were far better than the message they sometimes preached, and most of them even had a good deal to say, however inconsistently, about the love of God. When I compare my own childhood, moreover, with that of many others, including those who have suffered physical and sexual abuse of various kinds, I am keenly aware of just how good it was and just how important the Christian community was in making it good. Nonetheless, the *theology* I encountered, both in church and in high school, was essentially a message of fear, and God's love always turned out, within the context of that theology, to be conditional in one way or another.

As I came to understand it, the fundamental religious problem was to find an answer to the question of how I, a polluted sinner, might escape the vindictiveness and the wrath of God. How, in particular, might I escape everlasting torment in hell? Even

---

[16]Jonathan Edwards, "Sinners in the Hands of an Angry God," reprinted in Ola Elizabeth Winslow, *Jonathan Edwards: Basic Writings* (New York: The New American Library, Inc.), p. 159.

salvation I came to understand as essentially an escape from the wrath, even the hatred, of God, and I still have in my possession a "gospel" tract that begins with these ominous words in bold faced, capital letters: **"GOD HATES YOU."** The technique here, familiar to anyone who understands the art of brain washing, was especially evident at the church camps I attended: First evoke a terrible fear; then offer a means of escape. According to a host of teachers whom I encountered in my youth, Jesus Christ, who died for us and was subsequently raised from the dead, provided the means whereby we might escape the wrath of God; by enduring our punishment for us, by allowing God to vent his wrath on someone other than us, Christ successfully appeased the vindictive God. But then, according to that teaching, vindictiveness and wrath remain ultimate facts about God. If we accept Christ as our savior—if, that is, we respond to the preacher's altar call, or submit to the authority of some church—God's vindictive attitude towards us will change; but if we do not accept Christ, if perchance we should die in our sin, God's vindictive attitude will *never* change. First evoke a terrible fear; then offer a means of escape.

I'll probably never forget my first job as a teenager, when I worked for a contract paint company scraping walls, sand blasting, and cleaning gutters; I'll never forget that job, because I was terribly afraid of the boss. Nor was I alone in this. Many of the other workers, particularly those who liked to loaf, were likewise afraid of the boss, whose wrath, easily kindled, was something to behold. But we also had, fortunately, a good foreman who always stood by us, a kind of mediator between the boss and the working crew. Again and again, the foreman would deflect the boss' anger away from us, or pacify his wrath, or reconcile him to something we were doing. Still, though I was certainly relieved to have someone pacify the boss on my behalf and on behalf of the other workers, I never felt comfortable around that man and was always glad to see him leave; during that particular summer anyway, I never felt reconciled to that particular boss. And we have here, I believe, a parable of the twisted gospel, the message of fear, that I encountered in the churches of my youth. God in his wrath and his anger is essentially someone to fear, not because he means to perfect us, but because he may reject us and torment us forever and ever and ever. Because Jesus Christ provides a means of escape, we experience a sense of relief, perhaps, but not a heartfelt love for the one we have learned to fear.

Observe how easily a subtle shift of emphasis can twist the New Testament message of hope into a message of fear. As George MacDonald was so fond of pointing out, not one word in the New Testament implies that vindictiveness and wrath are ultimate facts about God, or that Christ's sacrifice was required in order to appease a vindictive God. A more accurate understanding would be that Christ's death and resurrection was God's sacrifice to us, the means whereby God changes *our* attitudes and reconciles *us* to himself (see, for example, II Corinthians 5:19); it is not a means whereby God's attitude towards us is changed. God's attitude remains the same yesterday, today, and forever. For God is love; that is the rock-bottom fact about God. But the history of organized religion, at least in the Western tradition, is a record of our human resistance to the proclamation that God is love, that his love extends to everyone, and that it is in no way conditioned upon human obedience or human faithfulness.

As a more recent illustration of such resistance, consider Kenneth Kantzer's claim that "the biblical answer [to the question of human destiny] does not satisfy our wishful sentiments. It is a hard and crushing word, devastating to human hope and pride."[17] It is "a hard and crushing word," Kantzer evidently believes, because it implies that, even if we should escape eternal perdition ourselves, some of our loved ones may not. And one could hardly imagine anything more "devastating to human hope" than that. Is it any wonder that so many well-meaning people have turned to persecution and violence? Is it any wonder that they have resorted to desperate means in an effort to protect their loved ones from a fate worse than death? Perhaps few Christians today would advocate, or even tolerate, the persecution of those whom they see as heretics; we may be thankful for that. But even today, the fears that have

---

[17]Kenneth S. Kantzer, "Troublesome Questions," *Christianity Today*, March 20, 1987.

led to such persecution in the past continue to do their evil work of making people miserable and of estranging one person from another—as the wife whose husband dies "in unbelief," or the mother whose teenage son leaves the faith, or the teenager whose closest friend commits suicide might testify. A church in the grips of fear has little to offer those most desperate for a word of consolation, little except more pain, more misery, more fear. Kantzer claims that this really is the Christian gospel—"a hard and crushing word, devastating to human hope"—but I shall argue in subsequent chapters that he is simply wrong about that. I shall try to set forth a radically different picture, according to which the gospel, if true, really would be, as the word itself implies, good news—indeed, the best possible news for those of us in our present human condition. The gospel presents, for our consideration, a vision of God and the world that makes one want to shout with joy, a vision that can free us from all of the fear and the guilt and the worry within which we so often imprison ourselves. That vision may not always satisfy our *wishful sentiments*—Kantzer is right about that—but it does satisfy our *deepest yearnings*; it may at times devastate human *pride*, but it could never, ever devastate human *hope*. It is a vision altogether worthy of being true, and that is also, I believe, an indispensable condition of its being true.

In her novel, *Jane Eyre*, the nineteenth century writer, Charlotte Bronte, captures with a haunting accuracy the coldness and emptiness that sometimes passes for Christian ministry. I could almost feel the hard wooden pews against my back when I first read this description of a sermon:

> Throughout there was a strange bitterness; an absence of consolatory gentleness; stern allusions to Calvinistic doctrines—election, predestination, reprobation—were frequent; and each reference to these points sounded like a sentence pronounced for doom. When he had done, instead of feeling better, calmer, more enlightened by his discourse, I experienced an inexpressible sadness; for it seemed to me—I know not whether equally so to others—that the eloquence to which I had been listening had sprung from a depth where lay turbid dregs of disappointment—where moved troubling impulses or insatiate

> yearnings and disquieting aspirations. I was sure St. John
> Rivers—pure-lived, conscientious, zealous as he was—had
> not yet found that peace of God which passeth all
> understanding; he had no more found it, I thought, than
> had I . . ..[18]

Perhaps few of us in this life *have* found the "peace of God which
passeth all understanding"; many who glibly claim to have found it
sooner or later prove by their actions that they have not yet found
it. But according to the Christian faith, as I have come to understand it, all of us *will* eventually find such peace, either in this life
or in some other, but only after we have finally learned the lessons
of love. As we learn our lessons, in some cases after much travail
and hardship, we will find that in the end "perfect love casts out
fear; for fear has to do with punishment, and whoever fears has not
reached perfection in love" (I John 4:18). And just as "perfect love
casts out fear," so also, I am persuaded, is the New Testament message of love, when rightly understood, the best corrective for a
theology that expresses our fear. In the following chapters, therefore, I shall try to create a context—biblical, theological, and philosophical—in which the grounds for hope and the groundlessness of
our fears might be more evident to us.

---

[18]Charlotte Bronte, *Jane Eyre* (New York: The New American Library,
inc.), p. 354.

PART II
UNIVERSAL RECONCILIATION AND THE NEW TESTAMENT

4. THREE PICTURES OF GOD IN WESTERN THEOLOGY

> "The practical issues at stake in any one intellectual controversy are always more than we realize. This is especially true where fundamentally contrary views of God are in conflict. When the paths diverge at the top, almost everything below will be different."
>
> John Piper

I have said that I know of no better place to begin our reflections than right in the middle of my own religious and philosophical concerns, and these arise primarily from my encounters with the history of Western theology. So let us try to acquire, rather quickly, a perspective on that history.

A cardinal doctrine of the Christian faith is that God, being a loving Creator, is at work in the world redeeming sinners--that is, reconciling to himself those who have fallen into moral corruption. But Christians have often disagreed among themselves about the extent and the ultimate success of God's redemptive activity, and these disagreements reflect surprisingly different conceptions of the divine nature. The conceptions are so different, indeed, that some might wonder whether all Christians in fact worship the same God.

Here is a relatively easy way to understand these issues and to organize our thinking about them. We begin with an inconsistent set of three propositions:

(1) It is God's redemptive purpose for the world (and therefore his will) to reconcile all sinners to himself;

(2) It is within God's power to achieve his redemptive purpose for the world;

(3) Some sinners will never be reconciled to God, and God will therefore either consign them to a place of eternal punishment, from which there will be no hope of escape, or put them out of existence altogether.

In calling this an inconsistent set of propositions, I assume, of course, that the following is necessarily true: If it is God's redemptive purpose to reconcile all sinners to himself and it is within his power to accomplish that purpose, then he will indeed reconcile all sinners to himself. If this is necessarily true, then at least one of the above propositions is false[1]

Next, we observe the following: Although at least one of the propositions above is false, we nonetheless find theological arguments in support of each of them; we also find texts in the Bible that may appear, at least initially, to support each of them. In support of proposition (1), for example, we find such texts as II Peter 3:9: "The Lord . . . is not willing that any should perish, but [wills instead] that all should come to repentance" (KJV); I Timothy 2:4: God "desires everyone to be saved and to come to the knowledge of the truth"; Romans 11:32: "For God has imprisoned all in disobedience so that he may be merciful to all"; Ezekiel 33:11: "As I live, says the Lord God, I have no pleasure in the death of the wicked, but that the wicked turn away from their ways and live . . ."; and perhaps the clearest of all, Lamentations 3:22 & 3:31-33: "The steadfast love of the Lord never ceases, his mercies never come to an end . . . For the Lord will not reject forever. Although he causes

---

[1]As I here use the expression, "God's redemptive purpose for the world," it includes everything that God regards as *most* important; hence, it is by definition a purpose that overrides all others. If God regards it to be of utmost importance that he achieve justice in the end, for example, then that is part of his redemptive purpose for the world; and if he also regards it to be of utmost importance that he preserve human freedom, then that too is part of his redemptive purpose for the world. In the latter case, we might describe his redemptive purpose this way: It is his overriding purpose (and therefore his will) to achieve a state of affairs in which all sinners *freely* repent of their sins. Whether God has the power to achieve this purpose is, of course, a further question. But if God desires the salvation of all in *any* intelligible sense and also desires to preserve human freedom in this matter, then his redemptive purpose for the world is simply a combination of the two: It is his overriding purpose of bringing it about that all are reconciled to him freely.

grief, he will have compassion according to the abundance of his steadfast love; for he does not willingly afflict or grieve anyone." All of these texts seem to suggest that God sincerely wants to achieve the reconciliation of all sinners, and that his failure to achieve this end would therefore be, in some important sense, a tragic defeat of one of his purposes.

Similarly, in support of proposition (2), we find such texts as Ephesians 1:11: God "accomplishes all things according to his counsel and will"; Job 42:2: "I know that you [the Lord God] can do all things, and that no purpose of yours can be thwarted"; Psalm 115:3: "Our God is in the heavens; he does whatever he pleases"; and Isaiah 46:10b & 11b: "My counsel shall stand, and I will accomplish all my purpose . . . I have spoken, and I will bring it to pass; I have purposed, and I will do it" (RSV). These texts seem to imply that God is able to accomplish all of his purposes--including, therefore, his redemptive purposes. And in addition to these texts, a number of others, which we shall examine more fully in the following chapter, seem to imply that God has *both* the will *and* the power to bring all things into subjection to Christ (I Corinthians 15:27-28), to reconcile all things in Christ (Colossians 1:20), and to bring acquittal and life to all persons through Christ (Romans 5:18).

But finally, in support of proposition (3), we also find such texts as Matthew 25:46: "And these will go away into eternal punishment, but the righteous into eternal life"; II Thessalonians 1:9: "These will suffer the punishment of eternal destruction, separated from the presence of the Lord and from the glory of his might . . ."; and Ephesians 5:5: "Be sure of this, that no immoral or impure man, or one who is covetous (that is, an idolater), has any inheritance in the kingdom of Christ and of God" (RSV). These texts may seem to imply that at least some persons will be lost forever and thus never be reconciled to God.

Lest there should be any confusion in the matter, I should perhaps point out at this point that I make no claim, in the present context, about the correct interpretation of any of the texts I have just cited. Neither do I make any claim about the appropriateness of lifting isolated texts from very different contexts and setting them side by side, as if one could somehow adduce evidence thereby for the content of revealed truth. I merely make the point that various texts in the Bible may initially appear to support, and in fact have been cited on behalf of, each of our three propositions. With respect to each of them, some theologians and Bible scholars have concluded that it is a fundamental--not a peripheral, but a fundamental--teaching in the Bible. But as a matter of logic, not all of them can be true; at least one of them is false. So if we consider the matter purely as an exercise in logic--that is, without considering any textual evidence at all--we confront this alternative: We can say, on the one hand, that the Bible teaches all three propositions and is not, therefore, infallible in all of its teachings; or we can say, on the other hand, that the Bible is indeed infallible in all of its *teachings*, but does not really teach all three propositions.[2] In either case, those who believe that God has revealed himself in the Bible will face essentially the same hermeneutical problem, that is, essentially the same problem of interpreting the Bible as a whole: They must provide an interpretive structure that avoids a fundamental logical inconsistency in what they take to be the revealed truth about God.

The Emergence of Three Different Pictures

Now a good way to classify Christian theologians and their theological systems, I want to suggest, is according to which of our three propositions they finally reject. Of course, a theologian could always remain a skeptic on this question, but such skepticism would tend to undermine the entire discipline of systematic theology; it is virtually nonexistent, therefore, among traditional theologians. Instead of skepticism, however, we sometimes do find a kind of subterfuge: A theologian may embrace, clearly and

---

[2]As an illustration, consider the proposition that the earth is flat, which we now know to be quite false. If we consider the matter purely as an exercise in logic, without considering any textual evidence at all, we can say one of two things: Either the Bible teaches that the earth is flat and is not infallible in all of its teachings, or it is infallible in all of its teachings and does not teach that the earth is flat.

emphatically, two of the propositions and then try to waffle on the third, either by redefining a crucial term or simply by pretending to hold the third proposition in abeyance. Someone who embraces our first two propositions, for example, may try to ignore the third or to dismiss it with the comment: "The ultimate fate of the wicked is a mystery to be left in the hands of God." Another may reject proposition (1), which states that it is God's purpose to reconcile all sinners to himself, and then try to identify some artificial sense in which we can still say that God *offers* salvation to all. The fact is, however, that a theologian must reject at least one of the three propositions; and when we look carefully at a given theologian's writings, it is usually rather easy to say which one the theologian in fact rejects. We can therefore distinguish between three different schools of thought: The Augustinians, because they believe strongly in both the sovereignty of God's will (proposition (2)) and the doctrine of eternal punishment (proposition (3)), finally reject the idea that God wills the salvation of all (proposition (1)); the Arminians, named after Jacobus Arminius (1560-1609) for his opposition to the Calvinistic understanding of predestination and limited election, finally reject proposition (2); and the universalists, because they embrace both (1) and (2), finally reject proposition (3).

A point to bear in mind here is that the universalists are no different from the Augustinians and the Arminians in this regard: *Every* reflective Christian who takes a stand with respect to our three propositions *must* reject a proposition for which there is at least some *prima facie* biblical support. Whichever proposition one rejects, moreover, will have important implications for one's concept of the divine nature. If one rejects proposition (1), then one can no longer regard lovingkindness as a part of God's very essence; one must concede, in other words, that God's love has definite limits and does not extend to all created persons. So the dispute over proposition (1), which implies that God loves all created persons enough to will their salvation, is perhaps the most important dispute concerning these propositions, because it goes to the very heart of who God is. But the dispute over propositions (2) and (3) also raises some important theological issues. Those who reject proposition (2) can no longer regard God as being sovereign or undefeated with respect to his own redemptive purposes; he simply does his best to cut his losses, to minimize the defeat, and to produce the most favorable balance of good over evil that he can. Those who reject proposition (3), however, can continue to believe *both* that God's love is unlimited *and* that his redemptive purposes are unthwarted.

So here, then, are three quite different pictures of God: According to the Augustinian picture, God's redemptive purposes are unthwarted, but he is limited in love; according to the Arminian picture, God's love is unlimited, but his redemptive purposes are thwarted by factors over which he has no control; and according to the universalist picture, God's love is unlimited and his redemptive purposes are unthwarted as well. Accordingly, a question that may now arise is, "Which of our three pictures best preserves the praiseworthy character and the glory of the divine nature?" And two additional questions are, "Which picture, if true, would provide the firmest foundation for hope?--and which seems the most likely to cultivate our fears?"[3]

Saving the Appearances

We thus approach the difficult task of interpreting the Bible as a whole. It stands to reason that, once one of our three pictures captures the imagination of a given Christian thinker, it will have a profound effect on how that thinker puts together biblical ideas and interprets specific texts in the Bible. For as I have said, every Christian thinker must reject a proposition for which there is at least some *prima facie* biblical support; so as almost a practical necessity, virtually every Christian thinker (who looks to the Bible

---

[3]My purpose in this chapter is to treat each of our three pictures as if they were equal in one important respect: Each of them requires that we deny a proposition for which we can find *some prima facie* biblical support. But I am not here claiming that the biblical warrant for each of our three propositions is equally strong. Quite the contrary. In Chapters 5 and 6, I shall argue, respectively, that the biblical warrant for propositions (1) and (2) is exceptionally strong and the supposed biblical warrant for proposition (3) largely illusory.

as an authority) will end up interpreting some texts, some documents, and some authors in light of others.

As an illustration, consider how St. Augustine tries to handle
the statement in I Timothy 2:4 that God "desires everyone to be
saved and to come to the knowledge of the truth." According to
Augustine, this text

> does not mean that there is no one whose salvation he
> [God] doth not will . . . but by "all men" we are to under-
> stand the whole of mankind, in every single group into
> which it can be divided . . .. For from which of these
> groups doth not God will that *some* men from every nation
> should be saved through his only-begotten Son our Lord?[4]

So it is not God's will, says Augustine, to save every individual
from every group and every nation; it is merely God's will to save
all kinds of people, that is, *some* individuals from every group and
every nation. In support of such an interpretation, Augustine points
to the context of I Timothy 2:4, which singles out a specific group
of people—namely, "kings and all who are in high positions" (2:2)
—on behalf of whom prayers and supplications are requested.
Seizing upon this reference, Augustine argues that God wills salvation only for the elect, only for some persons from all groups:
"kings and subjects; nobility and plebeians; the high and the low;
the learned and the unlearned; the healthy and the sick; the bright,
the dull, and the stupid," etc.[5] To those of us who are not antecedently committed to the Augustinian picture, such an interpretation
will no doubt seem fantastic; I think it fair to say, indeed, that it *is*
fantastic. The text begins with an exhortation to offer prayers and
supplications on behalf of "everyone" (2:1); it then singles out one
group for a special reason: We should pray for kings and those in
positions of authority, it says, so that "we may lead a quiet and
peaceable life" (2:2); and finally, it explains why it is fitting to pray
for all: The stated reason is that God himself "desires everyone to
be saved" (2:4). That the author had a special, and quite under-
standable, reason for singling out one group of people for special

---

[4]Augustine, *Enchiridion*, Ch. XXVII.

[5]*Ibid.*

mention—namely, those in positions of authority, whose job it is to keep the peace—hardly justifies the Augustinian claim that "all men" or "everyone" really means "some from all groups of people."

But suppose that, on the basis of other texts from other contexts, one were antecedently committed to the Augustinian picture and therefore antecedently committed to two propositions: first, that God's will cannot be defeated (proposition (2)), and second, that eternal damnation will be the terrible fate of some persons (proposition (3)). One might then find the following reasoning altogether tempting: Even though I Timothy 2:4 *appears* to say that God "desires everyone to be saved," its *real* meaning, when taken in the context of the Bible as a whole, is merely that God wills the salvation of all kinds of people. For is that not at least a *possible* interpretation? If so, then even if the author did not have it explicitly in mind, it nonetheless remains what the Bible as a whole *requires*. Or, if that approach seems too artificial, one might simply say with Augustine: "We could interpret it [I Timothy 2:4] in any other fashion, as long as we are not compelled to believe that the Omnipotent hath willed something to be done which was not done"[6]— and as long as we are not compelled to believe, Augustine would no doubt add, that no one will be eternally damned. For if propositions (2) and (3) are true, then proposition (1) is false. It is as simple as that.

We find the same pattern of interpretation in Calvin. Concerning I Timothy 2:4, Calvin writes:

> How did it happen that God deprived many peoples of the light of his gospel while others enjoyed it? How did it happen that the pure recognition of the doctrine of godliness never came to some, while others barely tasted some obscure rudiments of it? From this it will be easy to determine the drift of Paul's reasoning [in I Timothy 2:4]. . . .

---

[6]*Ibid.*

Paul surely means only that God has not closed the door to
any order [or class] of men . . ..[7]

And concerning Ezekiel 33:11, Calvin writes:

If God wills that all be saved, how does it come to pass that
he does not open the door of repentance to the miserable
men who would be better prepared to receive grace [than
some who do receive it]? . . . God is without doubt ready to
forgive, as soon as a sinner is converted. Therefore, in so
far as God wills the sinners repentance, he does not will
his death. But *experience teaches* [my emphasis] that God
wills the repentance of those whom he invites to himself,
in such a way that he does not touch the hearts of all.[8]

So for Calvin, even as for Augustine, God does not *really* will that
all be saved, and Calvin's argument may seem no less contrived
and *ad hoc* than Augustine's. For here Calvin gives, it seems, a
rather confused argument from experience merely for the purposes
of overpowering a text. There could be a thousand reasons why
God, even though he wills the salvation of all and will accomplish it
in the end, does not save everyone *at the same time*—a thousand
reasons why he leaves some in darkness longer than others. How is
our limited and impoverished experience of such matters even relevant to what God will do *in the end*? How is it even relevant to the
meaning of the text in question?

But however strained Calvin's argument may initially seem, we
must again place it in the context of his commitment to the Augustinian picture. Because he accepts propositions (2) and (3), he
draws the inference that God does not save some of those whom
God could have saved. He then merely asks the obvious question:
If God does not save some of those whom God could have saved—
if, for example, God has "deprived many peoples of the light of his
gospel while others enjoyed it"—how can anyone contend that God
really wills the salvation of all? In this way, Calvin simply deduces

---

[7]John Calvin, *Institutes of the Christian Religion*, Bk. III, Ch. XXIV,
Sec. 16.

[8]*Institutes*, Bk. III, Ch. XXIV, Sec. 15.

his interpretation of the text from the Augustinian picture that he brings to the text and thus imposes upon it.

Perhaps we are now in a position to see why exegetical disputes between those who operate from different theological frameworks are apt to seem so futile. To Arminians and universalists, it will no doubt seem as if the Augustinians have simply rejected the plain teaching of Scripture that God at least wills the salvation of all. To Augustinians and Arminians, however, it will likewise seem as if the universalists have rejected the plain teaching of Scripture concerning the reality of eternal punishment. And to Augustinians and universalists, it will seem as if the Arminians have rejected the plain teaching of Scripture that God is *almighty* in the sense that none of his redemptive purposes can be thwarted.

When fully developed, moreover, each of our three positions will include standard and well-rehearsed ways of handling its own set of difficult texts. Just as Augustine and Calvin interpret the statement that God "desires everyone to be saved" to mean something like: "God desires all of *the elect*--that is, some persons from all classes--to be saved," so the Arminians will interpret the statement that God "accomplishes all things according his counsel and will" to mean something like: "God accomplishes *everything he is able to accomplish* according to his counsel and will." And similarly for the universalists: They will interpret the statement that some sinners "will go away into eternal punishment" to mean something like: "In the coming age God himself will punish some sinners"; and they will deny in particular that the Greek expression "εἰς κόλασιν αἰώνιον," which the King James Bible translates as "into everlasting punishment," carries any implication of *unending punishment* (see below for a fuller explanation). Each position, in other words, will have a standard way of "saving the appearances," of explaining (or explaining away) its own set of difficult texts in the Bible.

Choosing Between the Three Pictures

There is, perhaps, a twofold reason why so many well-meaning Christians, all of whom look to the Bible as an authority, find it so difficult to come to an agreement on important theological matters: First, the Bible is not a single text with a single (human) author; it is instead a rich and diverse set of documents that appeal to the religious imagination in a variety of complex ways.   Given the diversity of interests and writing styles of its various authors, the history of some of its documents, and the variety of perspectives that it includes, a fertile imagination can almost always find a congenial way of putting things together.   Even wildly implausible interpretations of specific texts are apt to seem utterly compelling to some, as the adherents of various religious cults sometimes illustrate.   Second, the Bible is not a textbook in systematic theology either; it rarely, if ever, addresses our theological questions in a systematic way.   Not even St. Paul does this with any degree of persistence.   In any (traditional) systematic theology, you will find a systematic discussion of such Christian doctrines as the Incarnation, the Trinity, the Atonement, and the Final Judgment, but you will not find anything like that in the Bible, not even in the New Testament; and Christians now sometimes fail to appreciate, it seems to me, how easy it is simply to read the traditional formulation of these doctrines *back into* the New Testament.   Why, you might ask yourself, were the controversies over these doctrines in the early church so heated?—and why were they finally resolved (for a season) not by New Testament exegesis, but by the power of the sword?   Is not the obvious answer that honest and reasonable Christians, all of whom accepted the absolute authority of the Bible, began to read the New Testament in quite different ways?

I do not mean to suggest here that every reading of the New Testament--or, more specifically, every reading of St. Paul—is as good as any other; far from it.   Some things in the New Testament—for example, the Pauline claim that God raised Christ from the dead—seem to me clear and undeniable; and beyond that, the New Testament provides decisive grounds, I shall argue in subsequent chapters, for choosing between our three pictures of God. But I do mean to suggest this: A theological interpretation of the Bible as a whole is as much an art, as much a work of the imagination, and as much a product of philosophical reasoning as it is of historical and linguistic study.   Just as proponents of the geocentric theory of the solar system found many ways to account for the anomalous behavior of planets, so those who interpret the Bible from the perspective of a given system of theology inevitably find many ways to account for anomalous texts in the Bible. There is, no doubt, a point at which interpretation passes over into systematic distortion; indeed, I shall argue that Augustinian theology does just that. But even in cases of systematic distortion, one cannot document such distortion simply by pointing to this or that text in the Bible. Neither can one undermine the apparent biblical warrant for any of our three pictures simply by pointing to its own set of difficult texts. Instead, one must tackle an entire system of interpretation, a way of putting things together, including the theological and philosophical assumptions that lie behind it; and one must somehow demonstrate a better way of putting things together.

Accordingly, in the following chapters I shall try to demonstrate that one of our three pictures, namely the universalist picture, is superior to the other two in two crucial respects: (i) It both accords with and illuminates the theology of the New Testament better than the other two do, and (ii) it avoids some serious problems of inconsistency and incoherence implicit in the other two. I shall take up each of these points in turn. In the balance of Part II, I shall set forth a positive case for reading the New Testament along universalist lines. Most Christians today have some idea of how to read the New Testament from either an Augustinian or an Arminian perspective, but too few have any idea at all of how to read it from a universalist perspective. And that more than anything else explains, I believe, the widespread assumption that universalism is heretical. Then, in Part III of the essay, I shall explore some issues of coherence and logical consistency. I shall argue that Augustinian theology is deeply incoherent and riddled with logical impossibilities, that the Arminian alternative, though perhaps more reasonable, ultimately rests upon an incoherent conception of human freedom, and that only the universalist picture, therefore, can fully satisfy the demands of logical consistency.

5. ST. PAUL'S UNIVERSALISM

> "When all things are subjected to him, then the Son himself will also be subjected to the one who put all things in subjection under him, so that God may be all in all."
>
> St. Paul

Let us now begin to consider the positive case for a universalist reading of the New Testament. I shall contend that the universalism of the New Testament is not only all pervasive, but clear and obvious as well. It emerges most clearly, perhaps, in the letters of Paul, in part because Paul addresses the issue more systematically than other writers do, but it is also implicit in the theme of victory and triumph that pervades the entire New Testament. It is so clear, I shall argue, that in the end we must try to account for this mystery: Why is it that so many, including perhaps a majority of scholars in the West, seem to have missed it?

Perhaps "missed it" is the wrong expression, however. The real mystery is why so many have failed to *appreciate* the universalism of the New Testament and why so many have tried to *explain it away*. For no one who reads the New Testament carefully could possibly miss the many passages that display the theme of victory and triumph and at least *appear*, when taken in their own context, to have a clear universalistic thrust. Paul, for example, speaks eloquently of the triumph of God's sovereign love; again and again, we find in his letters explicit statements to the effect that God will eventually bring all things into subjection to Christ and reconcile all things in Christ and bring life to all persons through Christ. As we shall see, these statements are neither obscure nor incidental; indeed, the lengths to which some have gone to explain them away is itself a testimony to their clarity and power. But there is, of course, another prominent theme in the New Testament as well, namely that of God's judgment and wrath; and the failure to understand this second theme sometimes induces people to ignore, or even to explain away, the all-pervasive theme of victory and triumph. The irony is that Paul himself explains exactly how to harmonize the theme of judgment with that of victory and triumph, but his explanation is so unexpected and so counter to some deeply entrenched ways of thinking that we are apt to miss it altogether. And if we do miss it, we are not likely to appreciate fully the theme of triumph.

Accordingly, in this chapter I shall examine some of the passages in the Pauline corpus that display the theme of triumph. I shall argue, first, that the standard ways of explaining them away are untenable, and second, that Paul clearly did anticipate a time when all created persons would be reconciled to God. I shall argue further that, if we understand the theme of judgment in the way Paul does, we shall no longer be tempted to find a doctrine of everlasting punishment, or even everlasting separation, in it. Neither shall we be tempted to water down the all-pervasive theme of triumph. My aim in this and the following chapters, however, is not to refute every conceivable argument against a universalist interpretation of the New Testament; it is rather to illustrate a way of putting things together. For in the end, I believe, it is a failure of the imagination—an imagination crippled by fear—and an inability to see how to fit things together from a universalist perspective that lies behind many of the faulty and confused exegetical arguments in the Bible commentaries. Even more important than the details of specific arguments, therefore, is the matter of perspective, and it is a complete transformation of perspective that I would here hope to encourage.

"Justification and life for all"

I begin with a remarkable assertion found in the fifth chapter of Romans: "Therefore just as one man's trespass led to condemnation [or doom] for all, so one man's act of righteousness leads to justification and life for all" (5:18). How should we understand such an assertion? To all appearances, Paul here identifies one "all"—that is, all human beings—and makes two distinct but parallel statements about that one "all"; and to all appearances, the second of these statements implies that all human beings shall receive "justification and life" and hence shall eventually be reconciled to God. But our text is, of course, a single sentence, lifted from a context; and as we all know, we cannot finally determine the meaning of a sentence apart from the context in which it occurs. So let us ask this question: Are there good reasons either in the immediate context of our text or in the wider context of Paul's thought for believing that Paul did not intend to say what his sentence, taken in isolation, *appears* to say? I think not, but many are those who disagree.

A popular strategy among conservatives at this point is to do an exhaustive (and, I should think, exhausting) word study: Look at every use of the word "all" in the New Testament, and try to find instances where it either does not literally mean *all* or where there is an understood (but unstated) limit to its scope. Fortunately, we need not actually carry out such a study in order to predict its likely results. When a storefront sign declares, "Going out of business. Everything must be sold!" we understand that "everything" does not include the cash registers and sales personnel;[1] and similarly, when Jesus tells his disciples that "you will be hated by all because of my name" (Luke 21:17), we understand that "all" does not include John's hating Peter or, sillier still, Peter's hating Peter. So the desired examples are not difficult to find. According to Loraine Boettner, "In some fifty places throughout the New Testament the words 'all' and 'every' are used in a limited sense";[2] and though some of Boettner's examples seem to me confused, we can let that pass. After citing his examples, Boettner concludes, without further argument, that "the doctrine of universal redemption cannot be based on the words 'all' or 'every' or the phrase 'all men.'"[3]

But how does any of this bear on the correct interpretation of *our* text, namely Romans 5:18? There are several difficulties here.

---

[1]I borrow the example from one of my own teachers in graduate school, Merrill Ring.

[2]Loraine Boettner, *Studies in Theology* (Grand Rapids: Wm. B. Eerdmans Publishing Company, 1947), p. 321.

[3]*Ibid.*

First, Boettner lifts almost all of his examples from the gospel narratives, and narrative is just where one would expect to find uses of
"all" in which the scope of its reference is less than precise ("When
the Portland Trailblazers passed over the chance to draft Michael
Jordan, they disappointed all of Oregon"). Though Paul's theological arguments are riddled with statements about "all human beings"
and it is Paul's view that is supposedly at issue here, Boettner fails
to cite a single example from one of these contexts. And that is
surely unfortunate, to say the least. Suppose that a future racist
society should come to regard our country's Declaration of Independence as a sacred document, and suppose further that some
scholars in this society, being determined to explain away the statement that "all men are created equal," should scour other letters and
documents of the time in order to find instances in which "all" does
not literally mean *all*. We might suppose that they find "some fifty
places," perhaps in some narratives of the Revolutionary War,
where "the words 'all' and 'every' are used in a limited sense."
Would this have any bearing on the meaning of "all men" in the
statement, "all men are created equal," as it appears in the Declaration of Independence? It is hard to see why it should. And it is no
less hard to see how Boettner's strategy is even relevant to the
correct interpretation of either Romans 5:18 or any of the other universalistic texts in Paul.

Second, when we focus on the Apostle himself, we encounter
this interesting fact: Every time he uses "all" in the context of some
theological discourse, he seems to have in mind a clear reference
class, stated or unstated, and he refers distributively to every member of that class. When he says that God "accomplishes *all* things
according to his counsel and will" (Ephesians 1:11),[4] he is not, it is
true, literally talking about everything, including numbers and
propositions and sets of properties; he is talking about every *event*.
Everything that happens in the world, he is saying, falls under
God's providential control. And similarly for Paul's remark that

---

[4]Here I adopt the traditional assumption that Paul was the author of
Ephesians, but nothing of substance hangs on it, since the quotation
from Romans 8:28 is of similar form and unquestionably Pauline.

"*all* things work together for good to them that love God" (Romans 8:28—KJV); here he means not just *some* events, but *all* events. Or again, when Paul asserts that "God has put *all* things in subjection" to Christ (I Corinthians 15:27), he clearly has in mind all *created* things; and so, as he points out himself, this does not include the Father (15:28). But it does include every member of the class he has in mind. And the same is true of his assertion that "*all* have sinned and fall short of the glory of God" (Romans 3:23). This "all" may not include dogs and birds and unfallen angels, as well as human beings; but it does include all the descendants of Adam, or more accurately, all the *merely human* descendants of Adam. Paul excludes Jesus Christ from this "all," because he did not think of Christ as merely human—*fully* human, perhaps, but not *merely* human. In all of these cases, the scope of "all" is clear; indeed, I have been unable to find a single example, drawn from Paul's theological writings, in which Paul makes a universal statement and the scope of its reference is unduly fuzzy or less than clear. Paul's writing may be cumbersome at times, but he was not nearly as sloppy a writer (or a thinker) as some of his commentators, in their zeal to interpret him for us, would make him out to be.

Finally, and most important of all, we must do justice to the grammatical evidence that our text itself presents. Note first the parallel structure of the sentence: "Therefore just as one man's trespass led to condemnation for all, so one man's act of righteousness leads to justification and life for all." This is typically Pauline. In the eleventh chapter of Romans, Paul again writes: "For God has imprisoned all in disobedience so that he may be merciful to all" (11:32); and in the fifteenth chapter of I Corinthians, he writes: "for as all die in Adam, so all will be made alive in Christ" (15:22). In each of these texts, we encounter a contrast between two universal statements, and in each case the first "all" seems to determine the scope of the second. Accordingly, when Paul asserts in Romans 5:18 that Christ's one "act of righteousness leads to justification and life for all," he evidently has in mind every descendant of Adam who stands under the judgment of condemnation; when he insists in Romans 11:32 that God is merciful to all, he has in mind every human being whom God has "shut up" to, or has "imprisoned" in, disobedience; and finally, when he asserts in I Corinthians 15:22 that "all will be made alive in Christ," he has in mind everyone who has died in Adam. The grammatical evidence here seems utterly decisive; you can reject it only if you are prepared to reject what is right there before your eyes. And though there seems to be no shortage of those who are prepared to do just that, the arguments one actually encounters have every appearance, it seems to me, of a grasping at straws.

Here is an example of what I mean. Following Charles Hodge, a number of commentators have sought to avoid the clear universalistic thrust of Romans 5:18 in the following way: First, they point to at least one exception—namely the man Jesus—to the first "all"; as Hodge himself put it: "Even the *all men* in the first clause, must be limited to those descended from Adam 'by ordinary generation.' It is not absolutely all" human beings.[5] Then, after finding this one *unstated* exception to the first "all," they (in effect) hold out for a vast number of additional exceptions to the second. But a little reflection will reveal that this entire line of reasoning is spurious, because it attributes an unwarranted theological significance to a perfectly familiar way of talking.

Observe first that Paul excludes Jesus Christ from the "all" of *both* clauses; even as Paul did not regard Jesus as having been condemned in Adam, neither did he regard Jesus as someone who receives the salvation that Jesus himself brings. So Hodge's claim is utterly irrelevant to this point: According to Paul, the very same "all" who were condemned in Adam received "justification and life" in Jesus Christ. Consider, moreover, a perfectly familiar way of talking. If I were to say: "Adam was the father of the entire human race and hence the father (or progenitor) of all men and women," would anyone take this to imply that Adam was the father of himself (or even of Eve)? Of course not. In most contexts, others would simply take the expression "all men and women" to *mean* "all men and women except Adam and Eve"; hence, in most

---

[5]Charles Hodge, *Commentary on the Epistle to the Romans* (New York: A. C. Armstrong and Son, 1896), p. 269.

contexts I would have no need to state the two obvious exceptions. And similarly for Paul: In virtually any soteriological context—that is, any context in which Paul has in view Christ's saving activity—he treats the expression "all human beings" as if it were shorthand for "all human beings except Christ" or, as already stated, "all the merely human descendants of Adam." As the agent of salvation, Jesus Christ obviously is not included in the "all" who are the object of his salvific actions; but just because this is so obvious, Paul had no need to state it in an explicit way. Nor does that one obvious exception justify additional exceptions; much less does it justify Hodge's conclusion that "the *all men* of the second clause is [not] co-extensive with the *all men* of the first."[6]

Consider the context of Romans 5:18 more carefully. In 5:12 Paul identifies the group or class he has in mind with great clarity; it is, he says, all human beings, or more accurately, all human beings who have sinned. Then, in vs. 15, he distinguishes within that single group or class between "the one" and "the many"—"the one" being Adam himself, who first sinned, and "the many" being those who died as a result Adam's sin. As John Murray points out:

> When Paul uses the expression "the many", he is not intending to delimit the denotation. The scope of "the many" must be the same as the "all men" of verses 12 and 18. He uses "the many" here, as in verse 19, for the purpose of contrasting more effectively "the one" and "the many", singularity and plurality—it was the trespass of the one", . . . but "the many" died as a result.[7]

In the same context, moreover, Paul insists that "the one," namely Adam, was "a type" of Jesus Christ (vs. 14), presumably because Jesus Christ, the second Adam, stands in the same relationship to "the many" as the first Adam did. But with this difference: "if the many died by the trespass of the one man, how much more did

[6]*Ibid.*, p. 268.

[7]John Murray, *Epistle of Paul to the Romans*, Vol. I (Grand Rapids: Eerdmans, 1960), p. 192-193.

God's grace and the gift that came by the grace of the one man,
Jesus Christ, overflow to the many!" (vs. 15—NIV). It seems to
me indisputable, therefore, that Paul had in mind one group of
individuals—"the many," which includes all human beings except
for the first and the second Adam—and he envisioned that each of
the two Adams stands in the same relationship to that one group of
individuals. The first Adam's act of disobedience brought doom
upon them all, but the second Adam's act of obedience undid the
doom and eventually brings justification and life to them all.

"So all will be made alive in Christ"

The explicit universalism of the fifth chapter of Romans is so
clear that even the proponents of everlasting punishment have
sometimes conceded, as Neal Punt does, that "Romans 5:18 and its
immediate context place no limitation on the universalistic thrust of
the second 'all men.'"[8] In opposition to absolute universalism,
therefore, Punt argues from the so-called "analogy of Scripture":
He in effect tries to find grounds elsewhere in the Bible for making
exceptions to the second "all" of Romans 5:18. As our discussion
in the previous chapter should already have suggested, however,
arguments from "the analogy of Scripture" are tricky and fraught
with difficulty; more often than not, they amount to little more than
a deduction from the picture of God that someone brings to the text.
Still, a legitimate question concerning Pauline thought as a whole is
whether we can find elsewhere in Paul's writings grounds for rejecting a universalistic interpretation of Romans 5:18. Not a few have
claimed that we can. According to John Murray:

> When we ask the question: Is it Pauline to posit universal
> salvation? the answer must be decisively negative (cf. II
> Thess. 1:8, 9). Hence we cannot interpret the apodosis in
> verse 18 [of Romans 5] in the sense of inclusive universal-
> ism, and it is consistent with sound canons of interpreta-
> tion to assume a restrictive implication. In I Cor. 15:22

---

[8]Neal Punt, *Unconditional Good News* (Grand Rapids: William B.
Eerdmans Co., 1980), p. 14.

Paul says, "As in Adam all die, even so in Christ shall all be made alive". As the context will demonstrate the apostle is here dealing with the resurrection to life, with those who are Christ's and will be raised at his coming. The "all" of the second clause is therefore restrictive in a way that the "all" in the first clause is not. In like manner in Rom. 5:18 we may and must recognize a restriction in the "all men" of the apodosis that is not present in the "all men" of the protasis.[9]

Like Punt, Murray seems to recognize that nothing in the immediate context of Romans 5:18 justifies any restriction upon its universalistic thrust; so like Punt, Murray appeals to the wider context of Pauline thought. As his decisive evidence against attributing "inclusive universalism" to Paul, Murray cites a text that we shall examine ourselves in the following chapter, II Thessalonians 1:8, 9. But Murray also considers I Corinthians 15:22, whose parallel structure so resembles that of Romans 5:18, and concerning this text he argues in the following way: As the context demonstrates, the second "all" of I Corinthians 15:22 is restricted to those who belong to Christ; therefore, despite the parallel structure of the sentence, the second "all" is more restrictive than the first. Because the structure of Romans 5:18 is so similar to that of I Corinthians 15:22, moreover, we may also conclude that the second "all" of Romans 5:18 is likewise more restrictive than the first.

The first part of Murray's argument, however, is a simple *non sequitur*. From the premise that the second "all" of I Corinthians 15:22 is restricted to those who belong to Christ, it simply does not follow that the second all is more restrictive than the first. To get that conclusion, one must make the additional assumption that the first "all" includes persons who will never belong to Christ—an assumption that not only begs the whole question of the correct interpretation of the passage, but also contradicts Paul's explicit claim, in the following verses, that everything shall eventually be brought into subjection to Christ. If anything, the second "all" of I Corinthians 15:22 is *less* restrictive than the first; for in the

---

[9]Murray, *Op. cit.*, p. 302.

following verses Paul immediately *expands* the second "all" to include not only every descendant of Adam (except Christ himself), but every competing will as well. Christ must continue to reign, Paul insists, until he finally brings *all things*, including every will and opposing power, into subjection to himself (15:24-27), and there is but one exception to this "all things," the Father himself (15:28). The last enemy that Christ shall destroy is death (15:27), which in the larger context of Paul's thought includes all separation from God. When Christ finally overcomes all separation from God, all persons will then be in subjection to Christ *in exactly the same sense* that Christ places himself in subjection to the Father (15:28)—a sense that, as I shall argue in the following section, clearly implies spontaneous and glad obedience. Then and only then will the Father truly be "all in all," because then and only then will all persons belong to him, or at least *know* that they belong to him, through his Son.

The most natural interpretation of I Corinthians 15:22, then, accords perfectly with the most natural interpretation of Romans 5:18: The very same "all" who died in Adam shall be made alive in Christ. Against this interpretation, Larry Lacy has written:

> Talbott believes that the theme of 15:22 is the affirmation that all those who have died in Adam will be made alive in Christ. But a close examination of the immediate context reveals, I believe, that this is not the theme which is in Paul's mind. Rather, the theme in Paul's mind in the immediately preceding verses and in the immediately following verse is the theme that the resurrection of believers is dependent on the resurrection of Christ, that is, it is only *in Christ* that believers shall be made alive. . . . We see this confirmed in v. 23, where Paul says "Christ, the first fruits, then at his coming those who belong to Christ."[10]

Now Lacy is certainly right about this: One "theme in Paul's mind" when he wrote the fifteenth chapter of I Corinthians was that

---

[10]Larry Lacy, "Talbott on Paul as a Universalist," *Christian Scholar's Review* XXI:4 (June, 1992), p. 402.

"the resurrection of believers is dependent upon the resurrection of Christ . . .." But why should anyone believe that this theme somehow excluded from Paul's mind the additional idea that "all those who have died in Adam will be made alive in Christ"? Why not attribute *both* ideas to Paul? What Lacy evidently fails to appreciate is that in verses 20-28, or right in the middle of the discourse on resurrection, Paul works the theme of resurrection into a much larger context—one that includes, as we have just seen, the bringing of all things into subjection to Christ; indeed, the hope of the resurrection itself depends upon the hope that all things shall be brought into subjection to Christ. Like Murray and many other commentators, Lacy considers only two stages in a process that Paul describes as having three stages. After informing us that "in Christ shall all be made alive," Paul goes on to say: "But each in his own order" (vs. 24). It is as if Paul has in mind the image of a procession, and he quickly lists three segments of the procession: At the head of the procession is Christ, the first fruits; behind him are those who belong to Christ at his coming; and behind them are the remainder—that is, those at the end of the procession—who are there when Christ "hands over the kingdom to God the Father, after he has destroyed every ruler and every authority and power" (vs. 24). Of course Lacy would no doubt reject my assumption that "$\epsilon\overset{,,}{\tau}\alpha$ τὸ τέλος" (literally "then the end") is correctly interpreted as "then, the remainder." For though this *is* a documented use of the Greek expression, and it *is* what the structure of Paul's list of three stages suggests, it is also controversial; hence, I shall not insist upon it here. For even if we understand "then the end" to mean something like "then comes the end of the ages or the end of redemptive history," Paul makes one point absolutely clear: The end will not come until Christ's victory and triumph are complete; that is, until "he has put all his enemies under his feet" (vs. 25), until he has destroyed the last enemy, which is death (vs. 26), and until "all things are subjected to him" (vs. 28)

We thus approach the very crux of the matter: How did Paul himself conceive of Christ's triumph, of the defeat of Christ's enemies, and of the final destruction of sinners? As we shall see in the following sections, nothing short of universal reconciliation could possibly qualify, within Paul's scheme of things, as a triumph; and neither could anything short of personal redemption qualify as the defeat of an enemy or as the destruction of a sinner.

"And through him God was pleased to reconcile to himself all things"

I have claimed that universal reconciliation is a central and pervasive theme in Paul. So far, we have seen that in the fifth chapter of Romans Paul spells out his universalism with great care and precision, and in the fifteenth chapter of I Corinthians he anticipates a time when every competing will shall be brought into subjection to Christ and all those persons in subjection to Christ shall be made alive. Let us now consider two texts that may help us to understand somewhat better what all of this means. In his letter to the Philippians, Paul again anticipates a time when "at the name of Jesus every knee should bend, in heaven and on earth and under the earth, and every tongue confess that Jesus Christ is Lord" (2:10-11); and in his letter to the Colossians, he goes so far as to declare that the very same "all things" created in Christ—including "all things in heaven and on earth . . . visible or invisible, whether thrones or dominions or powers" (1:16)—shall in the end be reconciled to God in Christ (1:20).[11] One could hardly ask for a more specific statement; Paul here applies the concept of reconciliation, which is explicitly a redemptive concept, not only to all human beings, but to all the spiritual principalities and dominions as well.

It is within this context, I believe, that Paul himself understood the nature of Christ's victory, the defeat of Christ's enemies, and the destruction of sin. But consider how some have tried to limit and minimize the victory. A standard argument at this point is that in Colossians 1:20 and Philippians 2:10-11 Paul had in mind, not reconciliation in the full redemptive sense, but a pacification of evil powers, a mere subjugation of them against their will. Peter T.

---

[11]Even if Paul was not the author of Colossians, as some scholars have argued, the old hymn or creedal statement reproduced in 1:15-20 is surely one that Paul would have endorsed.

O'Brien, a respected New Testament scholar of conservative out-
look, puts the argument this way:

> The reconciliation of the principalities and powers is in
> mind. They are one category whatever others are included.
> Yet these forces are shown as submitting against their will
> to a power they cannot resist. They are reconciled through
> subjugation (cf. I Cor 15:28) . . ..
>
> Although all things will *finally* unite to bow in the name of
> Jesus and to acknowledge him as Lord (Phil 2:10, 11), it is
> not to be assumed that this will be done gladly by all. For
> as the words following the hymn (Col 1:21-23) indicate,
> the central purpose of Christ's work of making peace has
> to do with those who have heard the Word of reconcilia-
> tion and gladly accepted it. To assert that verse 20 [of
> Colossians 1] points to a universal reconciliation in which
> every man will finally enjoy celestial bliss is an unwar-
> ranted assumption.[12]

In the second paragraph of this quotation, we encounter the
same confusion that we previously observed in Murray. For like
Murray, O'Brien adopts a true premise: that in Pauline thought
only "those who have heard the Word of reconciliation and [have]
gladly accepted it" will experience reconciliation in the full redemptive sense. But that premise, which Christian universalists also
accept, hardly provides a *reason* for denying to Paul the view that
someday all will gladly bow before their Lord. So here we have, it
seems, just one more *non sequitur*. The argument of the first
paragraph, however, is perhaps more cogent and runs as follows:
According to Paul, at least some spiritual beings, such as Satan and
his cohorts, will never be reconciled to God in the full redemptive
sense. Therefore, when Paul speaks of the reconciliation of "all
things"—all things including these spiritual beings—he does not
have in mind reconciliation in the full redemptive sense; and when
he says that every tongue shall confess Jesus Christ as Lord, he
does not necessarily mean that everyone will do it gladly.

---

[12]Peter T. O'Brien, *Word Bible Commentary Volume 44: Colossians,
Philemon* (Waco: Word Books, Publisher, 1982), pp. 56-57.

Is O'Brien right about this? Does Paul in fact teach in I Corinthians 15:28 that some spiritual beings will merely be subjugated and not reconciled to God in the full redemptive sense? Before addressing the specific exegetical question, I want first to suggest that O'Brien has in fact attributed to Paul an incoherent idea. The contradiction in the very idea of reconciliation through subjugation is no superficial matter. If the powers and principalities of which Paul speaks are *competing wills*, then as a matter of logic these powers and principalities could never be *entirely* in subjection to Christ against their will; for if they should be subjugated against their will, then their *will* would precisely not be in subjection to Christ. Here one is reminded, perhaps, of John Milton's Satan who, even after God defeats him in battle, finds that "the mind and spirit remains / Invincible."

> What though the field be lost?
> All is not lost; the unconquerable Will,
> And study of revenge, immortal hate,
> And courage never to submit or yield:
> And what else is not to be overcome?
> That Glory never shall his wrath or might
> Extort from me.[13]

As Milton's Satan illustrates, perhaps contrary to Milton's own intention, there is but one way for God to defeat a rebellious will and to bring it into subjection to Christ; he must so transform the will that it voluntarily places itself in subjection to Christ. For so long as a single will remains in a state of rebellion against Christ, so long as a single person is able to cling to his or her hatred of God, at least one power in the universe—the power of that person's will—is not yet in subjection to Christ. As a paradigm of subjection, therefore, consider Christ's own subjection to the Father, as Paul depicts it in I Corinthians 15:28. If Christ's will were in conflict with the Father's on some important issue, if he *wanted* to act contrary to the Father's will but simply lacked the power, would he truly be in subjection to the Father? Of course not. The very

---

[13]*Paradise Lost*, Bk. I, 105-111.

suggestion seems incoherent. And yet, in the very passage O'Brien cites, I Corinthians 15:28, Paul draws a parallel between the subjection of all things to Christ and Christ's subjection of himself to the Father; so that very passage shows, it seems to me, that Paul did not in fact hold the incoherent idea that O'Brien attributes to him.

And similarly for Philippians 2:10-11 and Colossians 1:15-20. When Paul suggests that every tongue shall *confess* that Jesus Christ is Lord, he chooses a verb that throughout the Septuagint is used to imply not only confession, but the offer of praise and thanksgiving as well; and as J. B. Lightfoot points out, the verb has such implications of praise "in the very passage of Isaiah [45:23] which St. Paul adapts . . .."[14] Now a ruling monarch may indeed force a subject to bow against that subject's will, may even force the subject to utter certain words; but praise and thanksgiving can come only from the heart, as the Apostle was no doubt clear-headed enough to discern. Quite apart from the matter of praise, moreover, either those who bow before Jesus Christ and *declare openly* that he is Lord do so sincerely and by their own choice or they do not. If they do this sincerely and by their own choice, then there can be but one reason: They too have been reconciled to God. If they do not do this sincerely and by their own choice, if they are forced to make obeisance against their will, then their actions are merely fraudulent and bring no glory to God; a Hitler may take pleasure in *forcing* his defeated enemies to make obeisance against their will, but a God who honors the *truth* could not possibly participate in such a fraud.

There remains an even more important exegetical consideration. In Colossians 1:20, Paul himself identifies the *kind* of reconciliation he has in mind; he does so with the expression "making peace through the blood of his cross." Similarly, in Philippians 2:6-11, Paul himself explains the nature of Christ's exaltation; he does so by pointing to Christ's humble obedience "to the point of death—even death on a cross." Now just what is the power of the

---

[14]J. B. Lightfoot, *Saint Paul's Epistle to the Philippians* (Grand Rapids: Zondervan, 1963), p. 115.

cross, according to Paul? Is it the power of a conquering hero to compel his enemies to obey him against their will? If that had been Paul's doctrine, it would have been strange indeed. For God had no need of a crucifixion to *compel* obedience; he was quite capable of doing that all along. According to the New Testament as a whole, therefore, God sent his Son into the world, not as a conquering hero, but as a suffering servant; and the power that Jesus unleashed as he bled on the cross was precisely the power of self-giving love, the power to overcome evil by transforming the wills and renewing the minds of the evil ones themselves. And Paul not only endorses this idea; he also tells us exactly what he means by "reconciliation" in the two verses following Colossians 1:20, citing as an example his own readers: "And you who were once estranged and hostile in mind, doing evil deeds, he has now *reconciled* in his fleshly body through death, so as to present you holy and blameless and irre-proachable before him" (1:21-22—emphasis mine).[15] So the blood of the cross does bring peace, but not the artificial kind that some tyrannical power might impose; it brings true peace, the kind that springs from within and requires reconciliation in the full redemp-tive sense. It seems to me without question, therefore, that Paul did envision a time when all persons will be reconciled to God in the full redemptive sense.

"That he may be merciful to all"

I have already mentioned one reason so many find it difficult to take Paul's universalism seriously: Many think it impossible to square such universalism with the theme of divine judgment that we find not only in Paul, but throughout the Bible generally. The God of the Bible, they like to remind us, is not only merciful; he is also just. But where is the biblical warrant, I would ask in return, for thinking that divine justice requires something that divine mercy does not, or that divine mercy permits something that divine justice does not? Where is the biblical warrant for thinking that mercy and

---

[15]I leave it to the reader to puzzle out how anyone could cite this passage, as O'Brien does, on behalf of the view that Paul has in mind something less than reconciliation in the full redemptive sense.

justice are separate and distinct attributes of God? At this point, I fear, we sometimes read our own ideas (and our own philosophical misconceptions) into the Bible. *We* think that mercy is one attribute and justice another, so we read this into the Bible; *we* think that God's love is an attitude of one kind and his wrath an attitude of an opposite kind, so we also read this into the Bible; *we* think that God punishes for one kind of a reason and forgives for another, and we tend to picture God as a schizophrenic whose justice pushes him in one direction and whose love pushes him in another; so we again read all of this into the Bible. When we turn to St. Paul, however, we find that he challenges this whole way of thinking.

Perhaps the best example of such a challenge is the eleventh chapter of Romans. For here Paul explicitly states that God's severity towards the disobedient, his judgment of sin, even his willingness to blind the eyes and harden the hearts of the disobedient, are expressions of a more fundamental quality, that of mercy, which is itself an expression of his purifying love. In Romans 11:7 he thus writes: "What then? Israel failed to obtain what it was seeking. The elect obtained it, but the rest were hardened" (or blinded). He then asks, "have they [the nonremnant who were hardened or blinded] stumbled so as to fall?" and his answer is most emphatic: "By no means!" (11:11). By the end of the following verse, he is already speaking of their full inclusion: "Now if their stumbling means riches for the world, and if their defeat means riches for the Gentiles, how much more will their full inclusion mean!" (11:12).[16] And three verses later he is hinting that their

---

[16]In order to avoid the implication that God hardens the heart as an expression of mercy, some commentators have insisted that Paul here speaks of Israel as a corporate whole. John Piper thus writes: "Notice that this [i.e., the "they" in 11:11] is not a reference to all Jews but to Israel as a corporate whole conceived of as an entity that endures from generation to generation made up of different individuals from time to time" ("Universalism in Romans 9–11? Testing the Exegesis of Thomas Talbott," *The Reformed Journal*, Vol. 33, Issue 7, p. 12). But that will never do. For in 11:7 Paul mentions three groups of people: Israel or the nation as a corporate whole, "the elect" or the faithful remnant, and "the rest," that is, the nonremnant Jews who were hardened. Now the

acceptance will mean "life from the dead" (9:15). He then generalizes the whole thing: God blinded the eyes and hardened the hearts of the unbelieving Jews, we discover, as a means by which *all* of Israel might be saved (Romans 11:25-26)—all of Israel including those who were blinded and hardened. There is simply no way, so far as I can tell, to escape the universalistic implication here. The *specific* point that Paul makes in Romans 11 is this: Though the unbelieving Jews were in some sense "enemies of God" (11:28), they nonetheless became "disobedient in order that they too may now receive mercy" (11:31-NIV). But the general principle (of which the specific point is but an instance) is even more glorious: "For God has imprisoned *all* in disobedience so that he may be merciful to *all*" (11:32—my emphasis).

According to Paul, therefore, God is always and everywhere merciful, but we sometimes *experience* his mercy (or purifying love) as severity, judgment, punishment. When we live a life of obedience, we experience his mercy as kindness; when we live a life of disobedience, we experience it as severity (see 11:22). Paul himself calls this a mystery (11:25) and admits that God's ways are, in just this respect, "inscrutable" and "unsearchable" (11:33),

---

antecedent of "they" in 11:11 cannot be the faithful remnant; they are not the ones who stumbled and were hardened. Neither can it be the nation as a corporate whole, for Paul has just distinguished between two groups within that corporate whole: the faithful remnant who did not stumble and were not hardened, and "the rest" who did stumble and were hardened. Accordingly, the antecedent of "they" in 11:11 must be "the rest," the nonremnant Jews, the very ones whom God had hardened. Even John Murray admits this. Murray thus asks (*op. cit.*, p. 75, n. 18): "Is not the denotation of those in view [in verse 11] the same as those mentioned in verse 7: 'the rest were hardened'? And is not Paul thinking here of those in verse 22: 'toward them that fell, severity'?" The answer is, "yes" and "yes." But since Murray cannot believe that God's severity, or his hardening of a heart, is an expression of mercy, he insists that "those who stumbled did fall with ultimate consequences." The "denotation of those in view" in verse 11, however, is not only "the same as those mentioned in verse 7"; it is also the same as those mentioned in verse 12: those whose "full inclusion" will mean so much more than the stumble which makes their full inclusion possible.

but nothing could be clearer than his own glorious summation of the whole thing in 11:32. If the first "all" of 11:32 refers distributively to *all* the merely human descendants of Adam, if all are "imprisoned" in disobedience, then so also does the second; they are all objects of divine mercy as well. And if one should insist, as some have in an effort to escape universalism, that neither "all" literally means "all without exception," the obvious rejoinder is that here, no less than in Romans 5:18 and I Corinthians 15:22, the parallelism is even more important than the scope of "all." According to Paul, the *very ones* whom God "shuts up" to disobedience—whom he blinds, or hardens, or cuts off for a season—are those to whom he is merciful; his former act is but the first expression of the latter, and the latter is the goal of the former. God hardens a heart in order to produce, in the end, a contrite spirit, blinds those who are unready for the truth in order to bring them ultimately to the truth, "imprisons all in disobedience so that he may be merciful to all."

Romans 11:32, where Paul declares the full extent of God's mercy, is the culmination of a theological argument that begins in chapter 9 and extends through chapter 11. It is here that Paul takes up the problem of Jewish unbelief and systematically defends his view that, contrary to what many of his kinsmen believed, God has every right to extend his mercy to all human beings including Gentiles. But though his argument *as a whole* is an explicit argument against limited election, against the pernicious idea that God restricts his mercy to a chosen few, we also confront this irony: Many commentators have interpreted the early stages of his argument (in chapter 9) as precisely an argument *for* such a restriction. And perhaps that is not surprising. For in the early stages of his argument, Paul does say some things that, if removed from the context of his full argument, might seem to imply that God does indeed restrict his mercy to a chosen few. For one thing, Paul gives several examples here of the severity of God's mercy—as, for instance, when he reminds his readers that according to the story in Exodus God himself had hardened Pharaoh's heart (9:17-18). In addition, Paul appears to draw a sharp distinction between (what he calls) vessels of mercy prepared beforehand for glory and vessels of wrath fit for destruction (9:22), and some have read into this a distinction between the elect and the non-elect. But no one who follows Paul's argument to its conclusion in Romans 11 will likely confuse the *severity* of God's mercy with the *absence* of mercy; nor will they likely confuse the distinction between vessels of mercy and vessels of wrath with a distinction between those who are, and those who are not, objects of God's mercy.

Consider first the severity of God's mercy towards Pharaoh: the hardening of Pharaoh's heart. One can find, it seems to me, a good deal of nonsense about this in the literature. Some speak as if the hardening of Pharaoh's heart were an instance of God's causing a man to sin;[17] others, in an effort to do justice to our moral intuitions, insist that Pharaoh first hardened his own heart and then God hardened it further.[18] Before jumping to conclusions of any kind, however, one should perhaps first consider what God's hardening of a heart *means*. The Hebrew word most commonly used in the Exodus account to which Paul refers literally means "to strengthen"; it is the same word that appears throughout the Old Testament in the formula "Be of good courage."[19] God simply strengthened Pharaoh's heart and gave him the courage to stand in the face of the "signs and wonders" performed in Egypt. God consistently hardened (or strengthened) Pharaoh's heart in connection with a specific command: "Let my people go!" Why would a merciful God do that? In the context of the story in Exodus, one possibility is this: Though Pharaoh had exalted himself over the Hebrews for years, he was essentially a coward who could never have stood the pressure, apart from the strength that God gave him, once things began to get difficult in Egypt. It is often that way; cowardice often prevents us from doing the wrong that we in fact wish to do. In the case of Pharaoh, God gave him the strength not

---

[17]See, for instance, Loraine Boettner, *The Reformed Doctrine of Predestination* (The Presbyterian and Reformed Publishing Co., 1968), pp. 222-223.

[18]See, for example, Edward John Carnell, *Christian Commitment* (New York: The MacMillan Company, 1957), p. 236.

[19]See, for example, 2 Samuel 10:12, 1 Chronicles 19:13, Ezra 10:4, Psalm 27:14, 31:24, Isaiah 41:6 in the King James Version.

to be cowed too easily; God gave him the *courage* to sin, if you will, but it hardly follows that God was the sufficient cause of the sin itself. And the hardening of Pharaoh's heart was an expression of mercy in two respects: First, it revealed to Pharaoh the destructive nature of his own sin, and second, it revealed to the Egyptians something of the nature of God. For as the Lord declared to Moses, "The Egyptians shall know that I am the Lord, when I stretch out my hand against Egypt and bring the Israelites out from among them" (Exodus 7:5). These great historical events no doubt brought real hardship to the Egyptians, even as they did to the Israelites; but they were also a revelation to the Egyptians, even as they were to the Israelites. Within the context of Paul's own argument, moreover, God's actions towards Pharaoh and the Egyptians were no different from his actions towards the Israelites or anyone else; if, at one time or another, God "imprisons" all the descendants of Adam in disobedience and does so for a merciful purpose, it is hardly surprising that he should do the same thing to Pharaoh.

Consider next Paul's distinction between vessels of mercy and vessels of wrath and why he could not possibly have in mind a distinction between those who are, and those who are not, objects of God's mercy. In the first place, the vessels of wrath of which he speaks in 9:22 are the unbelieving Jews, the very ones concerning whom he later makes two claims: (i) that "as regards election they are beloved, for the sake of their ancestors" (11:28), and (ii) that "they have now become disobedient in order that they too might receive mercy" (11:31-NIV). In Paul's scheme of things, therefore, those who are vessels of wrath, no less than those who are vessels of mercy, are objects of God's mercy; it is just that, for a person's own good, God's purifying love sometimes takes the form of wrath. Secondly, if Paul was indeed the author of Ephesians, then he clearly assumes that the *same individual* can be a vessel of wrath at one time and a vessel of mercy at another; he also assumes that every individual who is now a vessel of mercy was at one time a vessel of wrath. For as he says in his letter to the Ephesians, using a slightly different metaphor, all Christians were at one time "children of wrath" (Ephesians 2:3). But then, if Paul himself is a vessel of mercy who was at one time a vessel of wrath (call him Saul), a paraphrase that captures part of the meaning of 9:22-23 is this:

> What if God, desiring to show his wrath and to make known his power, has endured with much patience Saul, a vessel of wrath fit for destruction, in order to make known the riches of his glory for Paul, a vessel of mercy which he has prepared beforehand for glory. . .?

And what this paraphrase illustrates is again only what Paul himself explicitly states in 11-32; namely, that those whom God has "imprisoned" in disobedience—the vessels of wrath whom he endures with much patience—are precisely those to whom he is merciful.   By literally shutting sinners up to their disobedience and requiring them to endure the consequences of their own rebellion, God reveals the self-defeating nature of evil and shatters the illusions that make evil choices possible in the first place.

Some Concluding Remarks

In this chapter, we have examined some of the passages in the Pauline corpus that display Paul's belief in the ultimate triumph of God's love and mercy. Though the weight of tradition lies on the side of those who would try to explain these passages away, the actual arguments we encounter in the tradition are remarkably weak.   One of the most common arguments rests upon a mere confusion. First, someone points out that, according to Paul, only those who belong to Christ, or only those who gladly confess that Jesus Christ is Lord, or only those who repent of their sin will be saved; no unrepentant murderer, for example, can enter the Kingdom of God.   Then, the person draws the faulty inference that, according to Paul, not all sinners will be saved. But as I have tried to show in this chapter, that is a simple *non sequitur*. Paul's whole point is that the day is coming when all persons will belong to Christ, all will gladly confess that Jesus Christ is Lord, and all will have repented of their sin. For though Paul nowhere endorses the absurd view that God will reward unrepentant sinners with eternal bliss, he does endorse the view that the same God who transformed

Saul, the chief of sinners, into Paul, a slave of Christ, can and eventually will do the same thing for every other sinner as well.

Now if God is truly merciful to all, as Paul insists in the eleventh chapter of Romans—if God's severity towards the disobedient, no less than his kindness towards the obedient, is an expression of his mercy—then we must adjust our understanding of divine punishment accordingly. We must come to appreciate that, according to Paul, God punishes sin for exactly the same reason he sent his Son into the world: to redeem or reclaim those who have fallen into sin. Such a view is logically compatible with many things, including fierce punishment in the next life; but it is *not* compatible with a doctrine of *everlasting* punishment. So the full weight of what we have argued in this chapter provides a powerful reason to deny that Paul himself believed in everlasting punishment. But at this point someone may ask: Does not at least one text traditionally attributed to Paul, namely II Thessalonians 1:9, speak of the "eternal destruction" of the wicked?—and does not this text seem to imply a doctrine of everlasting punishment? Certainly many commentators have thought so. As I have already mentioned, John Murray cites this text as his decisive evidence against a universalistic interpretation of Romans 5:18; and in a similar vein, Charles Hodge writes:

> As, however, not only the Scriptures generally, but Paul himself, distinctly teach that all men are not to be saved, as in 2 Thess. I.9, this [universalistic] interpretation [of Romans 5:18] cannot be admitted by any who acknowledge the inspiration of the Bible.[20]

What are we to make of such an argument? In the following chapter, I shall argue that Murray and Hodge have misinterpreted II Thessalonians 1:9 entirely: Not only does this text carry no implication that some persons will be lost forever; we have every reason to believe that, within the context of Paul's own thought, the concept of "eternal destruction" is itself a redemptive concept. Before turning to that matter, however, I want to consider Hodge's claim

---

[20]Hodge, *op. cit.*, p. 270.

that a universalistic interpretation of Romans 5:18 "cannot be admitted by any who acknowledge the inspiration of the Bible." On the face of it, that is a remarkable claim for two reasons: first, because many Christian universalists have believed as strongly as Hodge did in the inspiration of the Bible, and second, because one could just as easily, if one wanted to be uncharitable, use the same kind of argument against Hodge. For surely, the following argument is at least as strong, if not stronger, than the one that Hodge gives:

> Because not only the Scriptures generally, but Paul himself, distinctly teach universal reconciliation, as in Romans 5:18, Romans 11, and I Corinthians 15:20-28, Hodge's interpretation of II Thessalonians 1:9 cannot be admitted by any who acknowledge the inspiration of the Bible.

As this argument illustrates, the issue of inspiration is a distracting irrelevancy in the present context; it is the correct interpretation of a text, not the inspiration of the Bible, that is here at issue. And concerning that issue—the correct interpretation of Romans 5:18—the appeal of Murray and Hodge to II Thessalonians 1:9 suffers from a serious weakness. For without any trouble at all, we can simply reverse their argument and argue in the opposite direction.

We here touch upon a point that is perhaps more familiar to philosophers than to others, and it illustrates how something that comes naturally to a philosopher can help to clarify our interpretation of the Bible. The logic of the situation is this: At least one proposition in the following inconsistent set must be false:

(1)   Paul wrote both II Thessalonians 1:8-9 and Romans 5:18.

(2)   II Thessalonians 1:8-9 teaches that some persons will literally be punished forever and hence will never be reconciled to God.

(3)   Romans 5:18 teaches that Christ's one act of righteousness "leads to acquittal and life for all men" and

hence that all sinners will eventually be reconciled to God.

(4) There is no inconsistency in Paul's teaching.

Because we know that at least one of these propositions is false, we must also consider whether one of them is more plausible to deny than the others. Some would no doubt reject proposition (1), because some scholars have come to doubt the Pauline authorship of II Thessalonians; others may want to reject proposition (4) and simply admit that Paul was himself inconsistent. But those who accept a traditional view of the Bible, as Murray and Hodge both do, are unwilling to reject either (1) or (4); such persons must therefore reject either (2) or (3). So let us ask ourselves: Which of *these* propositions is the more plausible to reject. According to Murray and Hodge, (2) is true; therefore, (3) is false. These theologians allow, in other words, their understanding of II Thessalonians 1:8-9 to determine their interpretation of Romans 5:18 and the other universalistic texts in Paul. But one could just as rationally argue in the reverse direction and insist that (3) is true; therefore, (2) is false. One could just as rationally, in other words, allow one's understanding of the universalistic texts to determine one's interpretation of II Thessalonians 1:8-9. At the very least, therefore, Murray and Hodge owe us some explanation of why they prefer an argument in the one direction rather than an equally plausible argument in the other.

We have here but another instance of the hermeneutical problem discussed in the previous chapter. Whichever way we argue, we shall end up denying a proposition for which there is at least some *prima facie* support in Paul. But consider this: On the one side, we have such systematic discourses as Romans 5 and 11 and I Corinthians 15; on the other, we have a single incidental text whose translation, as we shall see in the following chapter, is by no means clear and whose interpretation is debatable on any translation. Is it not remarkable, therefore, that Murray and Hodge should think it sufficient merely to *cite* this text without so much as *discussing* it or defending their interpretation of it?

The proponents of everlasting punishment do not, of course, restrict themselves to a single text in Paul; like Neal Punt, most would appeal to the so-called "analogy of Scripture," placing great weight upon the words of Jesus as these words are recorded in the Gospels. Accordingly, in the following chapter, we shall examine not only the idea of "eternal destruction," as it appears in II Thessalonians 1:9, but also that of "eternal punishment," as it appears in the parable of the sheep and the goats. We shall find that, contrary to what some have read into them, neither of these ideas carries an implication of unending punishment and, as surprising as it may at first appear, both turn out to be redemptive ideas.

6. ESCHATOLOGICAL PUNISHMENT:
An Interpretation of the New Testament Teaching

> "When a baser metal is mixed with gold, refiners re-
> store the more precious metal to its natural brightness
> by consuming the alien and worthless substance with
> fire. . . In the same way, when death, corruption, dark-
> ness, and other offshoots of vice have attached them-
> selves to the author of evil, contact with the divine
> power acts like fire and effects the disappearance of
> what is contrary to nature. In this way the nature is
> purified and benefitted, even though the process of
> separation is a painful one. "
>
> St. Gregory of
Nyssa

In the previous chapter, I tried to convey something of the
clarity and scope of St. Paul's universalism. I also alluded to the
mystery of why so many scholars in the West have failed to appreciate it, and I suggested that the explanation of this mystery lies in
the way in which many scholars have misconstrued the New Testament theme of divine judgment. It is not that these scholars have
missed the theme of universal reconciliation altogether; many would
no doubt agree with Larry Lacy, who admits that "Taken apart
from the context of other aspects of Paul's teaching, . . . the most
reasonable interpretation" of certain texts in Paul "would be that
Paul was therein teaching universal salvation."[1] But like Lacy,
many scholars find themselves unable to square Paul's *apparent*
universalism with their reading of other texts in the New Testament—namely, those which they take to imply a doctrine of everlasting separation—so they end up reinterpreting or even explaining
away those passages that appear to teach universal reconciliation.

---

[1]Larry Lacy, "Talbott on Paul as a Universalist," *Christian Scholar's
Review* XXI:4 (June, 1992), p. 395.

As I have already suggested in Chapter 4, part of the problem here is what sometimes passes for biblical exegesis, particularly among opponents of universal reconciliation. Too often these opponents merely deduce their interpretation of specific texts from an antecedent set of assumptions. Consider, by way of illustration, how Leon Morris reacts to Jesus' statement, as recorded in John 12:32, that "I, when I am lifted up from the earth, will draw all people to myself." Morris writes:

> "All men" is something of a problem. In fact not every man is drawn to Christ and this Gospel envisions the possibility that some men will not be. We must take the expression accordingly to mean that all those who are to be drawn will be drawn. That is to say Christ is not affirming that the whole world will be saved. He is affirming that all who are to be saved will be saved in this way.[2]

Why does Morris regard the expression, "all men" or "all people" to be "something of a problem"? Does anything in the immediate context of John 12:32 render it problematic? Not at all. It is not the context, but the Augustinian picture that Morris brings to it—his conviction that the text simply could not mean what it says, because "In fact not every man is drawn to Christ"—which creates "something of a problem" for him. He does say, it is true, that the "Gospel [of John] envisions the possibility that some men will not be" drawn to Christ. But he nowhere tells us where the Gospel envisions this possibility,[3] and in fact not one word in this Gospel implies that Jesus lacks either the will or the power to draw all sinners to himself.

So in the end, Morris reduces a magnificent prediction of triumph: "I . . . will draw all people to myself," to a miserable

---

[2]Leon Morris, *The Gospel According to John* (Grand Rapids: Eerdmans Publishing Co., 1971), p. 598.

[3]Even if the Gospel did envision this possibility, that would in no way support Morris' interpretation of the text in question. For the mere possibility that Jesus would not draw all humans to himself is quite compatible with its being a revealed fact that he will indeed draw them all to himself.

tautology: "I will draw to myself all of those whom I draw to myself." He does this because he does not ultimately believe in the triumph, and he does not believe in the triumph because he cannot square a real triumph with an idea he thinks he finds elsewhere in the New Testament: that of everlasting punishment in hell. But just where in the New Testament do we find such an idea? Where is it clearly articulated? Given the clarity of Jesus' own statement just examined and of the Pauline statements examined in the previous chapter, not even an equally clear statement on the other side would successfully counter these clear statements; it would, to the contrary, merely establish an inconsistency in the text. But in addition to that, the statements commonly cited on the other side are anything but clear, as we shall see in what follows.

The Parable of the Sheep and the Goats

For all of the emotional fervor with which some Christians defend the doctrine of everlasting punishment, exegetical arguments on its behalf are extremely difficult to find. Even Christian philosophers, who should know better, sometimes seem content merely to make pronouncements at this point: According to William Craig, for example, "If we take Scripture [or the New Testament] seriously, we must admit that the vast majority of persons in the world are condemned and will be forever lost";[4] and according to Peter Geach, "if the Gospel account [of the teaching of Jesus] is even approximately correct, then it is *perfectly clear* [my emphasis] that according to that teaching many men are irretrievably lost."[5]

But remarkably, in the context from which the above quotations are lifted neither Craig nor Geach even tell us which texts in the New Testament, or which words of Jesus, they have in mind. They proceed instead as if this were unnecessary, as if their

---

[4]William Craig, "'No Other Name': A Middle Knowledge Perspective on the Exclusivity of Salvation Through Christ," *Faith and Philosophy*, VI, 2 (April, 1989), p. 176.

[5]Peter Geach, *Providence and Evil* (Cambridge: Cambridge University Press, 1977), p. 123.

pronouncements were utterly uncontroversial, as if no reasonable person could interpret the New Testament, or certain texts in it, any differently than they do. Bald assertions, however, are no substitute for an argument, and the mere fact that Geach appeals to the words of Jesus should perhaps raise a doubt in our minds. For even a superficial reading of the Gospels reveals one point very clearly: Jesus steadfastly refused to address in a systematic way abstract theological questions, especially those concerning the age to come. His whole manner of expressing himself, the incessant use of hyperbole and riddle, of parable and colorful stories, was intended to awaken the spiritual imagination of his disciples and to leave room for reinterpretation as they matured in the faith; it was not intended to provide final answers to their theological questions. Are we to take literally, for example, such words as these: "Whoever comes to me and does not hate father and mother, wife and children, brothers and sisters . . . cannot be my disciple" (Luke 14:26)? Clearly not. Most of us would recognize these words for what they are, hyperbole, and use our imagination to find a point that is compatible with our *loving* our "father and mother, wife and children, brothers and sisters." At the very least, Geach owes us some explanation of which words of Jesus he has in mind and why he takes them to imply, so decisively, that some persons will be "irretrievably lost"; he owes us something more than a dogmatic assertion at this point.

Another philosopher who appeals to the words of Jesus is Richard Swinburne, who writes:

> It seems to me that the central point of New Testament teaching is that an eternal fate is sealed, at any rate for many, at death, a good fate for the good and a bad fate for the bad. This appears to be the main point of such parables as the sheep and the goats.[6]

Now according to the parable of the sheep and the goats (Matthew 25:31-46), the Son of Man will one day return and separate the

---

[6]Richard Swinburne, "A Theodicy of Heaven and Hell," in Alfred J Freddoso, *The Existence of God* (Notre Dame: University of Notre Dame Press, 1983), p. 52.

nations even as a shepherd might separate the sheep from the goats, placing the sheep at his right hand and the goats at his left. Those at his right hand will "inherit the kingdom" prepared for them, but those at his left will depart into the "eternal fire prepared for the devil and his angels." The parable ends with the following parallel construction: "And these [the unrighteous] will go away into eternal punishment, but the righteous into eternal life" (25:46). Evidently, then, it is this parallel construction that Swinburne takes to imply that "an eternal fate is sealed, at any rate for many, at death."

Is Swinburne right about that? As he points out himself, Jesus never intended for anyone to take the details of a parable literally;[7] the details merely provided a colorful background for the main point, which itself is not always easy to discern. So as a first step towards understanding the parable of the sheep and the goats, we must try to discover its main point. Is the main point really a moral about the eternal destiny of the good and the bad, as Swinburne supposes? I doubt it. As I read the parable anyway, its main point is truly startling. When we feed the hungry and provide drink for the thirsty, says Jesus, it is as if we are offering food and drink to Jesus himself; and when we refuse to do this, it is again as if we are refusing to offer it to Jesus himself. In order to make this point in a forceful way, Jesus tells a colorful story in which those who are judged are utterly surprised to discover the true nature of their own actions. The righteous ask: "Lord, when was it that we saw you hungry and gave you food, or thirsty and gave you something to drink?" (25:37); and similarly, the unrighteous ask: "Lord, when was it that we saw you hungry or thirsty or a stranger or naked or sick or in prison, and did not take care of you?" (25:44). To which Jesus replies: "Truly I tell you, just as you did it to one of the least of these who are members of my family, you did it to me . . . [And] just as you did not do it to one of the least of these, you did not do it to me" (25:40,45). It is a powerful point about the inclusive character love: how the interests of Jesus are so tightly interwoven with those of his loved ones that any good that befalls them is a

---

[7]*Ibid.*

good that befalls him, and any evil that befalls them is an evil that befalls him. As is true of all parables, furthermore, we could easily draw all kinds of faulty inferences if we should take the details of this one too literally. We might conclude that eternal life is simply a reward for our own good works—something that Paul, at least, explicitly denies; or we might conclude that, whether we repent or not, any of us who have ever failed to meet our responsibilities to others—which is to say all of us—are destined for eternal punishment. Such inferences, however, would take us far beyond the main point of the story, as would the inference that everyone's "eternal fate" is sealed at death. The purpose of the story is to inform us that our actions, for good or ill, are more far reaching than we might have imagined, and that we shall be judged accordingly; it is not to warn us concerning the ultimate fate of the wicked.

Still, Jesus does say that the unrighteous go "into eternal punishment" ("$\epsilon i\varsigma$ $\kappa\delta\lambda\alpha\sigma\iota\nu$ $\alpha i\dot{\omega}\nu\iota o\nu$") even as the righteous go "into eternal life" ("$\epsilon i\varsigma$ $\zeta\omega\dot{\eta}\nu$ $\alpha i\dot{\omega}\nu\iota o\nu$"); and many, like Swinburne, do take that to be the main point of the parable. Their assumption here, in addition to an assumption about the main point of the parable, is that "eternal punishment" is *unending* punishment even as "eternal life" is unending life. In the following section, however, I shall argue that our text in fact carries no such implication. Not only does it not imply that the punishment and the life are of equal duration; it may even imply that the two are *not* of equal duration. To see why this is so, we must examine the relevant concepts more carefully.

Punishment in the Coming Age

The Greek adjective that our English Bibles translate as "eternal" or "everlasting" is "$\alpha i\dot{\omega}\nu\iota o\varsigma$," which literally means "age enduring" or perhaps "that which pertains to an age." As many commentators have pointed out, this adjective need not carry any implication of unending duration; in fact, the context may even preclude such an idea. When Paul speaks of a "mystery that was kept secret for long ages ($\chi\rho\delta\nu o\iota\varsigma$ $\alpha i\omega\nu\iota o\iota\varsigma$) *but is now disclosed*" (Romans

16:25-26—my emphasis), he clearly supposes that an age enduring mystery or a mystery that endures for "eternal times" can come to an end; and if an age enduring mystery can come to an end, so also, one might argue, can an age-enduring punishment.

One could perhaps make too much of this point,[8] however. For Paul's use of "*αἰώνιος*" in Romans 16:25—where it refers neither to God nor to the actions of God—seems clearly exceptional. Given its more normal usage in the New Testament, the term has a good deal of religious meaning that it does not have in Romans 16:25. For Plato, at any rate, "*αἰώνιος*" clearly did mean "eternal" as opposed to "temporal"; it designated the timeless realm, that which exists without any temporal duration or change at all. And this Platonic use probably did influence the New Testament use to some extent: As Paul himself put it, "what can be seen is temporary, but what cannot be seen is eternal" (II Corinthians 4:18). For the New Testament writers, no less than for Plato, "*αἰώνιος*" applies, paradigmatically, to God himself (see the reference to "the eternal God" in Romans 16:26), to that which distinguishes the incorruptible God and his incorruptible realm from the things that undergo change and corruption in time. I do not mean to imply that the New Testament writers took over the Platonic idea of an utterly timeless eternity, but I do mean to imply that their use of "*αἰώνιος*" was *roughly* Platonic in this sense: Whether God is eternal (that is, timeless, outside of time) in the Platonic sense or everlasting in the sense that he endures throughout all of the ages, nothing other than God is eternal in the primary sense. Other things—for example, the gifts, possessions, and actions of God—are eternal in the secondary sense that they have their causal source in the eternal God himself. Accordingly, when the letter of Jude describes the fire that consumed Sodom and Gomorrah as "eternal fire," the point is not that the fire literally burns forever without consuming the cities; it is not that the fire continues to burn even today. The point is that the fire is a form of divine judgment upon those cities, a foreshadowing of

---

[8]In the past, I have perhaps tried to make too much of this point myself. See "God's Unconditional Mercy: A Reply to John Piper," *The Reformed Journal*, June, 1983, p. 13.

eschatological judgment, that has its causal source in the eternal
God himself. And similarly for Jesus' reference to "eternal fire" in
Matthew 25:41 and to "eternal punishment" in Matthew 25:46.
The fire to which he alludes is not eternal in the sense that it burns
forever without consuming anything—without consuming, for
example, that which is false within a person (see I Corinthians
3:15)—and neither is the punishment eternal in the sense that it
continues forever without accomplishing its corrective purpose.
Both the fire and the punishment are eternal in the sense that they
have their causal source in the eternal God himself. For anything
that the eternal God does is eternal in the sense that it is the eternal
God who does it.[9]

---

[9]Here I should perhaps clarify one point. When I say, "For anything
that the eternal God does is eternal in the sense that it is the eternal God
who does it," I am not, of course, making an ontological claim about the
nature of a divine attribute, namely God's eternity; I am instead making
an exegetical claim about how the adjective "αἰώνιος," whose correct
translation has always been controversial, functions in certain contexts.
I am describing, in other words, a way of speaking found in the New
Testament. I stress this because an anonymous referee for *Faith and
Philosophy* once suggested that my notion of "eternal" is "rather thin."
The referee asked: "Why does Talbott's point apply to eternity but not
other divine attributes?" and the referee then commented: "'For any-
thing that the triune God does is triune in the sense that it is the triune
God who does it' is nonsense."

If my exegetical claim is correct, however, then it is not my notion
of eternity, but the biblical warrant for a doctrine of everlasting punishment, which is "rather thin." For if my exegetical claim is correct, then
in those contexts where "αἰώνιος" qualifies the actions of God, for example God's actions in time, it signifies neither timelessness nor unending temporal duration but divine causality of a special kind. And even
if "αἰώνιος" literally means "eternal," this might be a perfectly natural
way of speaking. When we say that God's plan for the ages is wise, we
do not mean that *the plan* itself has a high IQ; we mean that it manifests
the wisdom of God. And similarly, when the letter of Jude describes the
fire that consumed Sodom and Gomorrah as "eternal," the point is not
that *the fire* itself literally burns forever; the point is that it manifests the
eternal God in a special way. It is perfectly natural to think of God's

Even as "eternal punishment" is that form of punishment that has its causal source in the eternal God, so "eternal life" is that mode of living that has its causal source in the eternal God. In the Gospel of John, we thus read: "And this is eternal life, that they may know you, the only true God, and Jesus Christ whom you have sent" (17:3). Here too, then, the emphasis is upon the special *quality*, not the duration, of a life in proper relationship with God. But there is more. The Gospel writers thought in terms of two ages, the present age and the age to come, and they associated the age to come with God himself; it was an age in which God's presence would be fully manifested, his purposes fully realized, and his redemptive work eventually completed. They therefore came to employ the term, "αἰώνιος," as an eschatological term, one that functioned as a handy reference to the realities of the age to come. In this way, they managed to combine the more literal sense of "that which pertains to an age" with the more religious sense of "that which manifests the presence of God in a special way." Eternal life, then, is not merely life that comes from God; it is also the mode of living associated with the age to come. And similarly for

---

actions in time as manifesting his love, his justice, his wisdom, his power, and even his eternal Godhead (see Romans 1:20).

If the idea of God's triune nature, moreover, poses special problems in this regard, that is hardly surprising. For here we need to clarify what it might mean to say that the triune God does something. Christians have traditionally spoken as if it is the Son and not the Father who died on the cross; and it is the Father, not the Son, who declared, "This is my Son, the Beloved, with whom I am well pleased" (Matthew 3:17). Actions attributed to one person in the Trinity, in other words, are not always attributed to all three; indeed, that seems to be the whole point of distinguishing between different persons in the Trinity. But perhaps Christians would also want to attribute some actions to the Trinity as a whole. In that case, it would seem perfectly appropriate to say that whatever the Trinity as a whole does is itself triune in this sense: It expresses the united will and the causal activity of not just one person, but all three persons, in the Trinity. How much sense we are able to make of this will depend, of course, on how much sense we are able to make of the Trinity itself.

eternal punishment: It is not merely punishment that comes from God; it is also the form of punishment associated with the age to come.

Now in none of this is there any implication that the life that comes from God and the punishment that comes from God are of an equal duration. I stress this because people sometimes mistakenly argue in the following way: If eternal punishment does not literally last forever, then neither does eternal life. D. P. Walker puts the objection this way:

> it could be argued that the 'everlasting fire' and 'everlasting punishment' (τὸ πῦρ τὸ αἰώνιον, κόλασις αἰώνιος). . . did not necessarily mean that their torments would be eternal, since the word αἰώνιος or its Hebrew equivalent is often used elsewhere in the Bible in contexts where it cannot mean an infinite period of time, as for example in Jude 6, where it is applied to the fire which destroyed Sodom and Gomorrah. But this interpretation is highly improbable, since Christ is clearly drawing a parallel between the eternity of bliss awaiting the sheep and the eternity of misery awaiting the goats. It can only stand if one also denies eternal life to the saved . . ..[10]

There are, I believe, three mistakes here: First, Jesus is *not* comparing the *duration* of the punishment with the *duration* of the life; he is comparing a form of punishment that has its causal source in the eternal God with a mode of life that has its causal source in the eternal God. The issue of temporal duration is not at issue here and not relevant to the main point of the parable. Second, the Christian hope of immortality does not rest upon the translation of the Greek "αἰώνιος"; it rests instead upon the doctrine of the resurrection (see John 6:40) and that of God's unchanging love for us. And finally, when we look more closely at the relevant nouns, we encounter a strong reason to believe that the life lasts longer than the punishment.

---

[10]D. P. Walker, *The Decline of Hell: Seventeenth Century Discussions of Eternal Torment* (Chicago: University of Chicago Press, 1964), p. 20.

Whereas eternal *life*, being rightly related to God, is an *end in itself*, eternal *punishment* (κόλασις αἰώνιος) is a *means to an end*. As we shall see in chapter 9, a *just* punishment, even when it has a retributivist flavor to it, is always a means of correction. But quite apart from that, the Gospel writer employs a word that is, according to the Greek scholar William Barclay, specifically a word for remedial punishment; "in all Greek secular literature," says Barclay, "*kolasis* is never used of anything but remedial punishment."[11] The etymology of the word is especially intriguing, because it "was not originally an ethical word at all. It originally meant the pruning of trees to make them grow better."[12] According to this (relatively conservative) Greek scholar, therefore, "Eternal punishment is . . . literally that kind of remedial punishment which it befits God to give and which only God can give."[13] Being remedial, the punishment is intended as a means of correction, a means to the end of eternal life; so it is, if you will, *an eternal means of correction*. It is eternal both in the sense that its causal source lies in the eternal God himself and in the sense that its corrective effects last forever. But as a means to an end, it need not last any longer than is necessary to produce the end for whose sake it exists in the first place.

Accordingly, there are several senses, compatible with New Testament usage, in which a punishment of limited duration could still be eternal. There is even a perfectly natural sense in which such terms as "eternal," "everlasting," and "forever," particularly when used in the context of punishment or judgment, sometimes indicate the intensity (and quality) of an experience rather than its duration. ("The dull after dinner speech simply dragged on forever!") In the Old Testament story of Jonah, we thus find Jonah praying as follows from the belly of the great fish that had swallowed him: "I went down to the land whose bars closed upon me *forever* [my emphasis]; yet you brought up my life from the Pit, O

---

[11]William Barclay, *A Spiritual Biography* (Grand Rapids: Eerdmans, 1977), p. 66.

[12]*Ibid.*

[13]*Ibid.*

Lord my God" (Jonah 2:6). Do we not have here a perfect ana-
logue for a Christian understanding of hell? Jonah too was "cast
out" from the presence of the Lord (2:6); and like Jonah, whose
punishment, according to the story, included being cast into the
depths of the sea, perhaps a myriad others will one day exclaim: "I
went down into hell, whose gates closed upon me forever; yet you
brought up my life from the Pit, O Lord my God."

The Eternal Destruction of the Old Person

So far, we have found no grounds for a doctrine of everlasting
punishment in the words of Jesus, as recorded in the parable of the
sheep and the goats. So let us now return to the thought of St. Paul
and the question of how to interpret II Thessalonians 1:9. In the
previous chapter, we saw how Murray and Hodge, who both assume that Paul wrote this text, appeal to it in an effort to explain
away the clear universalistic thrust of Romans 5:18 and I Corinthians 15:22. But I shall now argue that such an appeal rests upon
a series of misunderstandings. In an effort to understand the text in
its own context, let us begin by putting two questions to it.

First, when the author of II Thessalonians speaks of "eternal
destruction" ("ὄλεθρος αἰώνιος"), does he have in mind a literal
punishment of some kind? The answer to that question is, I take it,
both obvious and noncontroversial. As is evident from the context,
the author is reacting in anger to the persecution of Christians; he
assures the afflicted that in the end God himself will vindicate them.
"For it is indeed just of God," he says, "to repay with affliction
those who afflict you" (1:6). When "the Lord Jesus is revealed
from heaven with his mighty angels in flaming fire," he shall inflict
his own vengeance upon the persecutors and upon all who "do not
obey the gospel of our Lord Jesus" (1:7-8); they shall receive a *just
penalty*, namely "eternal destruction" (1:9).

Second, if "eternal destruction" implies punishment of some
kind, does it also imply a final separation from God? Some of our
English Bibles certainly do leave that impression. The Revised
Standard Version thus translates II Thessalonians 1:9 this way:
"They [i.e., those who do not know God and do not obey the

gospel] shall suffer the punishment of eternal destruction and exclusion from the presence of the Lord and from the glory of his might . . .." Similarly, the New International Version translates it this way: "They will be . . . shut out from the presence of the Lord . . .." But these are inaccurate paraphrases, and the King James Version, which speaks simply of "everlasting destruction from (ἀπό) the presence of the Lord, and from the glory of his power," is both more literal and less theologically biased at this point. The sole reason other translators have for injecting the idea of being *excluded* or *shut out* from the presence of the Lord is that the Greek "ἀπό," like the English "from," can sometimes mean "away from." As Leon Morris points out, "This is certainly the meaning . . . in Isa. 2: 10,"[14] where we read: "Enter into the rock, and hide in the dust *from* the terror of the Lord, and *from* the glory of his majesty." It is also the meaning in Revelation 6:16, where the Kings of the earth and others cry out to the mountains and rocks, "Fall on us and hide us *from* the face of the one seated on the throne and *from* the wrath of the Lamb . . .." But in these texts, the verb "to hide" or "to conceal" determines the correct translation. When we try to hide or to conceal ourselves *from* the presence of the Lord—an impossible task—we are indeed trying to get *away from* that presence. In the context of II Thessalonians 1:9, however, we find no relevant verb, such as "to hide" or "to conceal," no relevant subject of the action, and no other grammatical device that entitles us to translate "ἀπό" as "away from." To the contrary, the context seems to render such a translation logically absurd for this reason: When the author speaks of "the presence of the Lord" in verse 9, he clearly has in mind the Lord's appearance "in flaming fire" (see verse 8); and similarly, when he speaks of destruction in verse 9, his figure suggests, not destruction *away from* the flaming fire, but destruction that precisely results from the flaming fire.

---

[14]Leon Morris, *The First and Second Epistles to the Thessalonians* (Grand Rapids: Wm. B. Eerdmans Publishing Co., 1959), p. 206n.

Like many prepositions, the Greek "$\overset{\text{'}}{\alpha}\pi\acute{o}$" has radically different meanings in different contexts; so the context, and only the context, must determine its meaning. In some contexts, it no doubt does mean "away from"; in others, it means something like "coming from." In II Thessalonians 1:2, for example, we encounter the familiar formula: "Grace to you and peace from ($\overset{\text{'}}{\alpha}\pi\acute{o}$) God the father and the Lord Jesus Christ." Here it is clear that the grace and the peace are not *away from* God the Father; rather, they *come from* God the Father. God is *the source*, the one who *brings about* the grace and the peace. And that, it seems to me, is the most natural interpretation of II Thessalonians 1:9 as well. The presence of the Lord in flaming fire, the glory of his power, is the *source* of, or that which brings about, the destruction of the wicked. No other translation seems to me even plausible. "Destruction *away from* the glory of his power" simply makes no sense, but "destruction that *comes from* the glory of his power" makes perfectly good sense.[15]

So the translation "eternal destruction and exclusion from the presence of the Lord" is doubly unfortunate: first, because the idea of exclusion or separation is simply not in the Greek text, and second, because the English expression "eternal destruction and exclusion" implies not only exclusion but *eternal* exclusion—and that is simply too much to read into the preposition "from." Even on the assumption that "$\overset{\text{'}}{\alpha}\pi\acute{o}$" means "away from" that is too much to read into the text. Paul no doubt believed that God would eventually destroy the wicked, but the question is: What does this mean? Just what is the concept of *destruction* here? Leon Morris writes:

> The nature of the punishment is "eternal destruction." The noun is used in I Cor. 5:5 of the destruction of the flesh with a view to the saving of the spirit. In that passage Paul clearly does not view destruction as annihilation, for there

---

[15]Compare Acts 3:19: "Repent therefore, and turn to God so that your sins may be wiped out, so that times of refreshing may come from ($\overset{\text{'}}{\alpha}\pi\acute{o}$) the presence of the Lord." Just as the presence of the Lord brings refreshing times upon the obedient, so it brings destruction upon the disobedient.

is no likelihood that he thought of such a one as being
saved in a disembodied state. This has its relevance to the
verse we are discussing, for it indicates that the word does
not signify so much annihilation as the loss of all that is
worthwhile, utter ruin.[16]

But this is surely confused. In the first place, Paul clearly does
view destruction as annihilation—that is, the annihilation of the
thing destroyed, namely the flesh. But in I Corinthians 5:5 the term
"flesh" does not mean "body"; hence the destruction of the flesh is
not the destruction of the body and does not imply disembodied
existence. It implies instead the destruction of sin or a sinful
nature. So Morris' remark about a disembodied state has no relevance at all in the present context. Neither does "destruction"
signify, for the individual whose flesh is destroyed, "the loss of all
that is worthwhile, utter ruin." It no doubt does imply the ruin of
something; but within the context of I Corinthians 5:5, it could not
possibly imply the ultimate ruin of the individual whose flesh is
destroyed. For *that* individual, it implies just the opposite: the
gain of all that is worthwhile, utter blessedness, for Paul here
presents "the destruction of the flesh" and "the salvation of the
spirit" as two sides of the same coin. So here, anyway, *destruction*
is explicitly a redemptive concept, and not only that: Paul presents
Satan himself as an (unwitting) agent of the redemption: "you are
to hand this man over to Satan for the destruction of the flesh, so
that his spirit may be saved in the day of the Lord."

Note also two additional points about the context of I Corinthians 5:5: First, the sin concerning which Paul is so exercised is
one that he regards as utterly heinous; it is "of a kind that is not
found even among pagans" (5:1). And second, the punishment he
prescribes has a real retributivist flavor to it: "Let him who has
done this be removed from among you" (5:2—RSV). Paul goes on
to pronounce judgment on the man in the name of the Lord Jesus
(5:4) and orders the Corinthians to deliver him "to Satan for the
destruction of the flesh." Given the harsh tone of Paul's remarks—
as harsh as anything we encounter in the first chapter of II

---

[16]*Ibid.*, p. 205.

Thessalonians—one might never have thought that Paul intended the punishment for the man's own good, had Paul not explicitly said so; his tone is not the kind that would suggest a mere chastening of a believer, something akin to parental chastisement. And yet, as frightening as the idea of delivering someone to Satan may be, the resulting destruction of the flesh is precisely what would make possible, Paul seems to think, the redemption of the man himself. Paul thus demonstrates how, on his own view, even harsh punishment, the kind that may appear vengeful and unforgiving, can in fact serve a redemptive purpose.

Similarly, if we look closely at Pauline theology as a whole, it is clear that, for Paul, every vessel of mercy represents the destruction of a vessel of wrath. For if, as we saw in the previous chapter, every individual who is a vessel of mercy, for example every Christian, first came into the world as a vessel of wrath, then in a perfectly straightforward sense God redeems an individual only when he destroys a vessel of wrath. There would seem to be, indeed, but two ways in which God might destroy a vessel of wrath: He might, on the one hand, destroy an individual's sinful nature and thereby redeem the individual who is a vessel of wrath, or he might, on the other hand, simply annihilate the individual who is a vessel of wrath. In either case, the vessel of wrath—that is, the object of God's wrath—would no longer exist.[17] As I shall argue in the following section, however, Paul nowhere seems to contemplate the annihilation of individuals; and he explicitly states in Romans 11 that even God's severity towards the disobedient is an expression of mercy, as we have seen. So we are left with the conclusion that, in Pauline theology as a whole, the destruction of a vessel of wrath

---

[17]Morris suggests another way in which God might destroy the wicked: He might bring all of their wicked plans and ambitions to ruin. But as Milton's Satan again illustrates, there is but one way for God to defeat a sinner entirely and to bring *all* of the sinner's wicked plans and am- bitions to ruin: He must redeem or reclaim the sinner. For consider Satan's plan to cling, for the duration of his life, to his hatred of God. There is but one way for God to bring that plan to ruin: He must transform Satan to the point where Satan is no longer filled with hatred and is instead is gladly defeated.

and the redemption of an individual are logically equivalent concepts.

More generally, we should, I believe, interpret all of the biblical ideas associated with divine judgment as redemptive ideas. It is not that every biblical writer saw clearly the deeper meaning in the symbols of divine judgment, or even that Paul saw this clearly all of the time; it would be as unrealistic to assume that as it would be to assume that every biblical writer (or even that *any* biblical writer) saw clearly the doctrine of the Trinity. But personal redemption nonetheless *is*, I claim, the deeper meaning in the symbols of divine judgment, and that is one reason why a name change in the Bible can sometimes acquire great theological significance. Depending upon the interests of the particular biblical writer at a particular time, the writer may describe one side of the redemptive process as divine judgment upon a sinner and the destruction of the old person (perhaps even in hell), or the writer may describe the other side as the birth of a new person. When the old person, the "vessel of wrath," is destroyed, the new person, the real person, the "vessel of mercy . . . prepared beforehand for glory" is unveiled. When Saul, an enemy of Christ, is defeated, Paul, a servant of Christ, is born. In a very real sense, therefore—the Pauline sense, if you will—both Abram and Saul were utterly destroyed and destroyed forever; what they had thought themselves to be, what they had *called* themselves, no longer existed, and so it was altogether appropriate that their names should be changed.[18]

Our question, then, is whether we can justifiably fit II Thessalonians 1:9 into such a redemptive framework? And the answer is: Of course we can. Nothing in the context of II Thessalonians 1:9 precludes the idea that the eternal destruction of the wicked—that is, the eternal destruction of the old person or the false self—also makes possible the eternal redemption of those individuals who are wicked. Indeed, the very image of the Lord appearing in flaming fire suggests both judgment *and* purification (see again I

---

[18]In the case of Paul, a more accurate statement would be: It is altogether appropriate that Christians no longer call him by his Hebrew name.

Corinthians 3:15). And though the author of this letter, particularly
if it were someone other than Paul, may not have had the idea of
purification explicitly in mind at the time of writing, that is
irrelevant. For the author does not provide a systematic discourse
on the exact nature and purpose of punishment; he merely reacts in
anger to the persecution of Christians, a crime of which Paul
himself had once been guilty. Though the author does employ the
language of retribution (even as loving parents sometimes do), such
language is in fact compatible with virtually any theory of punishment you please. So even if nothing in the first chapter of II Thessalonians *requires* the view that the destruction of the wicked and
the redemption of those who are wicked are logically equivalent
concepts, neither does anything there rule it out. I conclude,
therefore, that II Thessalonians 1:9 is quite compatible with the
clear universalistic thrust of Romans 5:18 and I Corinthians 15:22.

Redemption vs. Annihilation

I said above that Paul nowhere contemplates the annihilation of
individuals. But in fact annihilationism seems to have gained considerable favor in the conservative wing of the church, and it may
seem to offer an attractive middle ground for those who reject both
absolute universalism, on the one hand, and the barbaric idea of unending torment, on the other. Those who believe in the annihilation
of the wicked can at least anticipate a future time when all things
(that remain) are in subjection to Christ and all persons (who remain) are reconciled to him in the full redemptive sense, and that
would also be a time, so it may seem to some, when God has removed every stain and every blemish from his creation. So annihilationism clearly has some theological advantages over the traditional understanding of everlasting punishment.

Nonetheless, such a view also implies, in addition to a final
destruction of all evil, the destruction of something good, namely,
those persons who, however sinful, were created in the image of
God. That in itself, as we shall see in Part III, would leave a terrible stain and blemish on God's creation. But that is not our present
concern, which is Paul's own view of the matter. In support of the

claim that Paul did believe in the annihilation of individuals, Larry Lacy points to such texts as Romans 1:32, where Paul indicates that those who commit certain sins "deserve to die," and Romans 6:23, where Paul warns that "the wages of sin is death." Lacy argues that the death of which Paul speaks in these texts "is literal death, the ending of life, so that the wicked do not live forever";[19] he argues that such death implies, in other words, a complete obliteration of consciousness. He offers two considerations in support of that conclusion: first, that the death of which Paul speaks in these texts is a form of "eschatological punishment," and second, that Paul also refers to this punishment "as *perishing* in Rom. 2:12" and elsewhere.[20]

As an exegetical argument, however, neither point comes to very much. That Paul regarded death as a form of eschatological punishment is unquestionably true, but it in no way follows that he therefore had in mind a complete obliteration of consciousness; and similarly, that Paul regarded this eschatological punishment "as *perishing*" is also true, but again it in no way follows that he had in mind the annihilation of an individual. Lacy evidently supposes that Paul uses the verb "to perish" ("*ἀπόλλυμι*") in a sense utterly different from its use in the following New Testament contexts: In the parable of the lost sheep, the shepherd goes after the one sheep *having been lost* (or *having perished*) until he finds it (Luke 15:4); in the parable of the prodigal son, the father says of the prodigal that, *having been lost* (or *having perished*), he was found (Luke 15:24); in Matthew 10:6 Jesus commands his disciples to go to those sheep of the house of Israel *having been lost* (or *having perished*); and in Luke 19:10, we read that the Son of Man came to save (literally) "the thing *having been lost* (or *having perished*)." In none of these contexts does being lost or having perished imply the annihilation of an individual's consciousness, nor does it imply that salvation is no longer possible; to the contrary, being lost or having perished is just what makes one eligible for being found and thus for being saved.

---

[19]Lacy, *op. cit.*, p. 397.

[20]*Ibid.*

Our question, then, is whether Paul uses the same term in a radically different sense from the above. In support of his claim that Paul (in effect) does so use the term, Lacy cites I Corinthians 15:17-18: "If Christ has not been raised, your faith is futile and you are still in your sins. Then those also who have died [or have fallen asleep] in Christ have perished." Here, says Lacy, the "clear implication is that perishing would end the hope of life after death." But why is that clear? Does not Paul here say exactly the same thing about those "who have died [or have fallen asleep] in Christ" as he says about those who have not yet done so. *If* Christ has not been raised from the dead, then you and I, he says, remain in our sins; we are lost and have already perished. Similarly, *if* Christ has not been raised from the dead, then those "who have died [or fallen asleep] in Christ" remain in their sins; they are lost and have already perished. To remain in your sins, to be lost, and to be in a state of having perished in relation to God are, in Paul's scheme of things, logically equivalent concepts. And who can deny that, as Paul sees it, *perishing* means one thing on the assumption that Christ was *not* raised from the dead and something else on the assumption that Christ *was* raised from the dead? If Christ was *not* raised from the dead, then there would be, according to Paul, no redemption, no resurrection, and no kingdom of love; and if all of that were true, then those who have perished would indeed be in a hopeless condition: being lost, they would never be found, never be saved, and (if you will) never be resurrected from the dead. But if Christ *was* raised from the dead, then it remains possible, according to Paul, that those who have perished will be found, that they will be saved, and that (once they are dead and buried) they will be resurrected from the dead. That is just what it means to be lost. No one but the lost—no one but those who have perished—can be an object of God's redemptive activity. So Paul's use of the term "perish" in I Corinthians 15:18-19 is perfectly consistent with what we find in the other contexts mentioned above.

And similarly for the Pauline understanding of death. Though Paul certainly teaches that "the wages of sin is death" (Rom. 6:23), he also claims to have experienced such death himself: "when the commandment came, sin revived and I died, and the very commandment that promised life proved to be death to me" (Rom. 7:9-10). He goes on to say that, once sin had aroused within him, it deceived him and actually *killed* him (Rom. 7:11). Such death as he experienced, however, is not an obliteration of all conscious experience; it is the spiritual condition of being under the control of sin, of having set one's mind upon the flesh, as Paul himself explicitly states in Romans 8:6.

Within the context of Pauline thought, therefore, neither *perishing* nor *death* implies the complete obliteration of consciousness; hence, we have no reason to suppose that Paul believed in the annihilation of individuals. But neither do we have any reason to suppose that Paul regarded the state of having perished or having died as being the final word for some persons. To the contrary, Paul clearly believed that all death, even in the form of eschatological punishment, will one day be overcome or abolished; for as he says in I Corinthians 15:26, death is the last enemy that Christ shall overcome or abolish. In short, the Pauline understanding of death comes down to this: Death is the inevitable consequence of sin, but by the grace of God it is also the punishment for sin; and as such, it is a means of correction. As a means of correction, moreover, it will be abolished as soon as it is no longer necessary for the purpose of correction.

It is within this context, I suggest, that we must understand some of the paradoxical ways that Paul speaks of salvation. On the one hand, he speaks of death in the context of divine judgment: It is an inevitable consequence of, and indeed punishment for, the revival of sin in a life. But on the other hand, he also speaks of death in the context of salvation—as, for instance, when he writes in Romans 6:6-7: "We know that our old self was crucified with him so that the body of sin might be destroyed, and we might no longer be enslaved to sin. For whoever has *died* [my emphasis] is freed from sin." Here Paul implies that salvation involves the crucifixion and complete destruction of something so intimately connected with us that we can refer to it with the same personal pronouns that we use to refer to ourselves; we can also think of it as the death of a person. When the old self or the false self is crucified—that is, when *we* are crucified in our innermost being—then in a very real sense *we* die; and in dying, we are thereby made alive. Paul can thus write: "I have been crucified with Christ; and it is no longer I who live, but it is Christ who lives in me" (Gal. 2:19b-20). So in some sense the Paul that was no longer lives.

Now consider the two ways in which Paul employs the concept of death more closely. Does he really have in mind here two quite different kinds of death, as so many have supposed? It would be easy at this point to jump to an affirmative answer; after all, the revival of sin in a life implies separation from God, and the death that being crucified with Christ brings to a person implies union with God. But here we must be careful not to distort Paul's view. The death or the punishment that sin brings is as much a means of grace, on his view, as the death that being crucified with Christ brings, and in both cases death is a process whereby the old person or the false self is destroyed. The difference between the two kinds of death, then, is essentially a difference of perspective. From the perspective of those already crucified in Christ, the destruction of the false self is clearly a good thing; it is liberation, salvation itself. But from the perspective of those who continue to cling to the false self, its destruction will be a fearsome thing; it will seem like the very destruction of themselves. For how else could those who cling to the false self experience God's opposition to it except as opposition to themselves? They will encounter their God as a consuming fire, and they will experience his opposition to the false self as wrath and fury. For one way or another, God *will* destroy the false self and will destroy it forever.

All of which suggests the following picture. Once the consuming fire of God's love has destroyed, whether in this life or in hell itself, everything that is false within us, once nothing of the false self remains for us to cling to, then nothing of our opposition to God will remain either. For then we shall see through all of the illusions that made such opposition possible in the first place. And then we shall discover this glorious truth: All that sinners fear most about God—the wrath and the fearsome punishment associated with his righteous ordinances—was never anything more than a schoolmaster to bring us to Christ and thus to save us from ourselves. That picture, which accords so well with Paul's universalism, also accords very well, I have suggested, with his understanding God's wrath and judgment of sin.   In Pauline thought, God has one and only one motive for all of his actions towards us, and that motive is love; hence, even his severity towards sin is itself an expression of mercy.

Are Some Sins Unforgivable?

Perhaps we are now also in a position to bring a Pauline per-spective to the idea of an unforgivable or unpardonable sin. During my own high school days, my classmates and I sometimes worried about whether *we* had committed such a sin. For as we had read in Matthew 12:31-32 and elsewhere, Jesus himself identifies blas-phemy against the Holy Spirit—that is, speaking against the Holy Spirit—as an unpardonable sin; such a sin, he says, "will not be forgiven, either in this age or in the age to come" (12:32). Our teachers warned us, of course, not to suppose that *other* sins might be forgiven in the age to come, though their reasoning on this matter always seemed to escape me. But in any event, as the experience of a friend of mine illustrates, the fear that speaking against the Holy Spirit might carry the direst consequences sometimes produced special temptations and stresses. After a long and sleepless night just before his first junior varsity basketball game, my friend confessed that in his frustration during the early morning hours he had cursed the Holy Spirit. Had he not feared the consequences of such a curse, he presumably would never have uttered it in the first place; but once he had uttered it, he began to wonder whether his condition had then become hopeless. It is a wonderful example of how our own fears can sometimes consign us to a prison of our own making.

Not surprisingly, a burning question at the time came to be, "Just what is blasphemy against the Holy Spirit anyway?" But our energies were, I fear, misdirected. A better focussed question would have been: "Just what does it mean to say that God will never forgive or pardon a given sin?" Does it mean that God no longer loves the person who commits the sin in question?—or that he no longer seeks to reconcile this person to himself?—or that his attitude towards this person is no longer one of forgiveness? Not at all. The idea that Jesus seems to have in mind (and the Gospel writers signify with the Greek "ἀφίημι") implies far more than an attitude of forgiveness, which in God never ceases; it also implies a release from some obligation, or a canceling of some debt, or a setting aside of some prescribed punishment. It is very close to our idea of forgiving a debt or pardoning a criminal. If a debt is unforgiven, then it must be paid; and once it is paid, it no longer exists. Similarly, if a criminal is unpardoned, then the criminal must serve his or her sentence; and once the sentence is served, there is no longer any need for a pardon. An unforgivable or unpardonable sin, therefore, need not be an *uncorrectable* sin at all; it is simply one that God cannot deal with adequately in the absence of an appropriate punishment.

To put the whole thing in perspective, we might observe that most people probably *have* committed sins that are unpardonable in the relevant sense; indeed, Jesus elsewhere indicates that one of the most widespread of all sins—the refusal to forgive others—is so unpardonable that it renders all other sins unpardonable as well: "if you do not forgive others, neither will your father forgive your trespasses" (Matthew 6:15). That is hardly surprising. God could hardly be *for* forgiveness and, at the same time, tolerate our refusal to forgive others; he could hardly be *for* reconciliation and, at the same time, tolerate our refusal to repent of that which separates us from others; and similarly, he could hardly be *for* our ultimate perfection and spiritual regeneration and, at the same time, tolerate our willful opposition to the work of the Spirit within. Accordingly, God does not withhold punishment—that is, a harsher means of correction—when we sin in this way. As the author of Hebrews put it: "For if we willingly persist in sin after having received the knowledge of truth, there no longer remains a sacrifice for sins, but a fearful prospect of judgment, and a fury of fire that will consume the adversaries" (10:26-27).

If we adopt a Pauline perspective, however, then we must regard all punishment, even the harsh punishment to which the author of Hebrews alludes, as an expression of mercy. When we nurse old grudges, refuse to forgive others, and willfully oppose the Spirit within, we become adversaries—not only in our relationship to God and to others, but in our relationship to ourselves as well. We undermine the very conditions of our own happiness and, in the end, make ourselves utterly miserable. It is as if we thereby launch an attack upon ourselves and fling ourselves into a fiery pit. Only in this modern scientific age, perhaps, are we beginning to understand in full the devastating *physiological* consequences of refusing to forgive those who have wronged us. But God's mercy, according to Paul, consists in just this: He will continue to hold our feet to the coals until the adversary—that is, the false self—is utterly consumed. We "will be saved, but only as through fire" (I Corinthians 3:15).

A point worth re-emphasizing here is that God's refusal to pardon a given sin—for example, his refusal to pardon blasphemy against the Holy Spirit, whatever exactly such blasphemy might be—in no way implies a lack of compassion or mercy on his part. When *we* speak of forgiveness, we typically have in mind an attitude or state of mind in the one who forgives; that is, a state of mind that exists when a person gives up all resentment towards an offender. But when Jesus speaks of forgiveness in the present context, he has in mind, as we noted above, the canceling of some obligation, debt, or prescribed punishment. A little reflection will reveal that the two kinds of forgiveness are utterly different. A governor may pardon a criminal for reasons, such as political expediency, that have nothing to do with a forgiving attitude; alternatively, loving parents, despite their forgiving attitude, may judge it best to hold their rebellious child to a given punishment. Precisely because the parents do love and do forgive their child, they may refuse to forgive the punishment in the sense of setting it aside. And that, I want to suggest, is exactly how we should understand the idea of a sin that God will not forgive or pardon as well. Because a refusal to forgive others, a refusal to repent, and a willful opposition to the work of the Spirit within undermine the very possibility of reconciliation and are so contrary to the conditions of our own future happiness, God will require that we experience in full the painful consequences of, and hence the punishment for, such sins as these. He could not express his love for us—his concern for our future happiness—in any other way. For when mercy itself requires severity, or a harsh means of correction, that is just what we can expect, says Jesus, either in this age or in the age to come.

If sin is anything that separates us from God and from each other, then if God is to be "all in all," he must sooner or later destroy all sin, thus removing every stain from his creation. According to the New Testament as a whole, I want to suggest, God's strategy for accomplishing this end is two-fold: On the one hand, he sent his Son into the world to defeat, in some unexplained mystical way, the powers of darkness and to pioneer the way of salvation (see Hebrews 2:10)—a way of repentance, forgiveness, and personal sacrifice. On the other hand, for those who refuse to step into his ordained system of repentance, forgiveness, and personal sacrifice, he has an alternative strategy: In their estrangement from God, they will experience his love as a consuming fire; that is, as wrath, as punishment, and, in the end, as a means of correction. So in that sense, they will literally pay for their sin; and God will never—not in this age and not in the age to come—forgive (or set aside) the final payment they owe, which is voluntarily to step inside the ordained system of repentance, forgiveness, and personal sacrifice.

7. GOD IS LOVE

"God is love, and he who abides in love abides in God
and God abides in him."

I John 4:16b

One of my aims in the previous chapters has been to illustrate how to read the New Testament from a universalist perspective. In Chapter 4, I distinguished between three different pictures of God: the Augustinian, the Arminian, and the universalist picture; and I pointed out that each of them represents a radically different way of reading the New Testament. Then, in Chapters 5 and 6, I began to defend a universalist reading. In Chapter 5, I argued, first, that universal reconciliation is a clear and pervasive theme in the letters of Paul, and second, that the standard ways of explaining away this theme are untenable, even contrived. Finally, in Chapter 6, I argued that those who find, or think they find, a doctrine of everlasting punishment in the New Testament have misinterpreted, perhaps even have mistranslated, certain crucial texts that in fact carry no implication of unending punishment. In all of this, I have been more concerned with perspective—the "big picture," if you will—than with great thoroughness in matters of detail; above all, I have tried to illustrate a way of putting things together. For nothing works greater mischief in theology, I am persuaded, than a simple failure of the imagination, the inability to put things together in imaginative ways.

Now as I have also pointed out in the previous chapters, the universalist perspective rests upon two theological assumptions for which we find ample support in the New Testament: first, that God, being perfectly loving, wills or sincerely desires the redemption of all sinners, and second, that God, being almighty, has the power to achieve this end. If you accept both of these assumptions, then universalism follows as a deductive consequence. So if you reject universalism, then you must also reject at least one of these assumptions; that is, you must either deny that God wills (or sincerely desires) the redemption of all sinners or deny that he has the power to achieve it. The Augustinians deny the first assumption, and the Arminians deny the second. But St. Paul, I have argued, endorses both assumptions; and in some of his most systematic theological discourses, such as Romans 5 and 11 and I Corinthians 15, he explicitly endorses the idea of universal reconciliation as well.

I am also persuaded, by the way, that an Arminian reading of the New Testament is far more plausible than an Augustinian reading; indeed, the latter, it seems to me, passes well beyond the bounds of reasonable interpretation. For consider how much of the New Testament that the Augustinians (who would restrict God's mercy to a chosen few) must either reject outright or else explain away. They must, first of all, either reject or explain away all of the explicit Pauline statements, discussed in Chapter 5, that seem to imply absolute universalism. Then, after disposing of these texts, they must either reject or explain away a host of other texts that, although logically compatible with everlasting separation, nonetheless imply that God loves all persons equally: for example, the explicit statement in I Timothy 2:4 that God "desires everyone to be saved," the explicit statement in II Peter 3:9 that God is unwilling that any should perish; the explicit statement of Jesus that God is unwilling that a single child (and hence that a single human being who ever was a child) should perish (Matthew 18:14); and the repeated statement of Paul (Romans 2:11, Ephesians 6:9, and Colossians 3:25) and Peter (Acts 10:34) that God shows no partiality to any persons. But even more important, perhaps, than these explicit statements is the whole thrust of teaching concerning the *nature* of God: his essential righteousness and purity and love. What could be clearer than the declaration in I John 4:8 and 16 that God not only loves, but *is* love? If God *is* love, if love is a part of his very essence, then he cannot act in unloving ways towards anyone, not even his enemies. That is why, according to Jesus, we too should love our enemies and pray for those who persecute us (see Matthew 5:43-48): "You, therefore, must be perfect, as your heavenly Father is perfect" (vs. 48—RSV). We must love our enemies, in other words, because God loves his enemies and we are to be like the perfect God in this respect. Or, as it is put in the Gospel of Luke: "But love your enemies . . . and you will be children of the

Most High; for he is kind to the ungrateful and the wicked. Be merciful, just as your Father is merciful" (Luke 6:35-36).

Still, the Augustinians do manage to explain all of this away and to do so in ways that many sincere Christians have found persuasive. In the present chapter, therefore, I propose to treat the Johannine declaration that God is love as a sort of test case. I shall begin with a question: How do the proponents of limited election interpret the Johannine declaration and try to square it with their belief that God's love and mercy extends to some created persons, but not to all? I shall then consider the exegetical and theological merits of their interpretation.

In Search of an Augustinian Interpretation

When it first occurred to me, several years ago, to wonder how the proponents of limited election might interpret I John 4:8 and 16, I immediately encountered three difficulties as I began to search for an answer. First, not all the proponents of limited election seem to regard these texts as particularly important. Louis Berkhof, for example, managed to write an entire systematic theology without citing either of the texts in question;[1] and though John Calvin does comment upon them briefly in his commentary on I John, he evidently did not regard them as important enough even to mention in his *Institutes of the Christian Religion*. When one thinks about it, this is truly astonishing. Calvin's *Institutes* is a monumental work of over 1500 pages; in it he sought to provide an exhaustive summary of Christian doctrine, as he understood it, along with the biblical support for it. In the Westminster Press edition, the index of Bible references alone is 39 pages of small print with three columns per page. And yet, in this entire work, as massive and thorough as it is, Calvin never once finds the Johannine declaration that God is love important enough to discuss. How, one wonders, could this have happened? Here is a statement that, to all appearances at

---

[1]Louis Berkhof, *Systematic Theology* (Grand Rapids: Eerdmans Publishing Co., 1931).

least, provides a glimpse into the very nature of the Christian God,
and in his *Institutes* Calvin ignores it altogether; he does not even
find it important enough to explain away.

A second difficulty I encountered as I began my search was
that the proponents of limited election are sometimes inconsistent in
the various claims they make. When he contemplates God's relationship with the redeemed in heaven, for example, Jonathan Edwards writes:

> The Apostle tells us that God is love, I John 4:8. And
> therefore seeing he is an infinite Being, it follows that he is
> an infinite fountain of love. Seeing he is an all-sufficient
> Being, it follows that he is a full and overflowing and an
> inexhaustible fountain of love. Seeing he is an unchange-
> able and eternal Being, he is an unchangeable and eternal
> source of love.[2]

Here Edwards says that God is an "infinite," "overflowing," "inexhaustible," "unchangeable," and "eternal source of love." But
when he contemplates God's relationship to the damned, Edwards
also writes: "In hell God manifests his being and perfections only in
hatred and wrath, and hatred without love."[3] By "hatred without
love," he evidently has in mind an attitude quite incompatible with
love. So at this point, the question arises: How are we to reconcile
the second quotation with the first? Suppose Edwards had said, in
one place, that God's *righteousness* is "infinite," "inexhaustible,"
"unchangeable," and "eternal," and then had said, in another, that
God acts towards some people—say, the nonelect or the members
of some minority race—in some expedient way *without righteousness*. That would have posed a similar problem of interpretation.
How could God's righteousness be both infinite and eternal if it is
also limited in the sense that he sometimes acts without righteousness? And similarly, one wonders, how could God be an infinite,

---

[2]Jonathan Edwards, *Charity and its Fruits*, reprinted in Paul Ramsey
(ed.), *Works of Jonathan Edwards, Vol. 8: Ethical Writings* (New Haven
and London: Yale University Press, 1989), p. 369.

[3]*Ibid.*, p. 390.

inexhaustible, overflowing, and eternal source of love if his love is also limited in the sense that he sometimes acts without love?

Perhaps the most serious difficulty I encountered, however, was a seemingly intentional kind of subterfuge. Consider how J. I. Packer, a popular lecturer and influential writer in Reformed circles a couple of decades ago, handles the love of God in his book *Knowing God*.[4] A strong proponent of limited election,[5] Packer is one of the few recent proponents of such a doctrine who tries to provide a consistent interpretation of I John 4:8 and 16. He in effect asks whether the proposition, *God is love*, expresses "the complete truth about God." By way of an answer, he juxtaposes two assertions. He begins one section with this italicized sentence as a caption: "*'God is love' is not the complete truth about God so far as the Bible is concerned*";[6] then, three pages later, he begins his next section with this italicized sentence as a caption: "*'God is love' is the complete truth about God so far as the Christian is concerned.*"[7] From the perspective of a Christian who looks to the Bible as an authority, however, these captions are no less perplexing than Edwards' apparent inconsistency. If the proposition, *God is love*, does not express the complete truth about God so far as the Bible is concerned, but does express the complete truth about God so far as the Christian is concerned, it would seem to follow that either the Bible or the Christian is mistaken. And what, one wonders, does Packer mean by "the complete truth about God" anyway? In a perfectly obvious sense, the proposition, *God is love*, does *not* express the complete truth about God, not if God is also

---

[4]J. I. Packer, *Knowing God* (Downers Grove: InterVarsity Press, 1973), pp. 106-115.

[5]Packer, one of the consulting editors for *The New Bible Dictionary* (London: The Inter-Varsity Fellowship, 1962), sets forth his own understanding of limited election in several entries, including crucial ones on election, predestation, and justification; he also defends a doctrine of limited election in his book, *Evangelism and the Sovereignty of God* (Chicago: Inter-Varsity Press, 1961).

[6]*Ibid.*, p. 108.

[7]*Ibid.*, p. 111.

omnipotent and omniscient; but that would be true, I should think, both so far as the Bible is concerned (at least on Packer's account) and so far as the Christian is concerned. Does Packer really want to say that the Christian's perspective is different from that of the Bible?

Clearly not. Like Edwards, Packer has simply stumbled over a text that he finds difficult to incorporate into his overall theological perspective. As a close reading of his discussion will reveal, a recognizable pair of theses lie behind the confused forms of expression in the two captions quoted above. The thesis of his second caption is really this: "According to the Bible, God loves the Christian with a perfect form of love"; and the thesis of his first caption is really this: "According to the Bible, God does *not* love *all* human beings with a perfect form of love." We can show that these are indeed Packer's theses in the following way. Packer makes two excellent and very profound points. The first concerns the nature of God's actions: "This is what God does for those he loves—*the best He can*; and the measure of the best that God can do is omnipotence!"[8] The second concerns a condition of God's own happiness, which "will not be complete," says Packer, "till all His beloved ones are finally out of trouble . . .."[9] Accordingly, Packer leaves us with exactly three possibilities: Either (a) all persons will eventually be reconciled to God, or (b) God's own happiness will never be complete, or (c) God does not love all created persons. Now Packer clearly rejects both (a) and (b), and that leaves only (c), namely, that God does not love all created persons.

So far as I can tell, moreover, Packer sees all of this clearly, though he fails to make it explicit. His confusing caption—"'God is love' is not the complete truth about God so far as the Bible is concerned"—is merely his way of opting for (c) without calling too much attention to it. But in the end, his readers are bound to ask the obvious question: Does the Johannine declaration imply that God loves all persons, or does it not? To this question, Packer can

---

[8]*Ibid.*, p. 115.

[9]*Ibid.*, p. 113.

give one of three possible answers: "Yes," "No," and "I don't know." As we have just seen, the answer he in fact gives is, "No," but it almost seems as if he recoils from the very answer that he gives. He probably felt a burden to express himself with sensitivity and caution on a difficult matter, lest he put off his readers with a clear statement of his own position. So he ends up trying to conceal his position, even as he articulates it, behind a curtain of ambiguous and confusing language.

Love and the Essence of Divinity

It is hard to avoid the conclusion that those Christians who would restrict God's love and mercy to a chosen few really have no clear idea of what to do with I John 4:8 and 16. In his commentary on I John, however, Calvin sees more clearly than Packer does exactly where the issue must be joined. The issue is not, as Packer has caricatured it, whether the proposition, *God is love*, expresses the complete truth about God. The issue is whether it expresses a truth about the very nature or essence of God—whether, in other words, it ascribes (what a philosopher would call) an essential property to the person who is God.

Consider, by way of illustration, the proposition, *God is omniscient*. Many Christians have believed that, though this proposition in no way expresses the *complete* truth about God, it does express a truth about the essence of God. If they are right about that, then it is logically impossible that the person who is God should ever believe something false or fail to believe something true. Or consider also the proposition, *God is holy and righteous*. If this too expresses a truth about the essence of God, then it is logically impossible that the person who is God should act in an unholy or an unrighteous way. And similarly for the proposition, *God is love*. If this expresses a truth about the essence of God, then it is logically impossible that the person who is God should fail to love someone, or should act in an unloving way towards someone, or should do anything else that is incompatible with his love. So it is clear why, given Calvin's theological perspective, he must deny that *God is love* expresses a truth about the essence of God. For according to

Calvin, God *chooses* to make some persons, but not all, the object of his love; hence, it is possible for God to act, in the words of Edwards, "without love" and possible for him not to love someone; hence, the proposition, *God is love*, does not express a truth about the very essence of God.

But if, on Calvin's view, *God is love* does not express a truth about the essence of God, how does Calvin himself interpret I John 4:8 and 16? Unfortunately, his remarks in the commentary are not only brief and unsatisfactory; they appear to be flatly self-contradictory as well. He begins by observing, correctly, that the author of I John "takes as granted a general principle or truth, that God is love, that is, that his *nature* [my emphasis] is to love men." He then goes on to write:

> But the meaning of the Apostle is simply this—that as God is the fountain of love, this effect flows from him, and is diffused wherever the knowledge of him comes, as he had at the beginning called him light, because there is nothing dark in him, but on the contrary he illuminates all things by his brightness. Here then he does not speak of the essence of God, but only shows what he is found to be by us [i.e., by the elect].[10]

Having just told us that the Johannine declaration *is* a statement about the nature of God, Calvin here gives some additional reasons for taking it so: Just as God is light in the two-fold sense that "there is nothing dark in him" and "he illuminates all things by his brightness," so God is love in the sense that he is the very source or "fountain of love." But then, by way of a conclusion that seems to come from nowhere, Calvin flatly contradicts himself and takes it all back: In declaring that "God is love," he concludes, "the Apostle . . . does not speak of the essence [or the nature] of God, but only shows what he is found to be by us" [i.e., by the elect]. Nor does Calvin explain himself any further; he simply moves on to other matters.

---

[10]John Calvin, *Commentaries on the Catholic Epistles* (Grand Rapids: Eerdmans Publishing Co., 1948), p. 239.

Though such an explicit contradiction is no doubt bewildering, Calvin's final conclusion—namely, that the author of I John "does not speak of the essence [or the nature] of God" remains just what his overall theological perspective requires. So let us now consider the exegetical merits of this interpretation. Is there anything to be said on its behalf? Very little; indeed, there is much to be said against it. For as Packer himself points out, there are two other Johannine statements "of exactly similar grammatical form": "God is light" and "God is spirit," and the "assertion that God is love has to be interpreted in the light of what these other two statements teach . . .."[11] But these other two Johannine statements unquestionably *are* statements about the essence (or the nature) of God. In I John 1:5, we read that "God is light and in him is no darkness at all." That is not a declaration to the effect that, by a happy accident, God *happens* to be free from all darkness, all impurity, all unrighteousness; nor is it a declaration that God has *chosen* to remain free from all darkness in his relationship to some fortunate people only. It is instead a declaration about the very essence (or nature) of God. And similarly for the assertion in John 4:24 that God is spirit. As Calvin acknowledges in a comment upon this very passage, "Christ himself calls God in his entirety 'Spirit'"; and this implies "that the whole essence of God is spiritual, in which are comprehended Father, Son, and Spirit."[12] But then, if *God is spirit* implies that "the whole essence of God is spiritual," why should not *God is love* likewise imply that it is God's very essence (or nature) to love?

According to Packer, the latter proposition is a mere "summing up, *from the believer's standpoint* [my emphasis], of what the whole revelation set forth in Scripture tells us about its author."[13] But just what is that supposed to mean? Would Packer interpret the statement that God is spirit in the same way? Would he describe this as a mere "summing up, from the believer's standpoint," of the revelation about God? I doubt it. He would recognize that,

---

[11]Packer, *op. cit.*, p. 109.

[12]*Institutes*, Bk. I, Ch. XIII, 20.

[13]*Packer, op. cit.*, p. 108.

given the spiritual nature of God, the expression "from the believer's standpoint" adds little but confusion. Given Packer's own principle of interpretation, therefore, we are entitled to conclude that, in Johannine theology at least, God is love in exactly the same sense that he is spirit and is light; that is, it is as impossible for God not to love someone as it is for him to exhibit darkness rather than light.

Packer no doubt employs the expression "from the believer's standpoint" in an effort to contrast the way in which, as he sees it, believers and unbelievers are apt to *experience* an encounter with God. The idea seems to be that, whereas a believer typically encounters the love of God, an unbeliever is apt to encounter the justice, or the holiness, or even the wrath of God. Packer thus writes:

> It is perverse to quote John's statement, as some do, as if it called in question the biblical witness to the severity of God's justice. It is not possible to argue that a God who is love cannot also be a God who condemns and punishes the disobedient, for it is precisely of the God who does these very things that John is speaking.[14]

Though Packer here assures us that some "quote John's statement" in an effort to question "the severity of God's justice" and to deny that God "punishes the disobedient," it is perhaps worth asking, at this point, whom he might have in mind. One would be hard pressed, I suspect, to name a single Christian writer, even among the most liberal, who denies that a loving God sometimes punishes the disobedient or condemns their sin. How else could God's purifying love reach the disobedient? Certainly those who insist that God punishes the disobedient as an expression of his love for them could hardly be charged with denying that God punishes the disobedient. Neither could they be charged with denying "the severity of God's justice"—though what Packer attributes to "the severity of God's justice," Paul attributes to the severity of God's *mercy*. For as we saw in Chapter 5, Paul's whole point in the eleventh chapter

---

[14]*Ibid.*, p. 108.

of Romans is that *all* of God's actions, his severity no less than his kindness, are expressions of his boundless mercy, which is in turn an expression of his purifying love.

In at least one place, moreover, Packer seems to acknowledge all of this. For in one place, he writes: "To say 'God *is* light' is to imply that God's holiness finds expression in everything that He says and does. Similarly, the statement 'God *is* love' means that His love finds expression in everything that He says and does."[15] If God's holiness "finds expression in everything that He says and does," and his love likewise "finds expression in everything that He says and does," then in God there is no such thing as a holy act devoid of love or a loving act devoid of holiness. Accordingly, God's holiness and his love must be, at the very least, logically compatible;[16] and if that is true, then the presence of divine judgment and divine wrath—which are but particular expressions of God's holiness—would no more imply the absence of God's purifying love than the presence of his love would imply the absence of his holiness.

Perhaps we are now also in a position to clear up a possible misunderstanding. Even as Packer complains about those who deny "the severity of God's justice," so others sometimes inveigh against sentimental conceptions of love. But there is nothing sentimental about the kind of purifying love we are talking about here. A father who does nothing when his teen-aged son is caught swindling old ladies might be indifferent, but not truly loving; he would have no real regard for the future happiness of his son. And similarly for God: If he should condone our selfishness, our vicious attitudes, our tendency to promote our own interest (as we perceive it) at the expense of others, he would be indifferent, not loving; he would have no real regard for *our* future happiness either. Accordingly, though God's love no doubt does preclude positive *hatred*

---

[15]*Ibid.*, p. 111.

[16]In Chapter 9 I shall argue further that God has but one moral attribute, namely his love, and that his holiness is nothing but his love.

and does preclude a final rejection of the beloved, it in no way precludes our *experiencing* that love as punishment, or as harsh judgment, or even as divine wrath. For if God is love and his purifying
love, like a consuming fire (see Hebrews 12:29), destroys all that is
false within us, the very thing we *call* ourself, then for as long as
we cling to the false self we will continue to experience that love,
not as kindness, but as harsh judgment and even wrath.

"I have loved Jacob, but I have hated Esau"

So far, we have seen that the Augustinians seem to have no
plausible interpretation of the Johannine declaration that God is
love. If God not only loves, but *is* love, then it is not so much as
possible that he should fail to love someone. At this point, however, some might point out that in at least one place Paul explicitly
quotes Malachi to the effect that God hated Esau, and John Piper,
another proponent of limited election,[17] sees great significance in
this. Writes Piper:

> What stops him [God] from saving some is, in fact, *ulti-
> mately* his own sovereign will. "In order that the *purpose
> of God* according to election might remain" he loved Jacob
> and hated Esau (Rom. 9:12,13). Therefore, I also accept
> the inference that there are people who are not the objects
> of God's electing love.[18]

If I understand him correctly, Piper here adopts the view that,
according to Paul, God literally hated Esau in this sense: From the
very beginning, God willed that Esau should come to a bad end;
that is, even before Esau was born, God had already rejected him
and had destined him for eternal perdition. So God does not,
according to Piper's interpretation of Paul in Romans 9:13, love all

---

[17]Piper defends his understanding of limited election in *The Justification
of God: an exegetical and theological study of Romans 9:1-23 (Grand
Rapids: Baker Books, 1993).*

[18]John Piper, "How Does a Sovereign God Love? A Reply to Thomas
Talbott," *The Reformed Journal* (Vol. 33), April, 1983), p. 10.

persons equally; and neither, from Paul's perspective, does the proposition, *God is love*, express a truth about the very essence of God.

Has Piper interpreted the text in question correctly? Does it really teach that God hated Esau in some literal sense? It is important, at this point, to avoid distracting irrelevancies. Charles Hodge, among others, tries to ameliorate things a bit by suggesting that in Romans 9:13 "hatred" means merely *"to love less, to regard and treat with less favour."*[19] But that is not of much help. If God so much as loved Esau *less* than he did Jacob, that would itself suffice to diminish his holy character and to contradict the Pauline claim that God shows no partiality to anyone. Others—for example, F. F. Bruce—point out that the prophet Malachi, from which Paul takes his quotation, has in view, not the Old Testament characters who bore the names "Jacob" and "Esau," but the peoples of Israel and Edom.[20] It is doubtful, however, that even Malachi would have disassociated the individuals, Jacob and Esau, from their progeny, the latter being seen as but an extension of the former. And furthermore, when Paul indicates that the election of Jacob took place before the twins were "born or had done anything good or bad" (9:11), he does seem to have the individuals, Jacob and Esau, principally in view. I do not mean to deny that he *also* had in view the nations they fathered.[21] But the whole point of his

---

[19]Charles Hodge, *Commentary on the Epistle to the Romans* (New York: A. C. Armstrong and Son, 1896), p. 490.

[20] See F. F. Bruce, *The Epistle of Paul to the Romans* (Grand Rapids: Eerdmans Publishing Co., 1963). p. 110.

[21]As evidence that Paul also had in mind the nations, one might point to Genesis 25:23, where the Lord declared to Rebecca: "Two nations are in your womb, and two peoples, born of you, shall be divided; the one shall be stronger than the other, the elder shall serve the younger." That Paul had these words in mind is clear, since in Romans 9:12 he quotes, "the elder shall serve the younger." I think it significant, however, that in both this quotation and the one from Malachi, he omits everything that might have made it clear that he had in mind nations rather than the individuals. And in the end, it is *Paul's* context, not the context

discussion at this point is to illustrate "God's purpose of election": how it continues "not by works but by his call" (9:11), and the familiar struggle between Jacob and Esau for the birthright—the fact that the birthright went to the younger brother rather than to the older one—is just what illustrates his point in a forceful way.

But though Paul seems clearly to have had in mind the election of individuals, there remains the issue of the nature of that election. Just what is the connection between election, as Paul understood it, and personal redemption? It will not do, at this point, to suggest that, in Pauline theology, Abraham, Isaac, and Jacob were chosen *merely* for positions of national prominence or historical privilege, without any implication of personal redemption. When Paul speaks of God's "purpose of election" in Romans 9:11 and cites some historical examples in the previous verses, he seems precisely to have in mind the history of God's redemptive acts, the chosen means by which God fulfills his promise to Abraham. One could hardly separate the historical circumstances of a person's life from the chosen means by which God draws the person to himself anyway. So the real issue is not whether the elect are eventually redeemed on Paul's view; they are. The real issue is whether election is exclusive or inclusive. Does the election of Isaac and Jacob, for example, imply the rejection of Ishmael and Esau? For that matter, does the election of Abraham imply the rejection of all others, living at the time, whom God could have put in his historical position but did not? Though a thorough discussion of this issue would be a paper in itself, I want to suggest that Paul's understanding of election carries no implication of rejection at all. As Paul saw it, God does indeed elect or choose individuals for himself. But the election of an individual inevitably reaches beyond the elected person to incorporate, in a variety of ways, the community in which the person lives and, in the end, the entire human race. That is why the election of Abraham is ultimately a blessing to all nations (Galatians 3:8), including Esau and his progeny, and why the idea of a "remnant, chosen by grace" (Romans 11:5) plays such an important role in

---

from which he has lifted his quotations, that must determine *Paul's* meaning.

Paul's argument that God is merciful to all (11:32). The remnant is always a pledge on behalf of the whole; it is the proof that God has not rejected the whole (see 11:1-6) and also the proof that "the word of God" or his "purpose of election" has not failed (9:6). For even in the case of the nonremnant Jews—those who had defected and had been cut off for a season (11:17)—God never permitted them, says Paul, to fall with ultimate consequences (11:7);[22] instead, he permitted them to stumble, first, as a means of saving the whole (11:25-26), and second, so that the fallen ones, the very ones who had stumbled and were hardened, could themselves become objects of his mercy. For God is, in a word, merciful to all who fall into disobedience (11:32).

But if all of this is true—if, as I argued more fully in Chapter 5, Paul nowhere contemplates the final rejection of anyone including Esau—why does he attribute to God a hatred for Esau? I see no reason to suppose that he literally does. He merely adopts a perfectly natural way of talking. When he contemplates the election of Jacob, he clearly has in mind the struggle between Jacob and Esau for the birthright and for their father's blessing. Now, as the brothers themselves perceived the struggle, their interests had come into conflict; hence it was not possible that both should have their perceived interests satisfied. Any arbitration of the matter would have to favor one set of perceived interests over the other, so one of the brothers would inevitably seem to be favored and the other disfavored. According to Paul, moreover, God had already decided the matter even before the brothers were born: In the struggle for the birthright, Jacob would win, not because he deserved to win, but in order that God's "purpose of election"—that is, the means by which he extends his mercy to all, including Esau—might continue. So even before the twins were born, says Paul, Rebecca "was told, 'The elder shall serve the younger'" (9:12). That, I want to suggest, gives us the full meaning of God's so-called "hatred" of Esau. It is a thoroughly anthropomorphic idea, a *human* way of speaking—even as, so Paul tells us in Romans 3:5, his own talk about the wrath of God is merely a human way of speaking. God's

---

[22]See Chapter 5, especially footnote 14.

"hatred" of Esau implies nothing more than this: Esau lost—and
was destined to lose—in a struggle that he wanted, or thought he
wanted, to win.

Nor will it do to say with John Murray that God's "hatred" of
Esau implies, at the very least, "disfavour" or a "positive outflow
of his displeasure" towards a sinner.[23] That may be true enough,
but it is also beside the point. For God's "hatred" is no different
from his love in this respect. According to Murray, "the mere
absence of love or favour hardly explains the visitations of judgment mentioned" in Malachi 1:1-5,[24] to wit: "I have hated Esau; I
have made his hill country a desolation and his heritage a desert for
jackals. . . . I will tear down, until they are called the wicked country, the people with whom the Lord is angry forever."[25] But then,
neither would a "mere absence of love" explain such judgments as
these upon the house of Jacob: "The Lord God has sworn by
himself . . .: 'I abhor the pride of Jacob, and hate his strongholds;
and I will deliver up the city and all that is in it'" (Amos 6:8);
"Then the mountains will melt . . . and the valleys will burst open,
like wax near the fire, like waters poured down a steep place. All
this is for the transgression of Jacob and for the sins of the house of
Israel" (Micah 1:4-5). It is not the mere *absence* of God's perfecting love that explains such judgments as these; Murray is right
about that. It is rather the *presence* of such love that explains such
judgments as these. For does not God's love for Jacob imply a
rejection of all that is false within Jacob?—and does not his love
for Israel likewise require that he destroy her wickedness forever?
If so, then God's *love* for Jacob is no different, in that respect, from
his so-called *hatred* of Esau. For surely, God's "hatred" of Esau
also implies a rejection of all that is false within Esau, and his
"hatred" of Edom requires that he destroy her wickedness forever.
So if there is any difference at all between God's "hatred" and his
love, it lies only in this: From a certain human perspective, such as

---

[23]John Murray, *Epistle of Paul to the Romans*, Vol. II (Grand Rapids:
Eerdmans Publishing Co., 1965), p. 22.

[24]*Ibid.*

[25]Compare this use of "forever" with its use in Jonah 2:6.

Esau's perspective in his struggle with Jacob or Edom's perspective in her struggle with Israel, God's perfecting love will consume the very thing that, in our present condition, we continue to hold dear.

But even as God's perfecting love destroys, like a consuming fire, all that is false within us, so our perspective is bound to change. According to the account in Genesis, Esau eventually did forgive his cheating brother and the two did come to love each other as brothers. In fact, the account of their reconciliation is one of the most moving stories in the entire Old Testament: "But Esau ran to meet him [Jacob], and embraced him, and fell on his neck and kissed him, and they wept" (Genesis 33:4). So complete was their reconciliation and so sincere was Esau's forgiveness that Jacob declared: "for truly to see your face is like seeing the face of God—since you have received me with such favor" (33:10). Yet, this man—in whom Jacob was able to see the very face of God—is one whom, as some would have it, God had already rejected and had destined for eternal perdition even before he was born.

Exclusivism: The Perennial Heresy

The Pauline idea of inclusive election—the idea that the elect are chosen instruments through whom God's mercy will eventually reach those who have stumbled—sets Paul squarely against a temptation as old as religion itself: the temptation to distinguish between the favored few—to which, of course, we belong—and everyone else. We see the clearest manifestation of this temptation, perhaps, in some of the primitive religions, where people seek the favor of God (or the gods) in an effort to achieve an advantage over their enemies. Here the idea seems to be to possess the tribal god, or at least to pacify him with sacrifices, so that one can control him and even use him as a weapon against one's enemies. The last thing one may want, at this stage in one's religious development, is a God whose love and mercy extends to all persons including the members of enemy tribes, and the last commandment one may want to hear is that we must love our enemies as well as our friends.

It would be a mistake, however, to suppose that such attitudes of exclusivism are limited to primitive religion; to the contrary, they are widespread and persistent, and they lie behind some of the most important religious struggles in many different ages. In the Old Testament, no less than in the New, we encounter a prophetic tradition that not only condemns such attitudes, but testifies to their persistence and destructive power. A good early example is the story of Jonah and his refusal to preach to the people of Nineveh. According to the story, Jonah's disobedience arose from his hatred of these people: the fact that he simply did not want them to repent and be saved. When they did repent and the Lord therefore spared their city, Jonah became so angry and so distraught that he literally wanted to die:

> But this was very displeasing to Jonah, and he became angry. He prayed to the Lord and said, "O Lord! Is this not what I said when I was yet in my country? That is why I fled to Tarshish at the beginning; for I knew that you are a gracious God and merciful, slow to anger, and abounding in steadfast love, and ready to relent from punishing. And now, O Lord, please take my life from me, for it is better for me to die than to live" (Jonah 4:1-3).

So great, and so self-destructive, was Jonah's hatred for the Ninevites that he would have preferred to die himself than to see them spared. Observe his whining complaint: "for I knew that you are a gracious God and merciful, slow to anger, and abounding in steadfast love, and ready to relent from punishing." The very thing that should have been his greatest source of hope was transformed by his hatred into a source of despair. But in one respect, at least, he exhibits more insight than some. For as much as he detested—so he thought—God's loving and merciful nature, he did not try to explain it away; instead, he lashed out at God angrily and asked to die. So perhaps he recognized, on some level of consciousness at least, that what he really wanted—namely, for God to extend mercy to him, but not to the Ninevites—was an impossibility.

Even as Jonah did not want God's mercy to reach the Ninevites, so many of Paul's contemporaries did not want it to reach the Gentiles. We thus read in the book of Acts that, when Paul defended himself before a large gathering of his kinsmen, they listened respectfully until he declared that he had been called to preach to the Gentiles—at which point "they lifted up their voices and said, 'Away with such a fellow from the earth! For he should not be allowed to live'" (Acts 22:22). They were so angry that they also began "shouting, throwing off their cloaks, and tossing dust into the air" (vs. 23), in effect starting a riot. They no more wanted God's mercy to reach the Gentiles, it seems, than Jonah wanted it to reach the Ninevites, and they objected in particular to Paul's teaching that Gentiles could attain "righteousness through faith" (Romans 9:30) without converting to Judaism, without keeping the Jewish ceremonial law, and without having their males circumcised. For as they saw it, such teaching implied that God, having broken his promise to Abraham, was unjustly extending his mercy to the Gentiles. That God's original promise to Abraham, as recorded in Genesis, had already included a reference to all nations (see Genesis 12:3 and 18:18) seemed not to matter at all; whatever the original promise had stated, many in Paul's own day believed that the election of Israel implied the rejection of other nations (even as many Christians have also believed that the election of Jacob implies the rejection of Esau). Hence, if God were to extend his mercy to the Gentiles, that would imply, by the same twisted logic, a rejection of Israel.

Now it is against the background of this controversy that we must understand Paul's question concerning God's justice and the answer he gives in Romans 9:14-16. After reviewing briefly the election of Isaac and Jacob, Paul goes on to write:

> What then are we to say? Is there injustice on God's part? By no means! For he says to Moses, "I will have mercy on whom I have mercy, and I will have compassion on whom I have compassion." So it depends not upon human will or exertion, but upon God who shows mercy.

Why, first of all, did a question concerning justice even arise in the present context? Was it because Paul really did accept a seemingly unjust doctrine of limited election? Clearly not. It was Paul's opponents, not Paul, who believed in limited election; his opponents would have seen no injustice, for example, in the election of Isaac and Jacob, or even in a literal interpretation of "I have hated Esau."

It was not this reminder of history, in other words, that motivated the question about injustice; it was rather the implication in Paul's teaching that election depends not upon physical descent from Abraham (9:6-8) and not upon works (9:12), but upon God's sovereign mercy alone (9:16). What seemed unjust to Paul's contemporaries was precisely the implication in his teaching that the Gentiles, who are not descended from Abraham and have not kept the Jewish law, might nonetheless be an object of God's mercy.

Paul's question, then, is essentially this: "Has God acted unjustly in extending his mercy to Gentiles as well as to Jews?" Paul's remarks about Jacob and Esau, which occur just prior to the question, are not what generate the question, but part of his *answer* to the question. Like a good debater, he meets his opponents on their own ground and prepares them for his answer even before raising the question. For as we just saw, none of Paul's opponents would have denied God's right to violate human tradition and convention in the matter of Jacob and Esau. According to tradition—that is, according to the conventions governing ancient Semitic society—the birthright, the blessing, and the headship of the tribal family should have passed from Isaac to Esau rather than from Isaac to Jacob. But if none of Paul's opponents would have denied God's right to violate that tradition, then neither, Paul in effect argues, should they deny God's right to violate the tradition that would restrict God's mercy to the physical descendants of Abraham, or at least to the circumcised and to those who keep the Jewish law.

Having disarmed his opponents even before raising his question, Paul then sets forth his unassailable answer, a quotation from Exodus 33:19 in which the Lord declares: "I will have mercy on whom I have mercy, and I will have compassion on whom I have compassion." This is an idiomatic expression that stresses not the *indeterminacy* of God's mercy, as some Augustinians have supposed, but rather its *intensity* and *assuredness*. As one Old

Testament scholar, Frederick Bush, has pointed out,[26] "the meaning that the expression is normally given in English, i.e. an arbitrary expression of God's free, sovereign will, makes almost no sense in the context" of Exodus 33:19, where it is a revelation of the very name, or essence, or goodness of God. It is, says Bush, "equivalent to 'I am indeed the one who is gracious and merciful.'" And similarly for Paul's own context. To all of those who, having succumbed to the perennial heresy, insist that God has no right to extend his mercy to a given class of persons—whether it be the Ninevites in Jonah's day, the Gentiles in Paul's day, or the non-Christians in our own day—Paul in effect quotes the Lord as saying: "I will have mercy upon whomever I damn well please." There is absolutely nothing in view here except God's unlimited and inexhaustible mercy—a mercy that, although no doubt severe at times (as Esau and Pharaoh might well have attested), is none-theless utterly reliable and therefore secures our hope for the future. For as Paul had already contended in the first part of Romans 3, no human disobedience or unfaithfulness can nullify the faithfulness of God. He will continue to meet our true spiritual needs and to consume all that is false within us, regardless of what choices we make, good or bad. So however important these choices may be for the here and now, or even for the immediate future, our *destiny* "depends not upon human will or exertion, but upon God who shows mercy."

Conclusion

In this chapter, we have examined the Johannine declaration that God *is* love. The most plausible interpretation, I have con-tended, is that we have here something more than an assertion about the *experience* of believers; we have an assertion about the very nature (or essence) of God, an assertion to the effect that it is God's very nature to love. The interpretations of those, such as Calvin, Edwards, Packer, and Piper who seem to hold that God sometimes

---

[26]Frederick Wm. Bush, "'I Am Who I Am': Moses and the Name of God," *Theology, News and Notes* (Pasadena: Fuller Theological Semi-nary, Dec. 1976), p. 11.

acts without love are untenable, both from the perspective of Johannine theology and from the perspective of Paul's inclusive understanding of election. For according to Paul, God is merciful to all.

Paul's inclusive understanding of election also explains why
some of his contemporaries found his views so offensive. But in
the early Christian Church at least, Paul's view of the matter won
the day; as a result, the doctrine of a limited (or exclusive) election
virtually disappeared from the Church for several centuries. Of
course Paul combated the specific form that the doctrine had taken
in his own day: the idea that God restricts his mercy to a single
nation, namely, the nation of Israel. He did not address—or try to
anticipate—every conceivable form that it might take in the future;
he did not specifically discuss, for example, the Augustinian view
that restricts God's mercy to a limited elect drawn from all classes
and all nations. He did not discuss this view, because he had never
heard of it. For his purposes, it was enough to point out that God
will save everyone "who calls upon the name of the Lord" (Romans
10:13) and "everyone who has faith" (Romans 1:16), whether the
person be a Jew or a Greek. But though Paul did not explicitly
discuss the Augustinian view, he nonetheless did rule it out with his
doctrine that God is merciful even in his severity. Even in the case
of the disobedient, those who have refused to call upon the name of
the Lord, Paul insists that God permits them to stumble only as a
means by which they might receive additional mercy. So in Pauline
theology, no less than in Johannine, *all* of God's actions are, in the
end, an expression of his loving nature. Not only does God love; he
is love.

As we shall see in Part III, moreover, the view that God's
mercy extends to *some* persons, but not to *all*, is remarkably paradoxical. Consider this: According to Packer, God always does
"the best He can" for his own loved ones; but according to Packer,
not all human beings are to be numbered among God's loved ones.
So at this point a reflective person is bound to ask: How could God
do the best he can for Jacob without doing the same for Esau,
whom Jacob had learned to love? Or, how could God do the best
he can for Paul without doing the same for Paul's Jewish kinsmen?
Packer, like Augustine and Calvin before him, supposes that God

could do his best for one person without doing it for that person's loved ones, or without doing it for all others whom God has commanded that person to love. We shall examine this remarkable assumption, together with some of the logical absurdities it generates, when we turn to the logic of divine love in the following chapters.

PART III:
THE LOGIC OF DIVINE LOVE

8. THE PARADOX OF EXCLUSIVISM

> "The only victory love can enjoy is the day when its
> offer of love is answered by the return of love. The
> only possible final triumph is a universe loved by God
> and in love with God"
>
> William Barclay

In Part II of this work, I tried to explain why, in my opinion, a universalist reading of the New Testament as a whole is more plausible than either an Augustinian or an Arminian reading. I shall now turn to some logical issues concerning the nature of divine love and examine some questions of logical consistency. In this and subsequent chapters, I shall argue, first, that Augustinian theology gives rise to a serious logical paradox—the paradox of exclusivism, as I shall call it—and is therefore logically inconsistent; second, that Arminian theology, though it escapes the paradox of exclusivism, nonetheless embraces a logical impossibility as well; and finally, that only universalism can pass the test of coherence and logical consistency.

The Logic of Divine Love

As we have seen repeatedly, a fundamental precept of Augustinian theology is that God's love extends to some, but not to all, created persons; it extends to Jacob, but not to Esau, to the elect or the especially favored, but not to the human race as a whole. But such exclusivism, I shall now argue, is not only morally repugnant; it is logical inconsistent as well.

Consider again J. I. Packer's excellent statement of what it means to be an object of God's love: "This is what God does for those he loves—*the best He can*; and the measure of the best that God can do is omnipotence!"[1] In an effort to clarify the idea

---

[1] J. I. Packer, *Knowing God* (Downers Grove: InterVarsity Press, 1973), p. 115.

expressed here, let us suppose that God truly loves Jacob, the son of Isaac, and let us try to answer three questions. First, if God loves Jacob and therefore does the best he can for Jacob, does this include God's giving Jacob everything he wants, or *thinks* he wants? Does it include God's promoting all of Jacob's perceived interests—that is, all of Jacob's interests as Jacob himself perceives them? Clearly not. For what Jacob wants, or thinks he wants, may not be what is truly best for him, and his perceived interests may not be his real interests at all. Accordingly, if God loves Jacob, then God will promote not Jacob's perceived interests, but his true or real interests, what I shall call his best interest.

Second, if God truly loves Jacob, will he literally do *everything* within his omnipotent power to promote Jacob's best interest? I believe he will, but there is also a theoretical difficulty here. Suppose that God should love *both* Jacob *and* Isaac, and suppose further that Jacob's best interest were, in some important respect, logically inconsistent with Isaac's best interest. In that event, God himself would face a dilemma. If he did everything in his power to promote Jacob's best interest, he would fail to promote Isaac's best interest; and if he did everything in his power to promote Isaac's best interest, he would fail to promote Jacob's best interest. We can illustrate the dilemma here by talking about *wants*. As the story unfolds in Genesis, Isaac wanted to give his blessing and the birthright to Esau; but Jacob wanted this for himself. Isaac and Jacob therefore had inconsistent wants; hence, it was logically impossible for God to satisfy both their wants. Now my own view is that genuine conflicts of interest cannot occur at the most fundamental level. My wants and desires and even some of my narrowly defined interests, such as an economic interest, may indeed conflict with yours, but what is truly best for me could never conflict with what is truly best for you. If I am right about that, then God could always promote the best interest of one person without harming someone else over the long run; he would therefore do *everything* within his power to promote the best interest of each and every loved one. But even if I should be wrong about that—even if conflicts of interest sometimes do occur at the most fundamental level—we could still say something like this: If God truly loves

Jacob, then he will do everything within his power to promote Jacob's best interest, provided that the actions taken are consistent with his promoting the best interest of all other loved ones as well.

Finally (and most important of all), if God's love for Jacob implies a disposition to promote Jacob's best interest, how in general should we construe a person's best interest? We might note, initially, that a person's best interest must have *some* connection, however difficult it may be to specify, with the conditions of a happy life. But unfortunately, we may not always agree on what those conditions are; and as Richard Swinburne points out in an important discussion of this matter, not just anything that someone happens to call "happiness" will qualify as the relevant *kind* of happiness.[2] So what *is* the relevant kind of happiness, the kind that a loving God would seek to promote? Though it may include "the absence of unpleasant sensations," it is not, says Swinburne, essentially "a matter of having pleasant sensations."

> There are no pleasant sensations had by the man who is happy in reading a good book or playing a round of golf with a friend, or by a man who is happy because his son is making a success of the business which the father founded. Basically a man's happiness consists in doing what he wants to be doing and having happen what he wants to have happen.[3]

Nor can the relevant kind of happiness, what Swinburne calls "supremely worthwhile happiness," arise from a false belief or from an action that is morally wrong.

> However, although someone may be fully happy doing some action or having something happen, this happiness may arise from a false factual belief or from doing an action or being in a situation which, objectively, is not

---

[2]Richard Swinburne, "A Theodicy of Heaven and Hell," in Alfred J. Freddoso, *The Existence of God* (Notre Dame: University of Notre Dame Press, 1983).

[3]*Ibid.*, p. 39.

really a very good one. Happiness is surely more to be
prized according as the happy man has true beliefs about
what is happening and according as what is happening is
in fact of great value . . ..[4]

Nor can the relevant kind of happiness quickly lead to boredom
or quickly fade with the mere passage of time. It must be, surely,
the kind of contentment and sense of well-being that could quite
literally endure forever; the kind of happiness that, according to the
New Testament, one possesses only when one is loved by others
and likewise is filled with love for others. If that is true, if a
community of love is a condition of the highest form of human happiness—if love, and only love, makes life worth living forever—
then God must first purge us of all the selfishness and arrogance
and lust for power that separates us from others before he can
fulfill his own loving purpose for us.

One could, perhaps, enumerate many more conditions of the
kind of happiness that is supremely worthwhile, and some may
want to quibble over one or more of the conditions mentioned
above. For our purposes, however, it will suffice to insist upon two
points: first, that supreme happiness, unlike blissful ignorance,
cannot rest upon deception or false factual beliefs, and second, that
one who possesses such happiness must be filled with love for
others. The first point seems relatively uncontroversial, and the
second is one that no Christian would want to deny. Beyond that,
we need insist only upon one additional point: Whatever else
supremely worthwhile happiness might entail, it is the kind of happiness that a loving God would, of necessity, seek to promote in his
loved ones. If these minimal points are acceptable, then we are now
in a position to argue that Augustinian exclusivism is logically inconsistent.

The Inclusive Nature of Love

Consider first a curiosity about the nature of love. Not only is
a disposition to love essential for supreme happiness; it can also be

---

[4]*Ibid.*, p. 40.

an instrumental evil, making a person more miserable, not less. Indeed, the more one is filled with love for others, the more the unhappiness of others is likely to jeopardize one's own happiness— as Paul illustrates when he comments concerning his fellow worker, Epaphroditus: "He was indeed so ill that he nearly died. But God had mercy upon him, and not only on him but on me also, so that I would not have one sorrow after another" (Philippians 2:27). Curiously, the very thing that makes supreme happiness possible— namely love—also makes us more vulnerable to misery and sorrow. If I truly love my own daughter, for example, and love her even as I love myself, then I simply cannot be happy knowing that she is suffering or that she is otherwise miserable—unless, of course, I can somehow believe that, in the end, all will be well for her. But if I cannot believe this, if I were to believe instead that she has been lost to me forever—even if I were to believe that, *by her own will*, she has made herself intolerably evil—my own happiness could never be complete, not so long as I continued to love her and to yearn for her redemption. For I would always know what *could* have been, and I would always experience that as a terrible tragedy and an unacceptable loss, one for which no compensation is even conceivable. Is it any wonder, then, that Paul could say concerning his unbelieving kin whom he loved so much: "For I could wish that I myself were accursed and cut off from Christ for the sake of my people" (Romans 9:3)? Nor is there anything irrational about such a wish. From the perspective of Paul's love, his own damnation would be no worse an evil, and no greater threat to his own happiness, than the damnation of his loved ones would be.

Given the right circumstances, then, love can render happiness utterly impossible, and herein lies a paradox that the Augustinians would do well to ponder. If two persons are bound together in love, their purposes and interests, even the conditions of their happiness, are so logically intertwined as to be inseparable. That is why Jesus can say, "just as you did it to one of the least of these who are members of my family, you did it to me" (Matthew 25:40); it is also why the letter of I John can declare, "Those who say, 'I love God,' and hate their brothers and sisters are liars . . ." (I John 4:20). Jesus' interests are so tightly interwoven with those of the

children he loves that, if we do something to them, it is as if we
have done it to him; and God's own interests are likewise so tightly
interwoven with those of *his* loved ones that, as a matter of logic,
we cannot love God *and* at the same time hate those whom he
loves. Indeed, if we *say* that we love God whilst hating some of our
brothers and sisters, then we are liars. But the reverse is true as
well: Just as we cannot love God and hate those whom he loves,
neither can God love us and, at the same time, hate those whom we
love. If I truly love my daughter *as myself,* then God cannot love
(or will the good for) me unless he also loves (or wills the good for)
her. For I am not an isolated monad whose interests are distinct
from those of my loved ones, and neither is anyone else. If God
should do less than his best for my daughter, he would also do less
than his best for me; and if he should act contrary to her best
interest, he would also act contrary to my own.

Here we might try, as a thought experiment, to imagine the
impossible: what it would be like for God to love me without loving
my own daughter. If God were to deceive me concerning his indif-
ference toward, or hatred of, my daughter, then my blissful ignorance, being based upon a false belief, would not be the kind of
happiness that is supremely worthwhile; and if he were to bring it
about that I no longer love my daughter, that my attitude towards
her is as callous as his is, then he would again destroy the very
possibility of happiness that is supremely worthwhile. In either
case, he would be acting in unloving ways not only towards my
daughter, but towards me as well. And similarly for Jacob, who
finally came to love his brother, Esau, and to see in his brother's
own forgiveness a reflection of God. God could not both love (or
will the good for) Jacob and literally hate (or refuse to will the good
for) Esau; the whole thing is a *logical* impossibility, and it is an
impossibility that lies at the very heart of Augustinian theology.

At this point, however, one might begin to wonder about those
who are not our loved ones. Is it not at least theoretically possible
for God to love us without loving those whom we do not love? A
little reflection will reveal that this is not possible either. For if a
given person is *not* an object of my love, it will be for one of three
reasons: either I am ignorant of that person's existence, or I know

the person but not very well, or my capacity for love is not yet perfected. Now if I am ignorant of some person's existence, some person whom God despises, then either my blissful ignorance arises from the false belief that there are no such persons or my capacity for love is not yet perfected; if I know a person but not very well, then either I will continue to desire the good for that person—just as, for instance, I might desire the good for starving children in Somalia—or my capacity for love is not yet perfected; and finally, if my capacity for love is not yet perfected, as it certainly is not, and God wants me to experience supreme happiness, then he must continue to teach me the lessons of love until it is perfected. Is it not precisely for this reason that, according to the teaching of Jesus, God has commanded us to love our enemies as well as our friends? Of course love for a cruel and vicious person is difficult (perhaps impossible apart from the grace of God), and we must always express such love in appropriate ways; it may require that we oppose the actions of another or that, like Jonah, we preach repentance to one whom we regard as an enemy. But if, as the Christian religion has always taught, the highest forms of human happiness require that we love even those who wrong us, and wrong us badly, then God cannot truly love us without loving our enemies, those whom he has commanded us to love, as well.

It seems, then, that the Augustinians have embraced a logical impossibility. The idea that God loves some created persons but not all, or that he divides the human race into the elect and the non-elect, is, I contend, necessarily false. For even if, as Calvin insists, the proposition, *God is love*, does not express a truth about the essence of God—even if God could have chosen not to love us—he could not choose to love some of us without also choosing to love all of us. The reason, I have said, has to do with the inclusive nature of love, the way in which it binds people's interests together. For any two people you choose, either they will themselves be united in a bond of love, each willing the good for the other, or they will not be so united. If they are so united, then God cannot will the good for one of them without willing the good for the other as well. But even if they are *not* so united, God still cannot will the good for one of them unless he also wills that his loved one become the kind of person who is filled with love for, and therefore wills the good for, all others. And God cannot will all of that, I contend—cannot both will the good for someone and will that his loved one be the kind of person who wills the good for all others—unless God himself wills the good for all others as well. Hence God cannot love one person unless he loves all other persons as well.[5]

The Sin of Exclusivism

The argument of the previous section establishes, I believe, that exclusivism in theology is a logical absurdity. But there is another side to the argument, which I have not yet emphasized. So far, I have insisted upon this: If I love my daughter *as myself*, then God cannot truly love me without loving my daughter as well. An additional point is this: So long as I love my daughter as myself, I can neither love God nor worship him unless I at least *believe* that he loves my daughter as well; the idea that I could *both* love my daughter *and* love a God whom I know to hate her is also logically absurd. For consider what my love for God would have to entail: It would entail, first, that I respect God and approve of his actions, second, that I am grateful to God for what he has done for me, and third, that my will is, on the important issues at least, in conformity with his. But if I truly love my daughter, desiring the good for her, and God does not, then (a) my will is *not* in conformity with God's, (b) I could not consistently approve of God's attitude towards my daughter, and (c) neither could I be grateful to him for the harm he is doing to me. This is not merely to register a point about my own psychological makeup; the whole thing, I want to suggest, is *logically* impossible. As a matter of logic, either I do not love my daughter *as myself*, or I do not love God with all my heart, or I do not believe that God himself fails to love my own daughter.

---

[5]For a more rigorous statement of the argument, see my article, "The Doctrine of Everlasting Punishment," *Faith and Philosophy* (January, 1990), pp. 30-34 and pp. 40-41 (endnote 30).

Perhaps we are now in a position to appreciate the precise sense in which exclusivism in theology is a sin, a form of human rebellion. In the Gospels, Jesus declares:

> Thou shalt love the Lord thy God with all thy heart, and with all thy soul, and with all thy mind. This is the first and great commandment. And the second is like unto it. Thou shalt love thy neighbor as thyself. On these two commandments hang all the law and the prophets (Matthew 22:37-40—KJV).

Now suppose that I am a proponent of exclusivism in theology and believe, however sincerely, that God himself despises (or even just fails to love) some of those neighbors whom Jesus here commands me to love. For as long as I hold that belief, I will be unable to obey *both* commands. If I approve of a God who fails to love some of my neighbors (even though I know not which ones) and I am grateful for this fact, then I do not truly love or will the good for all of my neighbors; and if I *do* love them, then in the very act of willing the good for them I demonstrate my disapproval of any God who does not likewise will the good for them. Of course people are not always consistent and do not always see the moral implications of their own beliefs; neither do they always believe what they *think* they believe. I have known several people who, after some tragedy or the death of a loved one, have found that they did not really believe some of the terrible things they had always been taught about God and had previously thought they believed. But still, certain beliefs—a racist ideology would be an example—unquestionably do interfere with a person's capacity to love.

Consider the racist who sincerely believes that, because the African races are less than fully human, we must therefore treat them as an inferior species. If our racist is a Southern gentleman, he may be very gracious, very loving towards his family and friends, and a person of many good qualities; his demeanor may be utterly different from that of skinheads and members of the American Nazi Party. But his racist ideology will interfere with his capacity for love nonetheless, and the theological name for any belief that interferes with that capacity is sin. Our racist cannot *both* hold his racist beliefs *and* love his Black neighbor as himself. And what is true of a racist ideology is no less true of an exclusivist theology. One cannot *both* believe that God has divided the world into the elect, whom he loves, and the non-elect, whom he despises, *and* believe that this God is worthy of worship, *and*, at the same time, love one's neighbor as oneself.

I do hope I am not misunderstood here. My point is not that racists and exclusivists in theology are, on balance, worse than anyone else. I presume that when God has finally perfected our love for others, all of us will find that we have had to give up some deeply ingrained beliefs. For the fact is that some beliefs, particularly faulty beliefs about God, *are* an expression of sin; they undermine our capacity for love and therefore separate us one from another. When we finally learn to love our neighbor even as we love ourself, therefore, we shall then find that such beliefs have fallen away from us like the shackles they are.

9. PUNISHMENT, FORGIVENESS, AND DIVINE JUSTICE

> "I believe that justice and mercy are simply one and
> the same thing; without justice to the full there can be
> no mercy, and without mercy to the full there can be
> no justice."
>
> George McDonald

So far, I have argued that Augustinian theology, with its distinction between the elect and the non-elect, is logically inconsistent. But Augustinian theology also rests upon a particular conception of God and a particular way of understanding divine justice
and the purpose of punishment. If, as Augustine believed, the non-
elect are an object of God's justice and only the elect are an object
of his saving mercy,[1] then justice and mercy are distinct and very
different attributes of God;[2] and if, as Augustine also believed, the

---

[1]We see this clearly in the *Enchiridion* where, as I have already mentioned in Chapter 1, Augustine applies his understanding of limited
election even to children. Here he argues that all human beings, by
reason of their relationship to Adam, are part of "a corrupt mass" and
hence that all of them, the children no less than the adults, therefore
deserve everlasting punishment. He argues further that God selects
from this corrupt mass a limited elect to which he extends his mercy;
having made *them* a special object of his love, he saves them from their
sin. The rest God simply leaves in their sin and guilt, and they have,
Augustine insists, no grounds for complaint thereupon: For God merely
gives them the punishment they deserve [See *Enchiridion*, Chapter
XXV]. So the rest are objects of God's justice, but not his mercy.

[2]In some of his philosophical reflections upon the nature of God, Augustine does, it is true, endorse a doctrine of divine simplicity: the difficult
to understand (and, I suspect, finally incoherent) idea that each attribute
of God is identical with God himself and with every other attribute of
God. According to this idea, God's power, love, wisdom, self-suffi-
ciency, and independent existence are in fact one and the same attribute.
In *De Trinitate*, for example, Augustine writes: "God is truly called in
manifold ways, great, good, wise, blessed, true, and whatsoever other

condition of the damned is hopeless, but God nonetheless punishes
them for an eternity, then we can no longer conceive of their punishment as a means of correction. In this chapter, therefore, I propose to examine more fully the Augustinian understanding of divine
justice and the purpose of punishment.

I should perhaps clarify one point at the outset, however. The
Augustinians are by no means the only Christians who treat justice
and mercy as if they were distinct and very different attributes of
God; many Arminians—John Milton would be an example—have
conceived of God in the same way. For though Milton was a pas-
sionate opponent of limited election, he nonetheless spoke as if a
fundamental conflict, perhaps even a contradiction, exists in the
very being of God. In his great epic poem, *Paradise Lost*, he thus
described Christ's offer of himself as an atonement this way:

> No sooner did thy dear and only Son
> Perceive thee purpos'd not to doom frail Man
> So strictly, but much more to pity inclin'd,
> Hee to appease thy wrath, and end the strife
> Of Mercy and Justice in thy face discern'd
> Regardless of the Bliss wherein hee sat
> Second to thee, offer'd himself to die
> For man's offense.[3]

---

thing seems to be said of Him not unworthily: but his greatness is the
same as His wisdom; for He is not great by bulk, but by power; and His
goodness is the same as His wisdom and greatness, and His truth the
same as all those things; and in Him it is not one thing to be blessed,
and another to be great, or wise, or true, or good, or in a word to be
Himself" (VI, 7). But this too is inconsistent with Augustinian theology,
which, as we have seen, rests upon the assumption that justice and
mercy are different attributes of God.

Note also that Augustine identifies God's greatness, not with God's
love, but with God's *power*, and he identifies God's goodness with
God's greatness; hence he seems to reduce everything to mere power.
One can defend a doctrine of absolute simplicity *and* be faithful to the
biblical witness, however, only if one identifies God's power as the crea-
tive and transforming power of love (see Chapter 7).

[3]*Bk. III*, 403-410.

Here Milton suggests, first, that the fall of the human race produced a conflict within the heart of God, a "strife" between his mercy and his justice, and second, that Christ's atonement somehow managed to resolve the conflict. Presumably the source of the conflict was this: As a righteous judge, God willed something for the fallen human race that he could not possibly will in his role as a loving father; and as a loving father, he willed something that he could not possibly will in his role as a righteous judge. As a righteous judge, he willed that justice should prevail; and since justice requires retribution for sin, he was quite prepared to punish sin—in hell, for example—without any regard for the sinner's own good. But as a loving father, he also wanted to forgive sin and to permit his loved ones to escape the terrible punishment they deserved on account of their sin. Hence the strife within the heart of God, and hence the need for an atonement that would appease the wrath of God—that is, satisfy his justice—and put an end to the strife. It is almost as if, according to Milton, Christ died not to effect a cure in us, but to put an end to a bad case of schizophrenia in the Father. That may be a bit of a caricature, but it illustrates the point that, according to Milton and a host of other theologians, Christ died in order that God might be merciful to sinners without doing violence to his own sense of justice.

I have already pointed out in Chapter 3 how difficult it is to square such a view with the New Testament, which consistently presents the death and resurrection of Jesus Christ as the means by which God delivers us from sin and reconciles us to himself. The purpose of the sacrifice was not, in other words, to change God's attitude towards us, but to change our attitude towards him. I have also pointed out in Chapter 5 that, according to Paul, God's severity or justice is always an expression of his mercy; so from a Pauline perspective, divine justice could not possibly come into conflict with divine mercy. My present concern, however, goes beyond these exegetical questions to the philosophical merits of the idea that justice and mercy are distinct (and sometimes opposing) attributes of God. I shall begin with the Augustinian conception of divine punishment and point to some difficulties with it; I shall then contrast this Augustinian picture of God, as I shall call it, with a

radically different picture of the simplicity of God's *moral* character. According to the alternative picture, God's mercy and justice
are not distinct attributes that sometimes push him in opposite
directions, thereby creating a conflict within him that someone else,
namely his Son, must resolve for him; to the contrary, God has but
one moral attribute and that is loving kindness. It would even be
misleading, given the simplicity of God's moral nature, to say that
mercy and justice are different expressions of the one attribute,
loving kindness; for though God's love may indeed take different
forms at different times, his mercy demands everything his justice
demands, and his justice permits everything his mercy permits.
According to the alternative picture, in other words, "mercy" and
"justice" are but two different names for God's one and only moral
attribute, namely his love.

The Idea of Divine Retribution

According to Augustine, God's justice requires the punishment
of sin, whereas his mercy permits the forgiveness of sin. But just
what is the punishment that those who remain in their sin shall
eventually have to endure? As Augustine describes it, "deserved
and supreme misery shall be the portion of the wicked"[4]; the wicked
shall have to endure, first, everlasting separation from God, and
second, everlasting "physical" torment in the form of literal flames
that, although they produce the same experience as an earthly fire,
never consume those who writhe forever in them.[5] Similarly, John
Milton, despite his rejection of Augustinian predestination, describes the fate of those who freely reject the grace of God in Jesus
Christ this way:

> The second death, the punishment of the damned, seems to
> consist of the loss of the supreme good, that is, divine
> grace and protection and the beatific vision, which is com-
> monly called the punishment of loss. It consists also of

---

[4]*City of God*, Bk. XX, Chap. 1.

[5]*Ibid*, Bk. XXI, Chaps. 2-10.

eternal torment, and the usual name for this is the punishment of sense.[6]

Now behind any such doctrine of everlasting punishment lies a
particular philosophical theory about the nature of punishment and
the nature of moral guilt. We may call it, as many others have, the
retributivist theory of punishment. According to this theory, the
justification for punishment has nothing to do with deterring crime,
or with rehabilitating the criminal, or with protecting society from
criminal behavior; these may all be worthy goals, but they have
nothing to do with punishment *as* punishment. The only justification for punishment *as* punishment is that it serves the cause of
justice; hence the only question relevant to any given punishment *as*
punishment is whether the punishment in fact *fits* the crime. If
Judas betrayed Jesus for thirty pieces of silver, then the first question is whether Judas was truly responsible for his act and had
therefore acquired some measure of guilt; if he had, then justice
requires that he receive in return a certain penalty, perhaps suffering of some degree or a compensating loss of some specifiable kind.
St. Anselm, a clear proponent of such a theory, thus speaks as if
the sinner acquires a kind of debt; in the very act of disobeying
God, he or she fails "to render to God what is due" and thus "dis-
honors Him and removes from Him what belongs to Him".[7] So in
effect the sinner steals from God, or at least tries to steal, his honor.
But in the end, says Anselm, it is "impossible for God to lose His
honor. Either the sinner freely repays what he owes or else God
takes it from him against his will."[8] In the latter case, God restores
his own honor by punishing the sinner: "when because of his sin he
[the sinner] is deprived of every good, he is repaying from his own
possession (although against his will) what he has seized."[9] In that

---

[6]John Milton, *Christian Doctrine* reprinted in *The Complete Prose
Works of John Milton*, Vol. VI, (New Haven and London: Yale University Press, 1973), p. 628.

[7]*Cur Deus Homo* I, Chapter Eleven.

[8]*Ibid.*, Chapter Fourteen.

[9]*Ibid.*

way, the punishment of the sinner—that is, the infliction of suffering, or at least the removal of happiness—balances "the scales of justice" and makes up for, or is satisfaction for, the sin itself.

According to retributivists, then, the most important purpose of punishment is to satisfy the demands of justice, that is, to extract from the guilty a compensating loss; and according to many theists in the Augustinian tradition, that is also God's sole purpose in punishing the damned: to extract from them a compensating loss so that the scales of justice will balance.

Now I believe, for reasons I shall give below, that such a theory is fundamentally flawed. But within a certain legal context, the retributivist theory does have some strengths that we should perhaps appreciate, and retributivists have pointed to important difficulties in such utilitarian theories as the deterrence theory or even a simple rehabilitation theory. As retributivists are fond of pointing out, such theories tend to sever the concept of punishment from that of justice and thus to open the door for tyranny.[10] If the primary purpose of punishment were to deter crime, for example, and we should find that on certain occasions we can accomplish that by punishing an innocent person—perhaps a child of the guilty party or someone whom the vast majority believe to be guilty—then we would seem to have a justification for punishing the innocent. Or, if the primary purpose were to rehabilitate the criminal without regard for the criminal's own autonomy and rights as a person, we might feel justified in subjecting the criminal, against his or her will, to excessive "punishment"—that is, to prolonged and cruel treatment—for a minor offense, or even for no proven offense at all. According to the retributivist, however, the primary consideration in punishment should be justice, not deterrence and not rehabilitation. It is never *just* to punish an innocent person, whatever deterrent value such punishment may seem to have; nor is an excessive punishment ever just, whatever value such "punishment" may

---

[10]For a good popular treatment of this difficulty, see C. S. Lewis, "The Humanitarian Theory of Punishment," in *God in the Dock: Essays on Theology and Ethics* (Grand Rapids: Eerdmans Publishing Company, 1973), pp 287-294.

seem to have as a means of rehabilitation. And in addition to these important ideas—that a just judge never intentionally punishes the innocent and always tries to fit the punishment to the crime—retributivists make an even stronger point about the nature of law, namely this: The very difference between a law or a command on the one hand and a mere request on the other is that the former, unlike the latter, requires something like retribution in the case of disobedience. This is not really a point about when punishment is justified; it is a logical point about when a rule is, and is not, a law. You simply cannot have a law, except in name only, without also having some penalty in the case of disobedience. So if God wants to do more than simply make requests, if he wants to issue commands or to establish the rule of law, he must also ensure that those who disobey his commands or his laws suffer a punishment of some kind.

Accordingly, whatever defects the retributivist theory may ultimately have, retributivists have made an important contribution to our understanding of the relationship between law and punishment. They have also helped to clarify the idea of an excessive punishment. Contrary to popular belief, the Old Testament principle of retaliatory justice—"an eye for an eye and a tooth for a tooth"—was never instituted for the purpose of justifying harsh punishment for serious crimes, something that no one at the time would have questioned; instead, it was instituted for the purpose of eliminating excessive punishment, such as capital punishment in exchange for a tooth. The idea was very simple. We must measure the seriousness of a crime according to the degree of harm done, and we must proportion the punishment to the seriousness of the crime.

> He who kills a man shall be put to death. He who kills a beast shall make it good, life for life. When a man causes a disfigurement in his neighbor, as he has done it shall be done to him, fracture for fracture, eye for eye, tooth for tooth; as he has disfigured a man, he shall be disfigured (Leviticus 24:17-20).

This may seem harsh and unforgiving, as indeed it is, but it also has the effect of placing strict limits upon allowable punishment. And it raises an intriguing question: Given the principle of

equal retaliation (*lex talionis*), for what sort of crime might everlasting torment be a just retaliation? I think we can, if we are clev-
er, imagine such a crime. Consider a world in which one person
not only murders another but somehow manages to annihilate the
soul of the other, that is, somehow manages to put the other out of
existence altogether; or, consider one in which one person somehow
manages to inflict everlasting suffering upon someone else. If we
can imagine a world in which one person does *irreparable harm* to
another, then in such a world perhaps the one responsible for such
irreparable harm *would*, given the principle of equal retaliation,
deserve to suffer everlastingly in return. But if God is both omnipotent and perfectly loving, no such crime is even possible, it would
seem, in a world that God has created and therefore governs. For if
an action were so heinous, so dire in its consequences for others,
that its perpetrator would deserve to suffer everlastingly in return,
then a loving God would never permit it in the first place; his love
for the potential victims would require him to protect *them* from
such irreparable harm, and in so protecting them, he would likewise
be preventing others from *doing* irreparable harm. Insofar as the
degree of harm done determines the gravity of an offense, therefore,
God could never permit any offense that would warrant everlasting
torment as a just penalty.

So here we already have, I believe, an initial difficulty for the
doctrine of hell, as Augustine and Milton understand it. That doctrine clearly requires a retributivist theory of punishment, but it also
seems to contradict the retributivist's own principle of equal retaliation: the principle that punishment must be in direct proportion
to the degree of harm done. According to retributivists, certain
punishments are *intrinsically fitting* for certain crimes in that they
satisfy the demands of justice; a greater punishment would be
excessive, and a lesser one would fail to satisfy justice to the full.
But then, if that is true, those who endure the appropriate punishment for their crimes should then be free of guilt; having paid their
debt, they would no longer need forgiveness and no longer deserve
further punishment. And because God necessarily limits the harm
that anyone can do to others, all of us, including the world's worst

criminals, should therefore be able to pay over a finite period of time for all of the sins committed in this life. Even if we accept a retributivist theory, therefore, we are entitled to ask: Why should *everlasting* torment be an appropriate punishment for any actual crime? At the very least, it would seem, the Augustinians must either reject or modify the retributivist's principle of equal retaliation. They must defend a proposition that, on its face, seems indefensible: the proposition that, despite the limited harm we have done to others, our actions are so heinous (and our guilt of such magnitude) that we deserve a punishment, namely everlasting torment, which is far out of proportion to the harm we have actually done.

Concerning Guilt and the Question of Desert

One question for the Augustinians, then, is this: Even if we accept a retributivist theory of punishment, why should anyone suppose that some sinners actually *deserve* to suffer everlastingly for their sin? The question is especially acute when we consider the supposed source of guilt. For as I indicated above, Augustine appeals to the fall of Adam and to the doctrine of original sin in an effort to explain the source of our own guilt; he insists that this "one sin originally inherited, *even if it were the only one involved* [my emphasis], makes men liable to condemnation."[11] And following Augustine, John Calvin makes a similar appeal:

> Original sin . . . seems to be a hereditary depravity and corruption of our nature, diffused into all parts of the soul . . .. [As a result], we are so vitiated and perverted in every part of our nature that by this great corruption we stand justly condemned and convicted before God, to whom nothing is acceptable but righteousness, innocence, and purity.[12]

---

[11]*Enchiridion*, Chapter XIV, Section 50

[12]*Institutes*, Bk. II, Chapter I, Section 8.

From the perspective of a retributivist theory of punishment, however, the appeal to original sin merely compounds the difficulty. One of the most important intuitions underlying the retributivist theory is that we are neither responsible nor justly punished for the sins of another; and if we accept that intuition, then the idea of *inherited guilt* makes no sense at all. If, as Calvin suggests, we have inherited a depraved and corrupt nature, if we are subject to evil impulses not of our own making, then God has *less* to forgive us for, not more. He may have more to *deliver* us from, but not more to forgive us for. Consider how one author in the Augustinian tradition, Loraine Boettner, describes the effects of original sin:

> Man's fallen nature gives rise to the most obdurate blindness, stupidity, and opposition concerning the things of God. His will is under the control of a darkened understanding, which puts sweet for bitter, and bitter for sweet, good for evil, and evil for good.[13]

Observe that virtually every one of these supposed effects is, from the perspective of a retributivist theory of punishment, an excusing condition. Such conditions as "blindness," "stupidity," and a "darkened understanding," particularly when not self-imposed, can only *decrease* our personal guilt; they could hardly *increase* it. So if anything, the doctrine of original sin, as many have interpreted it, seems to provide an additional reason for *denying* that you and I deserve to suffer everlastingly for our sin. Such a doctrine merely pushes the crucial question one step further back anyway. For even if we set aside the problem of inherited guilt, the most fundamental question remains: Why should anyone think that everlasting torment is a just punishment for *any* act of rebellion, whether it be yours, or mine, or Adam's, or even that sometimes attributed to Satan himself? How could any finite being, limited in power and knowledge and wisdom, subject to deception and blindness, ever do anything that would deserve such punishment by way of a just recompense?

---

[13]Loraine Boettner, *The Reformed Doctrine of Predestination* (The Presbyterian and Reformed Publishing Company, 1968), p.63.

In an effort to answer such questions, St. Anselm argues that the gravity of an offense has nothing to do with the degree of harm done; neither does it have anything to do with potential harm, or even intended harm. He asks us to consider a simple example: Suppose that God were to forbid you to look in a certain direction, even though it seemed to you that by doing so you could preserve the entire creation from destruction.[14] If you were to disobey God and to look in the forbidden direction, you would sin so gravely, says Anselm, that you could never do anything to pay for that sin. As a good retributivist, Anselm first insists that "God demands satisfaction in proportion to the extent of the sin."[15] He then goes on to insist: "you do not make satisfaction [for any sin] unless you pay something greater than is that for whose sake [namely God's] you ought not to have sinned."[16] And this seems to imply that the greatness of the one against whom an offense occurs, not the degree of harm done, determines the extent, or the gravity, of the sin. So perhaps Anselm's argument is this: If God is infinitely great, then the slightest offense against God is also infinitely serious; and if an offense is infinitely serious, then no suffering the sinner might endure over a finite period of time could possibly pay for it. So either the sinner does not pay for the sin at all, or the sinner must pay for it by enduring everlasting suffering (or at least a permanent loss of happiness). And since, for Anselm, every sin is ultimately a sin against God, it follows that no sinner could ever pay for any sin over a finite period of time.

This is, in truth, the only argument I have been able to find in support of the view that all sinners deserve to suffer everlastingly for their sin. It seems to be the basic argument that people have in mind; though few are as explicit about the argument as Anselm is, many talk about the greatness of God and the heinous nature of any sin against *him*. But the argument is also rather strange, to say the least. First, why *should* the greatness of the one against whom an offense occurs determine *the degree of one's personal guilt*?

---

[14]*Cur Deus Homo*, Chapter Twenty-one.

[15]*Ibid.*

[16]*Ibid.*

Given a retributivist theory of punishment, the personal guilt of those who act wrongly must depend, at least in part, upon certain facts about *them*; it must depend, for example, upon the answer to such questions as these: to what extent are those who act wrongly responsible for their own rebellious impulses?—to what extent do they see clearly the choice of roads, the consequences of their actions, or the true nature of evil?—to what extent do they possess not only an implicit knowledge of God and his will for them, but a clear vision of the nature of God? Even the Augustinians admit the relevance of such questions when they insist that Adam's sin was especially heinous because he had special advantages, such as great happiness[17] and the beatific vision, which you and I do not enjoy. If Adam's sin was especially heinous because he had special advantages, then the sins of those who lack his special advantages must be less heinous; and if that is true, if some sins against God are less heinous than others, then the greatness of God cannot be the only, or even the decisive, factor in determining the seriousness of a given sin.

Second, if *every* sin is infinitely serious and thus deserves the same penalty as every other sin, namely everlasting torment, then once again the idea, so essential to the retributivist theory, that we can grade offenses collapses—as does the idea of an excessive punishment and that of fitting lesser punishments to lesser crimes. Many Christians do, it is true, speculate that gradations of punishment exist in hell; some, they suggest, may experience greater pain than others, and some places may be hotter than others. But even that seems inconsistent with the idea that *every* sin against the infinite God is infinitely grave and therefore equal to every other sin, and it does nothing to ameliorate the difficulty anyway. If all of the sinners in hell are dead in the theological sense, if all have lost *forever* everything that might make life worth living, then all have received essentially the same punishment: everlasting separation from God and a permanent loss of happiness. And the idea that all sins deserve essentially the same punishment undermines perhaps the most important intuition behind the retributivist theory: that

---

[17]See *Enchiridion*, Chapter XIV, Section 48.

some offenses merit less severe punishments than others do. We would hardly regard a king who executes every law-breaker, the jaywalker no less than the murderer, as just; nor would we feel much better if, in an effort to fit the punishment to the crime, the king should reserve the more humane forms of execution for the jaywalker.

Third, even if the slightest offense against God *were* infinitely serious, our fundamental question would remain: Why should anyone think that everlasting torment is a just penalty for any *possible* sin at all, even one that is infinitely serious? Retributivists do tend to believe that the more serious the offense, the more severe the punishment deserved, but even that is true only to a point. At some point additional punishment in the form of additional suffering seems diabolical and seems to have nothing to do with justice at all. Whether we believe in capital punishment or not, most of us probably would regard execution as a more fitting punishment for murder than for jaywalking; we so regard it, no doubt, because we regard murder as a more serious offense than we do jaywalking. But we also regard the rape and murder of many women over a period of years as even more heinous than the murder of one person; and we could devise—as many societies have—punishments far more severe than mere execution. We probably now have the technology to kill a person, inch by inch, over a period of years, all the while subjecting that person to such excruciating torment that death would seem like a blessing. Should we conclude that a mass murderer, such as Ted Bundy, deserves a more severe punishment than execution?—that a more just, or fitting, punishment would be to torture him to death over a period of years? I see no reason to draw any such inference, and neither have retributivists typically drawn such an inference. Even if we could justify such an inference, moreover, this would in no way justify the further inference that Ted Bundy deserves to suffer *everlastingly* for his crimes; far less would it justify the inference that those who inflict *less* suffering than Bundy did also deserve to suffer everlastingly for their sin.

Indeed, once you begin to measure the seriousness of a sin by some criterion other than the degree of harm done, you seem to undermine the retributivist rationale for proportioning the degree of

punishment to the seriousness of the sin. One can always challenge, of course, the moral intuitions that underlie the retributivist
idea of a fitting punishment; one can challenge, for example, the
widespread intuition that it is wrong to inflict upon wrong doers
greater suffering than they themselves have inflicted upon others.
But in challenging such intuitions, one also undermines the only
ground we have for accepting the retributivist theory in the first
place.

Is God a Retributivist?

We have seen so far that, even if we accept a retributivist
theory of punishment, there remain serious difficulties in the
Augustinian conception of divine punishment. But now we must
examine the retributivist theory more closely and consider some of
its difficulties.

I believe that Anselm himself points, unwittingly, to the fatal
flaw in this theory. Recall that according to Anselm no punishment
that a disobedient person might endure over a finite period of time
could possibly pay for the slightest offense against God. I shall
now argue that Anselm was right about this; if God should torment
us from now until the end of time, that would not successfully
cancel out a single sin. But unfortunately, Anselm never fully
grasped *why* he was right, because he never fully grasped this all-
important point: Punishment is simply not the sort of thing that
could pay for any offense; it is no equipoise at all for sin. Instead
of concluding, as he should have, that the retributivist theory is
mistaken, Anselm distorts the theory beyond recognition and thus
concludes that all offenses warrant essentially the same punishment; namely, everlasting torment in hell. His intuition seems to be
this: If no suffering of *finite* duration will satisfy the demands of
justice, perhaps suffering of *infinite* duration will do the trick. But
the truth is that no suffering of any duration will satisfy the demands of justice fully, because justice requires something of a different nature altogether.

We thus approach the fundamental weakness of the retributivist
theory. According to retributivists, justice requires that we suffer

some loss in return for every immoral action and in proportion to our degree of guilt; it requires punishment, not as a means to some other end, but simply for the sake of justice itself.   But though retributivists insist that, for every immoral action, some degree of retaliatory punishment is *intrinsically fitting*, they have failed to appreciate, I believe, the very limited legal and temporal contexts in which their theory has even a degree of plausibility.   Many are the contexts, perhaps, in which punishment is a fitting means to a desirable end, such as the protection of society or the redemption of the guilty, but very special are those—if there are such at all—in which it is, or even seems to be, intrinsically fitting.   Because punishment alone does nothing to make up for, or to cancel out, any crime, it seems intrinsically fitting only within a context in which real justice seems impossible to achieve; that is, only within a context in which we have to settle, or at least think we do, for the best possible alternative: a kind of partial, or even contrived, justice.

Consider this question: Exactly what is it that *real* justice would require in the event that one should do something morally wrong, something that harms another or even oneself?   I mean to ask here a very general question: What *sort of thing* would satisfy justice *to the full* in the event that one should do something morally wrong?   The answer, it seems to me, is obvious: If one could somehow make amends for the wrong action, that is, undo any harm done, repair any damage, in a way that would make up for, or cancel out, the bad consequences of the action (in one's own life as well as in the life of others), one would then satisfy justice *to the full*.   I fully appreciate that, when stated in such general terms, this answer may seem rather silly; it is doubtful, you might think, that a murderer could do very much in this life to make up for, or to cancel out, the bad consequences of a vicious murder.   But that is not to the point.   What would satisfy justice to the full is one question; whether a given person is in a position, or has the power, to accomplish this is another altogether.   So far as I know, few murderers have the power to resurrect their victims or to undo entirely (apart from God's help) the harm they have done; so if we move outside a theistic context, if we assume that physical death is the end of a person's conscious existence or that the murderer has done irreparable harm to others, then we can conclude only that perfect justice in the matter is impossible. In that event, those who believe in capital punishment may think it fairest simply to execute the murderer. Let the murderer suffer a loss in some ways comparable to that which he or she has inflicted on others. One reason, according to Herbert Morris, that such retaliatory punishment sometimes seems just is that it prevents one person from gaining an unfair advantage over others.

> A person who violates the rules has something others have—the benefits of the system—but by renouncing what others have assumed, the burdens of self-restraint, he has acquired an unfair advantage. Matters are not even until this advantage is in some way erased.[18]

But justice requires not only that a criminal's unfair advantage be erased; in many cases, it also requires that a victim's unfair *disadvantage* be erased. It even requires, I think, that the one responsible for a crime do something to make amends for it, something that might help to erase the victim's unfair disadvantage. In human society, of course, we cannot always achieve perfect justice; some may wonder whether even God has the power to achieve it. And when we cannot achieve perfect justice in a given case, such as cold-blooded murder, we then settle for the best possible alternative: a means of removing the murderer's unfair advantage. But whether we execute murderers, condemn them to a life sentence without possibility of parole, or punish them in some other way, our punishment does not in any way undo the harm they have done either to themselves or to others and does not, therefore, satisfy all the demands of justice.

Even the retributivists, I would also point out, recognize that punishment cannot, in and of itself, satisfy justice to the full. Richard Swinburne thus writes: "The taking of punishment removes all the effects of wrongdoing which someone other than the wrongdoer

---

[18]Herbert Morris, "Persons and Punishment," *The Monist*, 52, No. 4 (October, 1968), reprinted in Jeffrey G. Murphy, *Punishment and Rehabilitation* (Selmont: Wadsworth Publishing Co., 1973), p. 43.

can remove."[19] But that is not true either. If a mugger breaks my leg, the doctor who sets the leg may do more to remove the effects of the mugger's wrongdoing than punishing the mugger will ever do; and if God resurrects victims of murder, he may again do more to remove the effects of the murderer's wrongdoing than punishing the murderer will do. Of course, where punishment effectively encourages repentance or effectively achieves the goal of correction, it may do much to remove the effects of wrongdoing; but our present concern is with the sense we sometimes have that punishment is *intrinsically* fitting. And that sense, I have suggested, expresses a judgment something like this: If we cannot achieve perfect justice, if we must settle for partial justice as a kind of second best, then we should at least prevent the wrongdoer, in so far as it lies within our power to do so, from achieving an unfair advantage over others. Beyond that, there is also a tendency to objectify our desire for vengeance or revenge. When a criminal seems to have done irreparable harm to others and no one, not even the criminal, seems able to repair the damage, we have a natural urge to strike back; if we cannot achieve perfect justice, we can at least "even the score" a bit. And our legal system permits us to express that urge in accordance with a set of carefully defined rules, which a judge can indeed apply in a disinterested way. But whether it rests upon a desire to prevent wrongdoers from achieving an unfair advantage or upon the desire to avenge the victims with whom we sympathize, our sense that punishment is sometimes *intrinsically fitting* clearly presupposes a context in which the ideal of perfect justice is, or seems to be, impossible to achieve.

So now we must ask: What role might punishment of a retributivist kind have in a context—if there is such—in which perfect justice is *not* impossible to achieve? Presumably no *humanly* devised system of justice can escape altogether our human weaknesses and limitations. Unlike God, we humans have neither the data nor the wisdom nor the power to administer a perfect system of justice, and not only that: If we should try to institute a loftier

---

[19]Richard Swinburne, *Responsibility and Atonement* (Oxford: Clarendon Press, 1989), p. 107.

system than we are fit to administer, we would most likely institute a tyrannical regime and thereby produce even greater injustice. Accordingly, not even the best of the humanly devised systems of justice can be anything more than a distorted reflection of divine justice—limited, perhaps, to preventing wrongdoers from achieving an unfair advantage through their misdeeds and to regulating our human desire to strike back. But if we suppose that God, being supremely powerful, supremely wise, and supremely loving, *can* achieve and will settle for nothing less than perfect justice, then we must also suppose that he will settle for nothing less than a full *atonement* for sin—something that will actually make up for, or cancel out, sin; and as we have seen, punishment (in and of itself) has no power to do that.

So what, specifically, does perfect justice require? What sort of thing would make up for, or cancel out, sin? If we accept the Christian view, according to which sin is anything that separates us from God and from each other, then the answer to our question is clear: Perfect justice requires *reconciliation* and *restoration*. It requires, first, that sinners repent of their sin and turn away from everything that would separate them from others; it requires, second, that God forgive repentant sinners and that they forgive each other; and it requires, third, that God overcome, perhaps with their own cooperation, any harm that sinners do either to others or to themselves.

Some will no doubt balk at the idea that perfect justice in a theistic universe would lay so many requirements, however self-imposed, upon God himself, and some may find particularly offensive the idea that justice *requires* forgiveness. Do I really want to insist not only that sinners *ought* to repent, but also that God *owes* it to them to forgive them when they do?—that repentant sinners actually *deserve* God's forgiveness? In point of fact, I want to claim more than that. It seems to me that *all* sinners, repentant or otherwise, deserve God's forgiveness, not because they have earned it, which is impossible, but because it is their inalienable right as sons and daughters of God. Merit has nothing to do with it. Sinners are entitled to God's forgiveness for the same reason a newborn baby is entitled to parental care: because it is something they desperately need and cannot live without.

Even the Augustinians, I would note, seem prepared to acknowledge this much: Because God has forgiven us and has commanded us to forgive others, *we* have an obligation to forgive; *we* have no right, that is, not to forgive. But *why*, I would ask of them, has God commanded us to forgive others? Is it not because, given the Christian view of the world, forgiveness is the just and proper response to sin? Is it not because the sinner, who yet retains the image of God, deserves forgiveness?

With such questions as these, we approach a critical parting of the ways, a point at which our two pictures of God diverge dramatically. In part because they regard justice and mercy as distinct attributes of God, the Augustinians suppose that God could justly have refused to forgive sinners or to save them from their sin; as the Augustinians see it, this makes God's forgiveness a free gift and his mercy all the more glorious because it is supererogatory. But if, according to our alternative picture, God's moral nature is simple—if all of his moral attributes are identical with his love—then his justice will be altogether merciful even as his mercy is altogether just; he will punish sinners, in other words, only when it is merciful to do so, and he will always forgive them because that is the most loving and therefore the just thing to do. As I shall try to show in the following section, moreover, such a picture has several advantages over the Augustinian picture: It accords better with the New Testament analogy between God and a loving parent; it embraces a more radical conception of God's opposition to sin; and it provides, I believe, a more profound understanding of how God will finally vindicate his righteousness in the face of unjust suffering.

Why Divine Justice Requires Forgiveness

Those who set forgiveness over against punishment and confuse the forgiveness of sin with the tolerance of sin will inevitably reject the idea that divine justice requires forgiveness. But that surely *is* a misunderstanding. The woman who forgives her

adulterous husband does not merely tolerate his unfaithfulness; she
may also demand a change in his behavior and may even demand it
as a condition, not of forgiveness, but of continuing the marriage.
Just because she does forgive her husband and continues to love
him, she may refuse to continue in a dishonest relationship. And
similarly for the parents who discipline their children; those who
regard parental discipline as evidence of an unforgiving attitude
simply do not understand what the purpose of such discipline is.
So if, as our alternative picture suggests, forgiveness and just
punishment have the same object and the same goal (namely,
reconciliation), then the idea that sinners deserve forgiveness is no
more absurd than the idea that they deserve punishment.

Consider more closely, for a moment, the analogy to which the
New Testament directs our attention: that between God and a loving parent. Do not loving parents typically acknowledge an obligation to forgive their disobedient children? We see this most clearly,
perhaps, in cases of genuine repentance and remorse. Suppose that
the teenage daughter of a well-known televangelist is arrested for
drunk driving, and suppose that she is utterly heart-broken over the
embarrassment she has brought to her family and is prepared to do
anything within her power to make amends. Suppose further that,
when she begs her father's forgiveness, he refuses to be reconciled
to her and declares that, because she has disgraced the family, he
never wants to see her again. Has the father acted justly? Clearly
not, for he has failed, it seems, to discharge one of his obligations
as a father; indeed, given his special position of responsibility, his
own sin, in refusing to forgive, seems far worse than his daughter's
sin. In a case such as this, therefore, it seems quite natural to say
that the father *owes* it to his daughter to forgive her and that his
daughter *deserves* his forgiveness. And similarly for God; if he
should refuse to forgive repentant sinners—which, given the simplicity of his loving nature, he cannot do, because he cannot deny
himself—he would likewise fail to discharge one of his obligations
as the Creator. For one of these obligations, however self-imposed,
is to promote the welfare, including the spiritual welfare, of all
created persons; God could no more choose to create persons
without accepting that obligation than human parents can choose to

raise children without acquiring a similar obligation for the welfare of their children. And a God who refused to forgive repentant sinners could no more promote the welfare of those for whom he is responsible than a father who refuses to forgive his children can promote the welfare of the children for whom he is responsible. That is why, given the simplicity of God's moral nature, he forgives not only because he is merciful, but because he is faithful and just as well (see I John 1:9).

Let us now change the example a bit and suppose that the daughter is not particularly repentant. We might imagine that she is in a rebellious stage, that at this time in her life she desires, or seems to desire, the approval of her high school friends more than she does that of her parents; as a result, she becomes more and more defiant. Would that relieve her father of his obligation to forgive her? Again, it seems not. But in this case the father's forgiveness, however heartfelt, may not suffice to heal the broken relationship. So let us now ask a further question: What are the father's obligations in the event that his daughter's actions become more and more destructive to herself and more and more harmful to others? Here it seems clear that he must oppose his daughter's destructive behavior, and a well-chosen punishment may be the best means of communicating such opposition; on that score, at any rate, we can all agree. But insofar as such punishment expresses the father's continuing love for his daughter, it again implies no lack of forgiveness; to the contrary, it precisely *expresses* a forgiving attitude. Of course, any human father will also have to contend with his own weaknesses and limitations, and these may include feelings of resentment or even an unforgiving spirit. But in the case of God, the matter is quite different: We need have no fear that God, whose responsibility for the moral and spiritual welfare of created persons is far greater than that of any earthly father, might fail to discharge one of his obligations as the Creator. For if God is necessarily faithful and just and necessarily accepts, having created a world, all the obligations of the Creator, then his forgiveness, which is in no way opposed to punishment, will be unconditional and without limit of any kind.

As these examples illustrate, the idea that divine justice requires forgiveness accords very well with the New Testament analogy between God and a loving parent. It also illuminates in an intriguing way the nature of God's opposition to sin. As the Augustinians see it, God opposes sin enough to punish it, but not enough to destroy it altogether; instead of destroying sin altogether, he merely confines it to a specially prepared region of his creation, known as hell, where he keeps it alive for an eternity. According to our alternative picture, however, God forgives sin for this very reason: In no other way could he oppose it with his entire being. For as the St. Paul saw so clearly, our specific sins express a sinful condition, and the latter is a form of spiritual death; it is simply our condition of being separated or estranged or alienated from God and from each other. So the opposite of a sinful condition is a state of reconciliation; and if that is so, then God cannot be *against* sin, cannot oppose it with his entire being, unless he is *for* reconciliation. And he can hardly be for reconciliation unless he is prepared to forgive others even as he has commanded us to forgive them. Indeed, if God should refuse to forgive someone, as is not even possible given his loving nature, he would then separate himself from this person; and that is the very essence of sin as Paul himself understood it.

But there is, I believe, an even more subtle reason why divine justice requires the forgiveness of sin, namely this: Divine forgiveness is one of the essential means by which God protects the innocent from irreparable harm and will eventually vindicate his righteousness in the face of unjust suffering. Without any cooperation from us, God can deflect much of the harm that we might *intend* to do to others; he can resurrect victims of murder, for example, just as easily as he can victims of old age. He can even use the harm that we intend to do to others as a means of perfecting them and of promoting their good. But the real harm we do to others is another matter, because it rests upon the harm we do to ourselves, as the mother whose teenage daughter commits suicide illustrates so nicely; the agony the mother experiences rests upon the harm that the daughter has done to herself. Of course, in this case, God can always reunite the mother with her daughter in another life. But suppose that God should refuse to do this; suppose that he should refuse to do anything to reclaim the daughter and refuse to forgive her even on the condition of repentance.   If he should thus permit the daughter to harm herself irreparably, then he would also permit irreparable harm to befall all of those, such as the mother, who love her; and if he should refuse to forgive the daughter, even as the mother would forgive her, then he would separate himself not only from the daughter, but from the mother as well.   Nor would it make any difference if, instead of committing suicide, the daughter had committed murder or even if, like Ted Bundy and Jeff Dahmer, she had committed a series of brutal murders.   When the mother of Ted Bundy declared, so agonizingly and yet so appropriately, her continuing love for her son who had become a monster, she illustrated how in harming himself her son had also harmed his own mother. She also illustrated this all-important point: that not even God can impart supreme joy to such a mother or vindicate his righteousness in permitting her to suffer so, unless his forgiveness can find a way to reclaim her son.

More mysterious, perhaps, and therefore more difficult to appreciate is how God might vindicate his righteousness to the *victims* of a psychopathic killer or to, for example, the Jews who suffered in Nazi concentration camps.   Does God really forgive even those guilty of the most monstrous crimes including genocide?   Here two preliminary points are perhaps in order: First, we need not deny that giving the butchers a "taste of their own medicine" may have a place in the divine scheme of things, particularly when nothing else is likely to get their attention.   But as we have already seen, we simply deceive ourselves if we think that punishment of a retributivist kind would either make up for such atrocities or justify God's decision to permit them in the first place.   Such punishment might be a means to something that would vindicate God's righteousness, but it could hardly vindicate his righteousness in and of itself.   Second, the view that God necessarily forgives even the most monstrous criminals will inevitably make the most sense to those who see their own solidarity with such criminals, to those who fully appreciate their own potential for acting in truly barbaric ways. Most of us have never had the power or the opportunity to act in such ways, and neither have we suffered from the illusion that we could get away with such actions. Having never experienced the particular historical circumstances that existed in Nazi Germany, for example, we deal with our own fears, not theirs; our own torments, not theirs; our own twisted ideologies, not theirs. Most of us probably have no idea of how we would act if suddenly thrust into a set of terrifying circumstances. The moral realist or legalist asks but one question: What has a person actually done? But God, according to most theistic religions, looks at the heart, and he presumably sees in those of us who have *not* committed atrocities many weaknesses and many selfish impulses upon which, because of good fortune perhaps, we have never acted. That, at least, seems to be a prominent theme of the New Testament. To those who congratulate themselves for never having committed adultery, Jesus declares that "everyone who looks at a woman with lust has already committed adultery with her in his heart" (Matthew 5:28); and to those who congratulate themselves for never having committed murder, the letter of I John declares that "All who hate a brother or sister are murderers" (I John 3:15). In the same spirit, a prophet might declare that God sees all of the arrogance and lust for power, all of the fear and bigotry, that lurks in our own hearts as well. My point is not that such atrocities as the Nazi's committed may have been less heinous than we had thought; my point is that none of us should underestimate our own potential for acting in truly barbaric ways.

Be all of that as it may, our question is: How might God best vindicate his righteousness in the face of grossly unjust suffering? Insofar as we simply do not know why God has permitted certain horrors to occur in human history, we may find no answer to our question altogether adequate. But we can still exhibit an important advantage of our alternative picture. According to Augustine, God vindicates his righteousness by subjecting unrepentant souls to eternal torment; and though, as we have seen, such punishment does nothing to restore a just order, Augustine surely is right about one thing: At the very least, the ones responsible for terrible atrocities must learn a hard lesson; in particular, they must be made to appreciate the horror of their own actions. But the paradox is this:

Only someone on the road to redemption, only a forgiven sinner, can fully appreciate the horror of even the most monstrous acts. So long as an Adolf Eichmann remains merely a monster, an irrational remnant of a person, nothing he might endure spitefully, like a tormented animal, will teach him the hard lesson we want him to learn. Do we not want him to reclaim enough of his humanity to admit that he was wrong and to appreciate *why* he was wrong? Do we not want his illusions stripped away, so he can stand naked before his Creator? Only when the light finally breaks into his darkened understanding, only when the divine forgiveness begins its work of transformation, will he begin to appreciate the meaning of his punishment and the true nature of his evil deeds; and then, of course, he will already be on the road to redemption. According to our alternative picture, therefore, a just order will never fully be restored until Adolf Eichmann comes to love his victims so tenderly that he would gladly suffer on their behalf even as they have already suffered on his behalf.

So here, then, is the sum of the matter: If we suppose that God's moral nature is simple, we must also admit that his justice requires exactly the same thing his love requires: the absolute destruction of sin; it requires that sinners repent of any wrong they have done to others and that they be reconciled one to another. In the book of Acts, we thus find the Apostle Peter exhorting a crowd as follows: "Repent therefore, and turn to God so that your sins may be *wiped out*, that times of refreshing may come from the presence of the Lord" (Acts 3:19—my emphasis). Anything less than that would represent a defeat not only of God's love, but of his justice as well. Whether real justice, God's justice, will finally triumph, whether God will ever achieve a final restitution of all things (Acts 3:21) or the reconciliation of all things (Colossians 1:20) is, of course, another matter. But it is hard to see how anything short of such restitution and such reconciliation could possibly qualify as a triumph of justice.

10. OMNIPOTENCE AND THE MYSTERY OF EVIL

> "Aslan," said Lucy through her tears, "could you—
> will you—do something for these poor Dwarfs?"
>
> "Dearest," said Aslan, "I will show you both what I
> can, and what I cannot, do."
>
> C. S. Lewis, *The Last Battle.*

We have seen so far that the Augustinian idea of limited election entails a contradiction and is therefore logically impossible. Even if lovingkindness were not part of God's very nature (or essence), it would be logically impossible for God to make one person the object of his love without likewise making all persons the object of his love. We have also seen that, given the simplicity of God's moral nature, his justice requires exactly the same restoration, the same reconciliation of all things that his love requires. We are therefore entitled, I believe, to reject the Augustinian picture of God as untenable.

But there remains, of course, the Arminian picture. Because the Arminians believe that God truly loves all persons and sincerely wants to achieve the redemption of all sinners—because, in other words, they reject the Augustinian idea of limited election—they do not fall prey to the paradox of exclusivism set forth in Chapter 8. And though some Arminians, such as John Milton, do accept the idea that justice and mercy are different attributes of God, their understanding of hell as a tragic reality in no way requires this mistaken idea. It rests instead upon the assumption that God is unable to achieve the triumph that, given his love, he sincerely wants to achieve. He sincerely wants to reconcile all sinners to himself and is prepared to do anything within his power to achieve that end, but the reconciliation he wants also requires a free response on the part of the sinners themselves. So if a sinner refuses to give that free response or, worse yet, freely rejects God forever, then God, who would never himself reject anyone, is unable to achieve the kind of reconciliation he sincerely wants to achieve. As C. S. Lewis puts it, "I willingly believe that the damned are, in one sense, successful, rebels to the end; that the doors of hell are locked on the *inside*."[1] According to Lewis, then, the damned are precisely those who successfully defeat God's loving purpose for them and freely reject him forever.

A number of contemporary philosophers of religion have defended a similar view,[2] which stresses the role of free agency in the damnation of a soul. Indeed, such philosophers tend to treat the problem of hell in exactly the same way they do the more general problem of evil: In both cases, the crucial appeal is to free will. But while such an appeal is successful, I shall argue, in the latter case, it is not successful in the former. Accordingly, in the present chapter I shall try to show why a Free Will Defense successfully rebuts the anti-theistic argument from evil: the argument that the evil in the world is inconsistent with, or at least is evidence against, the existence of God.[3] Then, in the following chapter, I shall argue, first, that the very idea of someone freely rejecting God forever is deeply incoherent and, second, that an appeal to free will in defense of a doctrine of eternal separation is therefore unsuccessful. For some readers, I might add, the present chapter, in which I discuss the more general problem of evil, will be important for its own sake and will provide an essential foundation for what follows; but for

---

[1]C. S. Lewis, *The Problem of Pain* (New York: Macmillian, 1962), p. 127. See also *The Great Divorce* (New York: Macmillian, 1946).

[2]See, for example, Richard Swinburne, "A Theodicy of Heaven and Hell," in Alfred J. Freddoso (ed.), *The Existence of God* (Notre Dame: University of Notre Dame Press, 1983); Eleanore Stump, "Dante's Hell, Aquinas' Moral Theory, and the Love of God," *The Canadian Journal of Philosophy*, June, 1986; William Lane Craig, "'No Other Name': A Middle Knowledge Perspective on the Exclusivity of Salvation Through Christ," *Faith and Philosophy*, VI (April, 1989); *idem*, "Talbott's Universalism," *Religious Studies*, 27 (Sept., 1991); Jerry L. Walls, *Hell: The Logic of Damnation* (Notre Dame: University of Notre Dame Press, 1992); and Jonathan L. Kvanvig, *The Problem of Hell* (Oxford: Oxford University Press, 1993).

[3]See page 3 above for a succinct statement of the argument.

others, it may seem like an excursus into some rather abstract philosophical arguments. So if you find yourself getting bogged down here, I would simply invite you to move on to the next chapter and to pick up the thread there, which should not be difficult to do.

The Limits of Omnipotent Power

In chapter 1, I chronicled some of my own early struggles with the argument from evil: how my first philosophy class convinced me that I needed a better reply than I had at the time. It is now time to look more closely at this argument and how the appeal to free will figures in a successful reply. The crucial idea is, of course, that free will is incompatible with determinism and hence that not even God can causally determine our *free* choices.

If that is true, then even God, an omnipotent being, faces limits of a certain kind, namely *logical* limits, to what he can do. For though an omnipotent being can no doubt perform any logically consistent (or logically possible) task, not even an omnipotent being can do the logically impossible; that is, not even an omnipotent being can create square circles, or bring it about that two plus two equals five, or create a universe that has the property of being uncreated, or cause it to be the case that St. Paul freely repents of his sin. One way, though not the only way, that a proposition might be logically impossible is for it to include an explicit contradiction, but contradictions do not assert anything specific and therefore do not point to some obstacle in the world, or some competing power, over which God has no control. God's inability to do the logically impossible, therefore, remains quite compatible with his being all powerful in any *intelligible* sense. C. S. Lewis once put the point this way:

> If you choose to say "God can give a creature free will and at the same time withhold free will from it," you have not succeeded in saying *anything* about God: meaningless combinations of words do not suddenly acquire meaning

simply because we prefix to them the two other words
"God can."[4]

Now this is, to be sure, misleading in one respect. Self-contradictory statements are not meaningless combinations of words; if
they were, we would have no way of knowing that they are self-
contradictory. But because they exclude nothing, neither do they
say anything specific about the world; nor do we make them say
something specific "simply because we prefix to them the two other
words 'God can'." So Lewis is essentially right. If we attribute to
God the power to make contradictions true, we have not in fact
attributed to him any *intelligible* power at all; and similarly, if we
deny that God has such power, we have not denied that he has some
intelligible power that one would expect an omnipotent being to
have.

Still, despite anything we might say, some may yet object to the
idea of logical limits to omnipotent power; a being who could make
contradictions true may seem to them greater than one who could
not. But the point to bear in mind here is that the consequence of
such an objection is absolute theological nonsense, and nonsense
does nothing to enhance the greatness of God. If God could do the
logically impossible, then he could deceive all Christians as an expression of his faithfulness to them or subject each of them to eternal torment as an expression of his eternal love for them. That,
however, is nonsense; and as Lewis points out, "You may attribute
miracles" to God, "but not nonsense."[5]

A Fundamental Mystery: The Creation of Persons

Christians who remain uncomfortable with the idea of logical
limits to God's power can perhaps take comfort in the following:
Given these logical limits, two overwhelming difficulties confront
anyone who would try to put forth an anti-theistic argument from
evil.

---

[4]Lewis, *op. cit*, p. 28.

[5]*Ibid.*

The first difficulty arises because we cannot always tell what is, and is not, logically possible. That Smith should be a married bachelor clearly is *not* possible. But what about someone traveling backwards in time or an effect preceding its cause in time? Are these genuine logical possibilities? Whereas a few philosophers believe they are, many others disagree; so at least one side of this dispute is mistaken. But then, if we sometimes do make mistakes concerning what is, and is not, logically possible, we are especially likely to make such mistakes, I would suggest, when we contemplate the mystery of creation. For we really have no clear idea of the logical obstacles that God may have confronted in creating thinking, feeling creatures, who are conscious of themselves as distinct from our environment and from each other. Is it so much as possible, for example, that God should have brought "a society of free souls" into being outside the context of what C. S. Lewis calls "a relatively independent and 'inexorable Nature'?" I doubt it, even as Lewis does when he writes:

> There is no reason to suppose that self-consciousness, the recognition of a creature by itself as a "self," can exist except in contrast with an "other," a something which is not the self. It is against an environment, and preferably a social environment, an environment of other selves, that the awareness of Myself stands out.[6]

Being aware of myself, says Lewis, requires a contrast between myself and something other than myself; and if Lewis is right about that, as I believe he is, then we must consider how such a contrast might be realized. If I were always to get whatever I wanted as soon as I formed the wish, then I would see the entire physical universe, including other persons, as a mere extension of myself and would therefore never realize myself as distinct from my environment or from other people; and if I were not always to get whatever I wanted, then I would experience at least a degree of pain and frustration.[7] So perhaps a degree of pain and frustration is itself a

---

[6]*Ibid.*, p. 29

[7]I borrow this argument from Richard Purtill, *Thinking About Religion* (Englewood Cliffs: Prentice Hall, 1978), p. 20.

necessary condition of a society of independent persons who interact with each other; and if that is true, then perhaps it is not even possible that an individual consciousness should have emerged in what John Hick has called "a hedonistic paradise."[8] A newborn baby comes screaming into the world in what, from its own point of view, must be incredible frustration; and even in the most loving families, the baby will continue to experience many periods of frustration as its developing will comes into conflict with its surroundings. And for all we know, it could not have been otherwise; that is, perhaps not even an omnipotent being could have created an individual consciousness in the absence of all such pain and frustration.

Of course none of this speaks to the many evils in the world that make no contribution to an emerging consciousness and a developing will. But neither have we even scratched the surface of the relevant complexities. Consider a more far-reaching question: Is it so much as possible that a community of perfected saints should be created *ex nihilo* (out of nothing)? Again, I doubt it. If, as Lewis suggests, self-consciousness implies a contrast with an "other," then a sense of *separation*—perhaps an initial separation to be overcome—may be essential to the process by which God creates independent, conscious beings. Perhaps God had no choice, in other words, but to start us out in something like a fallen (or unperfected) condition. If a sinful nature, as some theologians would call it, is simply an *inherited propensity* to sin (literally, to miss the mark), if such a propensity is an inevitable concomitant of a sense of separation (and the ambiguity it implies), and if a sense of separation is essential to the creation of independent, conscious persons, then the very idea of such a person springing into existence in a state of perfection may be deeply incoherent. And if so, then perhaps the dilemma for God in creating independent, conscious persons is this: His love must somehow overcome in the end the very conditions of ambiguity and separation that are essential to their creation in the first place.

---

[8]John Hick, *Philosophy of Religion*, 4th ed., (Englewood Cliffs: Prentice Hall, 1990), p. 45.

Or consider these related questions: Is it possible that *created* persons should achieve supreme happiness, the kind that endures forever, in the absence of something like redemption from a fallen condition?—or possible that they should achieve such happiness without acquiring some of the higher moral virtues?—or possible that, without the freedom to inflict harm, or apparent harm, upon others, they might nonetheless acquire the higher moral virtues? Once again, I see no reason to suppose that any of these are genuine possibilities. But even if I am wrong about that, the most telling point of all remains: In many cases, we cannot be certain what is, and is not, logically possible; hence, we cannot be certain what God's options were in creating individual centers of consciousness and in meeting the conditions of their ultimate happiness. For all we know, God had no choice, if he truly loves us and wants us to achieve supreme happiness in the end, but to start us out in an environment in which we confront some very real evils.

Human Freedom and the Quantity of Evil in the World

One difficulty, then, for any anti-theistic argument from evil is that of knowing what kinds of worlds are, and are not, genuinely possible. A second difficulty is even more serious, but also more difficult to grasp. If it is not within God's power to do the logically impossible, then neither is it within his power to make actual every *possible* state of affairs that he might like to make actual. Many philosophers, following Leibniz, have assumed that an omnipotent being could create (or make actual[9]) any possible world he pleased,

---

[9]If by "world" one means a possible world and by "possible world" one means (roughly) a way things might have been, then God does not, strictly speaking, create a world; indeed a possible world is an abstract entity that has no beginning in time. Rather, God creates the physical universe and all the dependent beings in it and thereby brings it about that one of the possible worlds is the actual world. For this reason, some philosophers would say that God *actualizes* a world and does so, in part, by creating the heavens and the earth. (See, for example, Alvin Plantinga, *The Nature of Necessity* (Oxford: The Clarendon Press, 1974), p.

where a possible world is (roughly) a complete description of the way things might have been. As the philosopher, Alvin Plantinga, demonstrated[10] a couple of decades ago, however, Leibniz's assumption is clearly false. If there are logical limits to what an omnipotent being can do, then many *possible* states of affairs, no less than impossible ones, lie outside the bounds of his direct causal control.

The reason for this has to do with the nature and the possibility of human freedom, or the relevant *kind* of freedom. I perform a given action *freely* in the relevant sense only if it is within my power, at the time of acting, not to perform it; and it is within my power not to perform a given action only if, first, it is logically possible that I not perform it and, second, nothing outside my control causally determines (or necessitates) that I do perform it. So if my act of writing this page is free in the relevant sense, then it must have been possible for me not to write it; and if it *was* possible for me not to write it, then there is a possible world in which I do not write it. That world—call it W—might be the same as the actual world (at least in certain relevant respects) up to the time of my writing, but in that world I choose to spend my time in another way. But though W is truly a possible world (a way things might have been), it is a world that God was powerless to create; had he tried to create it, he would have failed. He could, of course, have *caused* me to refrain from writing, but then I would not have refrained *freely*. In the exact circumstances that obtained, only I could bring it about that I freely refrain from writing. Since I could have chosen not to write, W is indeed a possible world; but since I did not make that choice and God was powerless to bring it about that I did, he was also powerless to create W. If free will (of the relevant kind) is so much as possible, therefore, there are probably an infinite number of possible worlds that God was powerless to create.

169.) In what follows, however, I shall continue to speak as if God creates a world.

[10]See *The Nature of Necessity*, pp. 180-184. See also *God, Freedom, and Evil* (Grand Rapids: Eerdmans, 1977)., pp. 32-34.

I could hardly over stress just how devastating this point is for any anti-theistic argument from evil. Before thinking the matter through carefully, most people probably assume that an omnipotent being could have improved the overall balance of good over evil quite easily; he need only eliminate a bit of pain or a bit of misery or an evil choice here, and perhaps add in a bit of pleasure there. But in fact we have no good reason to suppose that any such procedure would have improved things at all. The point is not that ours is the best of all possible worlds, which may be an incoherent idea anyway;[11] nor is it that every evil is logically required for some greater good. The point is that, for all we know, every *possible* world with less evil than ours *and* a more favorable balance of good over evil belongs to the set of worlds that God was powerless to create; hence, for all we know, God could not have improved things by eliminating some of the evil that actually exists. The genius of this claim, which is apt to seem wildly implausible when one first hears it, will perhaps become clearer if we consider an argument on the other side.

John Beversluis writes:

> The claim that not even Omnipotence can create the kind of world the skeptic has in mind depends for its plausibility on the mistaken assumption that certain [contingent] facts that are true of our world are necessarily and "inexorably" true of *any* world. . . . But an omnipotent God is bound neither by the present properties of matter nor by the causal laws now in operation. He could have created the universe in any way he saw fit. Man could have been created without the capacity for pain or with a much higher pain threshold. While the resulting creature would have been different from us, it would in no way have had to be self-contradictory.[12]

---

[11]No matter how large the universe is, God could, perhaps, have made it larger; and similarly, no matter how much good there is, God could, perhaps, have created more good.

[12]John Beversluis, *C. S. Lewis and the Search for Rational Religion* (Grand Rapids: Eerdmans, 1985), p. 110.

As Beversluis rightly points out, "an omnipotent God is bound neither by the present properties of matter nor by the causal laws now
in operation." It simply does not follow, however, that God "could
have created the universe in any way he saw fit"; at least this does
not follow if free agents are a possible part of the created universe.
For suppose that God had wanted to create a universe just like ours
in this respect: the same laws of nature govern it, the same physical
properties characterize it, and the same persons exist in it; but
suppose also that God had wanted the universe to be different from
ours in this respect: the persons in it always freely refrain from
murder, warfare, and every act of violence against another human
being. Even if we grant that such a world is genuinely possible, it
in no way follows that God could have created it. Take the story of
Cain and Abel, as recorded in the book of Genesis, and treat it, for
purposes of illustration, as an accurate historical account. There is
no logical impossibility, so far as I can discern, in the following
revision of the story: When God puts Cain and Abel in the circumstances described in Genesis and gives Cain the opportunity to kill
Abel, Cain freely chooses not to kill his brother but to express his
anger in some other way. Could God have made this version of the
story true? On the assumption that Cain *freely* slew his brother,
God has already done everything within his power to make our revision of the story true; and yet, on the assumption that Cain freely
chose to murder his brother, it is not true. Accordingly, it was not
within God's power to make it true; and if not, then neither was it
within his power to create a universe of free agents "in any way he
saw fit."

Still, as Beversluis points out, God *could* have created a radically different kind of universe. He could have eliminated *all* pain
and suffering, for example, by the simple expedient of creating a
universe devoid of sentient creatures, and he might have "considered" other possibilities as well: perhaps a universe in which created persons never encounter each other and therefore never harm
each other, or perhaps one in which, because of a different physical
body or different laws of nature, created persons are incapable of
harming each other physically. We can presumably imagine many
possible changes in the structure of the physical universe. But why

assume that the result of any such changes would have been a better world?—that the result would have included greater possibilities of joy and happiness, more interesting life situations, more enduring friendships, better examples of moral courage and self-giving love, or a more favorable balance of good over evil than God will eventually produce in the universe that actually exists? If God did create free agents, remember, the free choices of these free agents will help to determine the overall balance of good over evil in the actual world; so how does Beversluis presume to know that God could have improved the overall balance of good over evil by making structural changes in the physical universe? How does he know what life would be like and what free choices would have been made in very different circumstances from those that actually exist?

Perhaps Beversluis thinks that God could have improved things immeasurably simply by eliminating all cancer from his creation. But in fact no one (who is not omniscient) could possibly know this or even have reason to think it true. Try this thought experiment. Try to imagine what God might have achieved if he had eliminated all cancer from his creation while retaining exactly the same persons in it. Our experiment will not be at all technically accurate and may even be incoherent, but it may also be pedagogically useful. To begin with, then, let us delete from the world (in our imagination) all the pain and suffering caused by this terrible disease as well as all the psychological torment that both cancer victims and those who love such victims have experienced; then, let us delete all those goods—such as the courageous endurance of certain specific pains—for which the cancer is a logically necessary condition; then, let us delete all the free choices—and all the consequences of such free choices—that either would not have been made at all or would have been made differently if our world had been devoid of all cancer. As one can see, things quickly get complicated. If God exists and there is an afterlife, some of the choices deleted may be choices that result in eternal joy and happiness for some persons. But that is just the beginning of our experiment. To fill out our world, we must also *add in* all the options, all the free choices, and all the consequences of such free choices that would have been different. If some persons would have become more arrogant and vicious, that must be added in; and if others would have become more humane and charitable, that too must be added in. At this point our experiment breaks down completely. We cannot possibly know what free choices people would have made in a world without cancer, whether they would have become more vicious or less; nor can we know what options God might have had in working with these people. And that is just the point. Trying to figure what a world of free persons would be like in the absence of cancer is not like calculating where the planets would be today if they had been in certain specified positions last year. Even if we restrict our attention to physical suffering, we cannot *know* that the total quantity of such suffering would have been less had there been no cancer. If, in the absence of cancer, more people would have become more vicious, more likely to engage in warfare or to inflict suffering on others, the elimination of cancer might have *increased* the total quantity of suffering in the universe. God could, to be sure, have created different people or have placed those he did create in different circumstances or have given them different bodies. But once again, we face the same difficulty as before: How are we to know what the consequences of these more radical moves would have been?—whether, for instance, in other bodies we would have become more loving or less loving, more bored with life or less bored with life? Unless Beversluis has a kind of knowledge that some philosophers deny even of God—knowledge of how each free person *would respond* in purely hypothetical situations that don't even exist—he cannot possibly know that a good and omnipotent God would have created things differently.

Once one begins to think through such complexities as these—which we have barely touched upon—the anti-theistic argument from evil begins to look less and less plausible. To make any case at all, a nontheist must defend two claims: first, that some worlds with less evil than ours *and* with a better overall balance of good over evil are logically possible, and second, that at least one of these worlds belongs to the set of worlds within God's power to create. The first claim is difficult enough to defend, as we saw in the previous section, but the second seems utterly impossible to defend. Only an omniscient being, or perhaps someone who receives a clear revelation from such a being, could have any reason to believe the second claim. Accordingly, the so-called Free Will Defense does provide the foundation, albeit an abstract one, for a successful reply to the anti-theistic argument from evil. But a fully satisfying reply requires, I believe, something further; it requires, first of all, the idea of a future compensation for present miseries, and secondly, some idea, if only a glimpse, of the *kind* of future good that might provide such compensation. As we shall see in our final two chapters, moreover, only the universalist is in a position to meet these additional requirements.

11. GOD, FREEDOM, AND HUMAN DESTINY

> "No matter how many eons it takes, he will not rest
> until all of creation, including Satan, is reconciled to
> him, until there is no creature who cannot return his
> love with a joyful response of love."
>
> Madeleine L'Engle

In the previous chapter, we saw something of the importance that Arminians attribute—correctly, in my opinion—to the idea of free choice. Insofar as freedom and determinism are incompatible, free choice introduces into the universe an element that, from God's point of view, is utterly random in that it lies outside of God's direct causal control. Accordingly, if I should freely act wrongly— or worse yet, freely reject God's grace—in a given set of circumstances, then it was not within God's power to induce me to act otherwise, at least not in those precise same circumstances. So in that sense, our free choices, particularly the bad ones, are obstacles that God must work around as he tries to bring his loving purposes to fruition.

Now so far, the Arminian picture seems to me essentially correct. But Arminians hold not only that our free choices are sometimes obstacles that God must work around; they hold also that we are free to defeat God's loving purpose for us altogether. They hold not only that we can reject God for a season, during the period of time we are mired in ambiguity and illusion, but also that we can reject him forever. They deny, in other words, that God is *almighty* in the sense that he is able in the end to accomplish *all* of his loving purposes. According to William Craig, for example, it is quite possible, given the nature of free will, that some created persons are utterly irredeemable in this sense: Nothing God can do—that is, no revelation he might impart, no punishment he might administer, and no conditions he might create—would ever induce them to repent freely or successfully reconcile them to himself.[1] It is also possible,

---

[1]See William Lane Craig, "'No Other Name': A Middle Knowledge Perspective on the Exclusivity of Salvation Through Christ," *Faith and*

Craig insists, that some persons would repent freely only in a world
in which others were damned forever; it is even possible that God
must permit a large number of people to damn themselves in order
to fill heaven with the redeemed. Craig himself puts it this way:

> It is possible that the terrible price of filling heaven is also
> filling hell and that in any other possible world which was
> feasible for God the balance between saved and lost was
> worse. It is possible that had God actualized a world in
> which there are less persons in hell, there would also have
> been less persons in heaven. It is possible that in order to
> achieve this much blessedness, God was forced to accept
> this much loss.[2]

As this passage illustrates, Craig accepts at least the possibility
that, because of free will, history includes an element of irreducible
tragedy, and he exploits this supposed possibility in defense of a
doctrine of everlasting hell. For it is possible, says Craig, that in
order to fill heaven, God had to pay the "terrible price" of "filling
hell" as well. So perhaps God, who is omniscient on Craig's view,
knows from the outset that his triumph will never be complete, and
perhaps he merely does the best he can to minimize his defeat and
to cut his losses.

Now to some, it may appear as if Craig's picture of a defeated
God is but a logical extension of some of my own remarks in the
previous chapter. For as I insisted there myself, the Arminian is
right about this: It is quite possible that, given the reality of free
will, God could not have created a world with less evil in it *and* a
better overall balance of good over evil than exists in the actual
world. But if that is true, one might wonder whether Craig is not
also right. For is it not likewise possible that, given the reality of
free will, God could not have created a world in which no one is

---

Philosophy, VI (April, 1989), pp. 172-178. It is possible, claims Craig,
that some persons suffer from what he calls "transworld damnation"
(and what I have called "transworld reprobation"). For a further discussion of this idea, see Thomas Talbott, "Providence, Freedom, and Human Destiny," *Religious Studies*, XXVI (1990).

[2]*Ibid.*, p. 183.

damned *and* some are saved? And is it not possible that, if fewer people were damned, then fewer would be saved as well? If so, then perhaps God had no choice but to permit some persons to damn themselves freely in order to achieve a better overall balance of good over evil.

In what follows, however, I shall argue that Craig is quite mistaken about the range of possible free choice. But first I want to point out that his picture of a defeated God is in no way a logical extension of anything I have conceded in the previous chapter. For according to Craig, God willingly permits *irreparable* harm to befall at least some of his loved ones, and my own view carries no such implication. To the contrary, I assume that God permits no evil, however horrendous it may appear to us in the present, that he cannot eventually turn to good; and he permits no harm to befall his loved ones that he cannot in the end repair. I also assume that, given a long enough stretch of time, the Hound of Heaven can overcome all of the obstacles that our wrong choices present and can thus achieve *all* of his redemptive purposes; in that respect, he is like the grand chessmaster who, though exercising no direct causal control over the moves of a novice, is nonetheless able to checkmate the novice in the end.

We thus approach the fundamental point of dispute between the universalists and the Arminians. Both agree that God is a perfectly loving being. But they disagree over the question of whether God is *almighty* in the specified sense. As the universalists see it, God's love will eventually triumph; he will thus destroy evil completely and thus remove every stain from his creation. But as the Arminians see it, evil will defeat the love of God in some cases; and in these cases, God will try to minimize the defeat by confining evil to a particular region of his creation, known as hell, where he will keep it alive throughout eternity. Accordingly, against the Arminian picture of a defeated God, I shall now defend three propositions: (i) The very idea of someone freely rejecting God forever is deeply incoherent and therefore logically impossible; (ii) even at the price of interfering with human freedom, a loving God would never permit his loved ones to reject him forever, because he would never permit them to do irreparable harm either to themselves or to others; and (iii) the Arminian understanding of hell is, in any case, utterly inconsistent with the New Testament teaching about hell. Then, in our final chapter, I shall consider again Paul's understanding of Christ's victory over sin and death, and examine the problem of human suffering in light of that victory.

(I) Free Will and the Concept of Damnation

Suppose that the parents of a young boy should discover, to their horror, that they must keep their son away from fire, lest he thrust his hand into the fire and hold it there. Suppose further that their son has a normal nervous system and experiences the normal sensations of pain; hence, the boy not only has no discernible motive for his irrational behavior, but also has the strongest possible motive for refraining from such behavior. Here we might imagine that when the boy does thrust his hand into the fire, he screams in agony and terror, but he nonetheless does not withdraw his hand. Nor does he show, let us suppose, any sign of a compulsion to get to the fire and thrust his hand into it; he sometimes just does it for no discernible reason and in a context in which nothing seems to force him to do it.

Is the story I have just told coherent? I doubt it, though perhaps more would have to be said to settle the matter decisively. But whether coherent or not, the story nonetheless illustrates an important point. If someone does something in the absence of any motive for doing it *and* in the presence of an exceedingly strong motive for not doing it, then he or she displays the kind of irrationality that is itself incompatible with free choice. A necessary condition of free choice, in other words, is a minimal degree of rationality on the part of the one who acts freely. Even on the assumption that nothing causes the boy to thrust his hand into the fire, his totally inexplicable act would be more like a freak of nature or a random occurrence than a choice for which he is morally responsible. Would his parents attribute to him some sort of moral guilt for his bizarre behavior? Not if they are thinking clearly. For moral guilt can arise only in a context in which there are discernible, albeit selfish, motives for what one does. We have imagined, however, a case where the boy has no motive at all, not even a spiteful or a selfish one, for his bizarre behavior.

Now as we have seen, the Arminians insist, correctly, that free will is incompatible with determinism; that is, I perform an action freely, on their view, only if conditions outside my control do not causally determine that I perform it. But too often the Arminians have been content to leave it at that, to proceed as if there were no other necessary conditions of a free act, which there clearly are. As our story above illustrates, a free choice implies not only indeterminism of a certain kind, but a minimal degree of rationality as well. The latter is required in order to distinguish a free choice from a purely random event or chance occurrence, such as the unpredictable change of state of a radium atom, and it also limits the range of possible free choice. That which is utterly pointless, utterly irrational, and utterly inexplicable will simply not qualify as a free choice for which one is morally responsible.

So with that understanding, let us now consider what it might *mean* to say that someone freely rejects God forever. Is there in fact a coherent meaning here? Religious people sometimes speak of God as if he were just another human magistrate who seeks his own glory and requires obedience for its own sake; they speak as if we might reject the Creator and Father of our souls without rejecting ourselves, oppose his will for our lives without opposing, schizo-phrenically perhaps, our own will for our lives. Craig thus speaks of "the stubborn refusal to submit one's will to that of another".[3] But if God is our loving Creator, then he wills for us exactly what, at the most fundamental level, we want for ourselves; he wills that we should experience supreme happiness, that our deepest yearn-ings should be satisfied, and that all of our needs should be met. So if that is true, if God wills for us the very thing we *really* want for ourselves, whether we know it or not, how *then* are we to under-stand human disobedience and opposition to God?

---

[3]William Lane Craig, "Talbott's Universalism," *Religious Studies*, 27 (Sept., 1991), p. 301.

As a first step towards answering this question, let us distinguish between two senses in which a person might reject God. If a person refuses to be reconciled to God and the person's refusal does not rest upon ignorance, or misinformation, or deception of any kind, then let us say that the person has made a *fully informed* decision to reject God; but if the person refuses to be reconciled to God and the person's refusal *does* rest upon ignorance or deception of some kind, then let us say that the person has made a *less that fully informed* decision to reject God. Now no one, I take it, would deny the possibility of someone's making a less than fully informed decision to reject God; it happens all the time. Even St. Paul, before his conversion to Christianity, presumably saw himself as rejecting the Christian God at one time. But what might qualify as a motive for someone's making a fully informed decision to reject God? Once one has learned, perhaps through bitter experience, that evil is always destructive, always contrary to one's own interest as well as to the interest of others, and once one sees clearly that God is the ultimate source of human happiness and that rebellion can bring only greater and greater misery into one's own life as well as into the lives of others, an intelligible motive for such rebellion no longer seems even possible. The strongest conceivable motive would seem to exist, moreover, for uniting with God. So if a fully informed person should reject God nonetheless, then that person, like the boy in our story above, would seem to display the kind of irrationality that is itself incompatible with free choice.

In an effort to establish a motive for a *fully informed* decision to reject God, Craig quotes the famous passage in Book I of *Paradise Lost*, where Milton's Satan declares that he would rather rule in hell than serve in heaven. But that will never do. Even if Milton's Satan were a believable character—which, in my opinion, he isn't[4]—we have no reason to believe that such a character, with so

---

[4]Milton's portrayal of Satan, though enormously insightful in specific contexts, seems to me in the end as unrealistic as his depiction of the war in heaven (in which immortals fight each other with cannons and the like). Milton's artistic challenge was to portray Satan both as the Arch Fiend and as a free and morally responsible agent. That he was

many illusions yet to be shattered, could possibly hold out for an eternity against the love of God. Observe the many ways in which Satan comforts himself: with the illusion that he "Can make a heaven of Hell," with the illusion that in hell he is at least free (despite his bondage to destructive desires), and with the illusion that in hell he "may reign secure." He evidently never even considers the outer darkness (where he would have no one to rule and no world to experience); nor has he yet come to terms with the fact that his willful opposition to God, his desire for revenge, is in reality an attack upon himself. It is a tribute to Milton's art, however, that by Book IV Satan has already lost most of the illusions that made the "heroic" speech of Book I possible; and had Milton's art not been the slave of his theology, I have no doubt that the more pitiful (and even human) character of Book IV would have repented.

Far from illustrating a fully informed decision to reject God, then, Milton's Satan in fact illustrates the essential role that ignorance, deception, and bondage to unhealthy desires must play in any intelligible decision to reject God. But ignorance, deception, and bondage to unhealthy desires are also obstacles to free choice of the relevant kind. If I am ignorant of, or deceived about, the true consequences of my choices, then I am in no position to embrace those consequences freely; and similarly, if I suffer from an illusion that conceals from me the true nature of God, or the true import of union with God, then I am again in no position to reject God freely. I may reject a caricature of God, or a false conception, but I would be in no position to reject the true God himself. Accordingly, the very conditions that render a less than fully informed decision to reject God intelligible also render it less than fully free; hence, God should be able to remove these conditions—the ignorance, the illusions, the bondage to unhealthy desires—without in any way interfering with human freedom.

As a counter to this, Craig makes the following suggestion: If God should shatter all of my illusions, remove all of my ignorance, resolve all of the ambiguities I face, and impart to me an absolutely

---

unable to unite both portraits into a believable whole in no way diminishes his artistic achievement.

clear revelation of himself, then that too would effectively remove any freedom I might have to reject him. Writes Craig: "It may well be the case that for some people the degree of revelation that would have to be imparted to them in order to secure their salvation would have to be so stunning that their freedom to disobey would be effectively removed . . .."[5] But if Craig is right about that, then the very idea of someone freely rejecting the true God is simply incoherent. If both ignorance and the removal of ignorance are incompatible with the relevant kind of freedom, then there can be no freedom of the relevant kind. So it seems that Craig is impaled on the horns of a dilemma. Either I am fully informed concerning who God is and the consequences of rejecting him, or I am not. If I am not fully informed, then I am in no position to reject the true God, as we have seen; and if I am fully informed, then (as Craig himself insists) I am incapable of rejecting God *freely*. So in neither case am I free to reject the true God.

Perhaps this is but one more reason why, according to Paul, we do not choose our own destiny, which "depends not upon human will or exertion, but upon God who shows mercy" (Romans 9:16). The Arminians rightly stress the importance of human freedom and choice, of choosing "this day whom you will serve" (Joshua 24:15). But they are quite mistaken, I believe, in their assumption that we choose our eternal destiny; we no more choose that than we choose to come into existence in the first place. We choose instead which path we shall follow today, and it is God who determines where that path ultimately leads. As the proverb says, "The human mind plans the way, but the Lord directs the steps" (Proverbs 16:9).

As we saw in Chapter 5, moreover, Pauline theology provides a clear picture of how the end of reconciliation could be foreordained even though each of us is genuinely free to choose which path we shall follow in the present. The picture is this: The more one freely rebels against God in the present, the more miserable and tormented one eventually becomes, and the more miserable and tormented one becomes, the more incentive one has to repent of one's sin and to give up one's rebellious attitudes. But more than that, the

---

[5]"Talbott's Universalism," p. 300.

consequences of sin are themselves a means of revelation; they reveal the true meaning of separation and enable us to see through the very self-deception that makes evil choices possible in the first place. We may think that we can promote our own interest at the expense of others or that our selfish attitudes are compatible with enduring happiness, but we cannot act upon such an illusion, at least not for a long period of time, without shattering it to pieces. So in that sense, all paths have the same destination, the end of reconciliation, but some are longer and windier than others. Because our choice of paths in the present is genuinely free, we are morally responsible for that choice; but because no illusion can endure forever, the end is foreordained. As Paul himself puts it: We are all predestined to be conformed to the image of Christ (see Romans 8:29); that part is a matter of grace, not human will or effort.

(ii) Irreparable Harm and the Limits of Permissible Freedom

We have seen so far that the idea of someone freely rejecting God forever—of someone rejecting the true God, as opposed to a caricature of God—is deeply incoherent. I shall now argue further that, even if there were a coherent motive for such a choice, a perfectly loving God would never grant his loved ones the freedom to make it; his love would require him to prevent any choice that would, in the end, undermine the very possibility of supreme happiness not only in the one making the choice, but in everyone else as well.

The issue here concerns the limits of permissible freedom. Consider first the two kinds of conditions under which we humans feel justified in interfering with the freedom of others. We feel justified, on the one hand, in preventing one person from doing irreparable harm—or more accurately, harm that no *human being* can repair—to another; a loving father may thus report his own son to the police in an effort to prevent the son from committing murder. We also feel justified, on the other hand, in preventing our loved ones from doing irreparable harm to themselves; a loving father may thus physically overpower his daughter in an effort to prevent her from committing suicide.

Now one might, it is true, draw a number of faulty inferences from such examples as these, in part because we humans tend to think of irreparable harm within the context of a very limited time-frame, a person's life on earth. Harm that no human being can repair may nonetheless be harm that God can repair. It does not follow, therefore, that a loving God, whose goal is the reconciliation of the world, would prevent every suicide and every murder; it follows only that he would prevent every harm that not even omnipotence can repair, and neither suicide nor murder is necessarily an instance of that *kind* of harm. So even if a loving God could sometimes permit murder, he could never permit one person to annihilate the soul of another or to destroy the very possibility of future happiness in another; and even if he could sometimes permit suicide, he could never permit his loved ones to destroy the very possibility of future happiness in themselves either. Just as loving parents are prepared to restrict the freedom of the children they love, so a loving God would be prepared to restrict the freedom of the children he loves, at least in cases of truly irreparable harm. The only difference is that God deals with a much larger picture than that with which human parents are immediately concerned.

So the idea of *irreparable* harm—that is, of harm that not even omnipotence can repair—is critical; and if one fails to distinguish between that kind of harm and others, then one will miss the whole point of the above argument. Jonathan Kvanvig, for example, clearly misses the point when he writes: "Contrary to what Talbott claims, freedom is sometimes more important than the harm that might result from the exercise of freedom."[6] For of course I have never claimed otherwise. I have claimed only that a *certain kind of harm*—that is, harm that omnipotence can neither repair nor compensate for—would outweigh not only the value of freedom but also the value of any conceivable good that God might bring forth from the misuse of freedom. Suppose, by way of illustration, that

---

[6]Jonathan L. Kvanvig, *The Problem of Hell* (Oxford: Oxford University Press, 1993), p. 85.

God should know the following: If he should grant me the freedom to annihilate the soul of my brother and I should exercise that freedom, then thousands of people who otherwise would not freely repent of their sin would, under these conditions, freely repent of their sin. We might imagine that the horror of such irreparable harm would induce these people to re-examine their own lives. Even so, God could not permit such irreparable harm to occur; an injustice such as I have just imagined—the complete annihilation of an innocent person—would outweigh any conceivable good that God might use it to achieve. In the end, it would also undermine the possibility of supreme happiness in everyone else, as we have seen in previous chapters (especially Chapters 8 and 9).

And similarly for the kind of case that William Craig asks us to imagine. Even if someone's damnation *would* induce thousands of people to repent of their sin freely, God could not permit, I contend, such irreparable harm to befall one of his loved ones. Some will no doubt want to drive a wedge between the kind of case where one does irreparable harm to *oneself*, perhaps by freely choosing to damn oneself, and the kind where one does irreparable harm to *another*. That seems to be what Jonathan Kvanvig has in mind when he first concedes that one might justifiably interfere with someone's freedom to commit murder, and then goes on to criticize my example of suicide in the following way:

> Talbott has not . . . correctly analyzed the case of suicide. Sometimes interference in cases of suicide is justified, but it is not justified solely because suicide causes irreparable harm. . . Rather, what justifies our intervention is the fact that the person will come, or will likely come, to see that his choice of death was not what he really wanted or would have wanted if he had reflected carefully. Alternatively, if we are fully convinced and it is true that the person is competent to choose, is rational in choosing suicide, and cannot be persuaded otherwise, then, from a purely moral point of view, interference is not justified (except insofar as

the suicide has consequences for other persons such as dependent children).[7]

But this criticism rests upon a pair of misunderstandings. Observe first that Kvanvig imagines a case where a "person is competent to choose" and "is rational in choosing suicide." Such a case is not difficult to imagine. If a person suffers from a terminal illness such as Alzheimer's disease, or suffers persistent and excruciating pain for which there is no treatment, or possesses information that an enemy could use against comrades in arms, then it may be quite rational to see suicide as the lesser of two evils. In at least some such cases as these, those who love the suicide victim may view the suicide with relief or even as a noble act; and in all such cases God would retain the power to re-unite the suicide victim with his or her loved ones at some future time. The relevant cases for our purposes, however, are those in which the suicide is quite irrational, even as a fully informed decision to reject God would be quite irrational. In these cases, we can reason in one of two ways: We might insist that the decision to commit suicide, being irrational, is not truly free; or if we grant, for the sake of argument, that the decision is free despite its irrational character, we might then insist upon an obligation to interfere, where possible, with the freedom of others to harm themselves in a way that is both irrational and irreparable.

Observe second Kvanvig's final proviso concerning the consequences of a suicide for other persons. In conceding the relevance of such consequences, he in effect concedes the very argument he has set out to criticize. For a person is not an isolated monad whose happiness, or lack of same, is independent of other persons; as we have seen repeatedly, it is simply not possible that one should destroy every chance of future happiness in oneself without, at the same time, undermining the future happiness of others as well. If I truly love my daughter as myself, for example, then her damnation would be an intolerable loss to me and would undermine my own happiness every bit as much as it would undermine hers. One simply cannot drive a wedge, therefore, between the kind of case

---

[7]*Ibid.*, p. 84.

where one does irreparable harm to oneself and the kind where one does irreparable harm to others. And if a loving God must prevent the latter, as Kvanvig himself concedes, then he must prevent the former as well.

This argument seems to me utterly decisive. But in an heroic effort to defeat it and to defend an Arminian conception of hell, Craig insists that God could indeed damn some without harming others; he could do so by foisting upon the redeemed an elaborate deception, thereby maintaining them in a state of blissful ignorance. For it is possible, Craig suggests, that God simply "obliterates" from the minds of the redeemed "any knowledge of lost persons so that they experience no pangs of remorse for them."[8] Here the suggestion seems to be that God performs a kind of lobotomy on the redeemed, expunging from their minds any memory that might interfere with their future happiness. In the case of those whose entire family is lost, this would mean, I presume, that God expunges from their minds every memory of parents and other family members; and I doubt that Craig has any conception of how much of a person's mind that would likely destroy. He is right, of course, about one thing:

> We can all think of cases in which we shield persons from knowledge which would be painful for them and which they do not need to have, and, far from doing something immoral, we are, in so sparing them, exemplifying the virtue of mercy.[9]

But withholding information for a season is one thing; obliterating part of a mind forever is something else altogether. The latter reduces God's victory over sin to a cruel hoax; his hollow "victory" consists not in his making things right, but in his concealing from the redeemed just how bad things really are. Though utterly defeated in the end, God simply conceals from us the enormity of the defeat.

---

[8] "Talbott's Universalism," p. 306.

[9] *Ibid.*

Nor has Craig analyzed correctly the conditions under which it is appropriate to withhold painful information from a loved one. In every case, I would suggest, this is either a concession to someone's poor physical health—as when a doctor conceals from a woman, critically injured in a traffic accident, that her child was killed—or a concession to someone's psychological or spiritual immaturity. The blissful ignorance that results from such deception is not only not supremely worthwhile; it is even inferior to the experience of misery under certain conditions.   For no one who truly loves another would want to remain blissfully ignorant of the other's fate, however painful the knowledge of such a fate might be. No loving father, for example—not even one whose daughter endures a brutal rape and murder and not even one whose son commits suicide— would want to remain blissfully ignorant about what happened. It is far better, he would judge, to know the truth of the matter; he might even take elaborate steps to discover the truth. And the idea that he might prefer to have all memory of a son or a daughter obliterated from his mind—that he might prefer this over his anguish—is simply preposterous.

On Craig's account, at any rate, God is the author not merely of a *temporary* deception, but of an *everlasting* deception as well. Now I have no doubt concerning this: In order to meet the needs of his loved ones, God sometimes does employ a temporary deception as a means of redemption; as Paul himself teaches, God sometimes deceives those who are unready for the truth in order to bring them ultimately to the truth (see Chapter 5). But here the goal of the deception is to prepare people for an ultimate unveiling of truth; as Jesus said, we shall know the truth, and the truth (not an elaborate deception) shall set us free (John 8:32). If the truth itself (and not an elaborate deception) is what ultimately sets us free, then that tells us something important about the nature of the truth. It tells us that the truth about the universe is ultimately glorious, not tragic; it is something that God can gladly reveal to us, not something that he must conceal from us, lest it should undermine our happiness in the end.   But even if the truth about the universe were ultimately tragic, it would be far better, I believe, for God to reveal to us the full dimensions of the tragedy. For even then we might find *some* consolation in sharing our eternal grief with others; and from love's point of view, honest grief is far better than blissful ignorance.

(iii) Free Will and the Misery of Hell

The theological and philosophical arguments, just considered, for preferring the universalist picture of a triumphant God over the Arminian picture of a defeated God are enough, I believe, to decide the issue in favor of the former. For those Christians who look to the New Testament for guidance and inspiration, however, I also want to point out how far removed the Arminian picture is from anything we encounter in the New Testament. In Part II of this essay, I tried to set forth the positive case for a universalist reading of the New Testament. Let us now examine, more specifically, the Arminian understanding of hell in light of the New Testament teaching.

As we have seen, the fundamental Arminian idea is that created persons are free to reject God forever (and therefore to defeat his love forever); and as we have also seen, the fundamental difficulty here is to discern any conceivable motive for a fully informed decision to reject God. Beyond that, there is this additional difficulty: The misery of hell, as depicted in the New Testament, would seem to provide the strongest conceivable motive for leaving the place *if* one were truly free to do so. According to C. S. Lewis and a host of others, God does not reject the damned; the damned, being successful rebels to the end, reject him. Hence, the gates of hell are closed from the inside; that is, though the inhabitants of hell are indeed free to repent and to vacate this place at any time they choose, at least some of them will never choose to do so. But here we must ask once again: How could anyone who is rational enough to be morally responsible for his or her actions prefer the misery of hell over the joys of reconciliation? What motive, what greater good from the perspective of the damned, would make the miseries of hell seem like the lesser of two evils?

A popular strategy among Arminians at this point is to suggest that, from the perspective of the damned, hell really isn't that bad a

place to be; at the very least, it is apt to seem far superior to heav-
en. The first step is to challenge the traditional image of a fiery
furnace and torture chamber as overly barbaric and superstitious;
the second is to suggest a motive for preferring hell over heaven.
According to Jerry Walls, for example, "hell may afford its inhabitants a kind of gratification which motivates the choice to go
there."[10] More than that, the damned may even experience a kind
of illusory happiness.

> Those in hell may be almost happy, and this may explain
> why they insist on staying there. They do not, of course,
> experience even a shred of genuine happiness. But per-
> haps they experience a certain perverse sense of satisfac-
> tion, a distorted sort of pleasure.[11]

Though Walls denies that the damned are *genuinely* happy, he does
not deny that they *believe* themselves to be happy; to the contrary,
he insists that, for some lost souls, the illusion of happiness may
endure forever and with sufficient conviction to explain why they
never leave their preferred abode in hell.

> Those who prefer hell to heaven have convinced them-
> selves that it is better. In their desire to justify their choice
> of evil, they have persuaded themselves that whatever sat-
> isfaction they experience from evil is superior to the joy
> which God offers.[12]

This line of thought leads naturally to a conclusion that Eleanore Stump has explicitly defended:[13] Because God knows that he
can do nothing, short of removing their freedom, to induce the
damned to repent, he simply employs his omnipotent power to make
them as comfortable as possible and to prevent them from harming

---

[10]Jerry L. Walls, *Hell: The Logic of Damnation* (Notre Dame: University of Notre Dame Press, 1992), p. 128.

[11]*Ibid.*, p. 126.

[12]*Ibid.*, p. 129.

[13]See "Dante's Hell, Aquinas' Moral Theory, and the Love of God,"
The Canadian Journal of Philosophy, June, 1986.

others. But this entire line of thought also seems far removed from the images and language of the New Testament, which are far more suggestive of a chamber of horrors than many would like to believe. Is it not precisely the New Testament that pictures hell as a "furnace of fire, where there will be weeping and gnashing of teeth" (Matthew 13:42) and where people will pray for the mountains to fall upon them (Revelation 6:16)? In the parable of the sheep and the goats (Matthew 25:31-46), Jesus alludes not to a freely embraced condition, but to a form of *punishment*, as we have seen; and in some cases at least, the punishment will come as a complete surprise. And in the parable of the rich man and Lazarus (Luke 16:16-31), the rich man wants to warn his five brothers "so that they will not also come into this place of torment" (16:28). As depicted in the New Testament, in other words, hell is not the kind of place that even the wicked would freely choose to inhabit forever. For it really is a place of unbearable suffering and torment.

We can appreciate, of course, why the Arminians might want to water down the New Testament picture of hell as a place of unbearable suffering; an eternity of such suffering would be, after all, utterly pointless, and a god who would actually inflict such suffering forever would be unspeakably barbaric. But here, I would suggest, the universalists are in a far better position to accept the images and the language of the New Testament than the Arminians are. For the universalists can regard hell as a genuine form of punishment or correction, rather than a freely embraced condition; hence, they have no need to water down the New Testament image of unbearable suffering. Perhaps a period of such suffering is just what a Hitler or a Goebbels needs; and for that matter, perhaps it is just what they began to experience during the final days of their earthly life. So if, as John Hick has suggested,[14] hell is but the continuation of the purgatorial sufferings of this life, then we have no reason to reject the language of unbearable suffering. Nor even to reject the image of a fiery furnace, which is as good a representation of God's purifying love as there is. When people

---

[14]See John Hick, *Philosophy of Religion,* 4th ed. (Englewood Cliffs: Prentice Hall, 1963), p.125.

deceive themselves and beat their heads against the hard rock of
reality, they suffer and sometimes suffer unbearably. They may not
choose to suffer any more than Hitler chose to be defeated in battle,
but their suffering is an inevitable consequence of their misguided
actions. And in the end, the unbearable nature of their suffering
will shatter their illusions and reveal to them the error of their
ways.

     One reason that some Arminians reject the New Testament lan-
guage of unbearable suffering and the image of a fiery furnace is
this: If the consequences of living a sinful life include unbearable
suffering, at least over the long run, and if unbearable suffering
will, in the end, successfully shatter those illusions that make a
sinful life possible in the first place, then no one is truly *free* to live
in sin forever. As Jerry Walls puts it, "no finite being can continue
endlessly to choose greater and greater misery for himself. So in
the end, the knowledge which makes impossible the choice of damnation is not acquired through free choice, but is itself impossible to
avoid."[15] That is correct. But consider the alternative. The only
alternative would be for God to protect people forever from the
consequences of living a sinful life and to do so for the purpose of
sustaining the illusions that make such a life possible. That, it
seems to me, would be incompatible with God's moral character.
Suppose that I should act upon the illusion that I can benefit myself
at the expense of others. If God should protect me forever from the
bitter consequences of such actions, then in a very real sense I
would not be acting upon an illusion at all. I would be right on the
most important matter. For I could indeed act selfishly with a degree of impunity. It is as if I should bring my hand near to a flame
and God should protect me from the excruciating pain of the flame.
In that event, my belief that I could so act with impunity would not
be an illusion.

     The fact is, moreover, people have their illusions shattered
against their will all the time. A man who, upon entering into an
adulterous affair, makes a total mess of his life may in time learn a
hard lesson, one that he in no way *chose* to learn; and having

---

[15]Walls, *op. cit.*, p. 132.

learned his lesson, he may be utterly unwilling to repeat the experiment. And similarly for Paul's conversion on the road to Damascus: As I read the account in *Acts*, Paul in no way *chose* to have his illusions shattered; and neither did he choose to receive a revelation that would in a very brief time transform this "chief of sinners" into a Christian missionary. Indeed, his own experience on the road to Damascus probably explains why Paul consistently regarded redemption as no less a work of God than creation itself. But Pauline theology in no way excludes human freedom and moral responsibility altogether. For even if redemption is a work of God, free choice and the correction of wrong choices could still be, as I believe it is, an essential part of the process whereby God reveals his true nature to us and teaches us the (occasionally hard) lessons we need to learn as we travel the road to redemption.

12. LOVE'S FINAL VICTORY

> "For I am persuaded, that neither death, nor life, nor angels, nor principalities, nor powers, nor things present, nor things to come, nor height, nor depth, nor any other creature, shall be able to separate us from the love of God, which is in Christ Jesus our Lord."
>
> St. Paul

Tradition holds that hell has two crucial features: It is a place (or perhaps a condition) of unbearable suffering, and the suffering will quite literally last forever. But suffering that is *both* unbearable *and* unending seems utterly pointless, as we have seen; it also seems clearly inconsistent with the love of God. We therefore confront the following alternative: Either we must deny, as some Arminians do, that hell is a place of unbearable suffering, or we must deny, as the universalists do, that the suffering will literally last forever. Now the New Testament seems clear and decisive on the matter of unbearable suffering; its brief allusions to punishment in the next life seem explicitly to rule out the idea that those who endure such punishment will nonetheless believe themselves to be in a happy state. So why not, I have asked, interpret this to mean that the sufferings of hell are temporary?—that these sufferings are the way in which those who cling to their illusions experience the final shattering of their illusions?

As I have suggested, such a view accords very well with the picture of hell that we encounter in the gospels; it also accords just as well with Paul's understanding of Christ's ultimate victory over sin and death. Consider again Paul's words in the fifteenth chapter of I Corinthians:

> Then comes the end, when he hands over the kingdom to God the Father, after he has destroyed every rule and every authority and power. For he must reign until he has put all his enemies under his feet. The last enemy to be destroyed is death. . . . When all things are subjected to him, then the Son himself will

also be subjected to him who put all things in subjection under him, so that God may be all in all (15:25-
26, 28).

Here Paul does seem to endorse *part* of the Arminian view. If *competing wills* lie behind "every rule and every authority and power" that Christ eventually destroys, then these competing wills are no doubt genuine obstacles that God must work around and overcome. For if the power in these competing wills is real, then presumably not even God can overcome that power by fiat; he must first produce conditions under which the competing wills themselves will cooperate in their own transformation. But Paul also speaks with great confidence concerning the assuredness of Christ's ultimate victory. Competing wills may successfully resist God for a season, but Christ will defeat all of them in the end and eventually bring all things, including every competing will, into subjection to himself. Then, after subduing every power and authority and bringing every competing will into conformity with his own loving will, Christ will subject himself to the Father, and the Father will then truly be "all in all." At this time, after all separation from God has been eliminated, nothing will exist except God and those who are united with him in love.

It seems clear, then, that Paul's understanding of Christ's ultimate victory leaves no room for the Arminian idea that some sinners, being successful rebels to the end, will defeat the love of God forever. According to the Manichaein theory, to which Augustine subscribed for a time prior to his conversion to Christianity, good and evil are eternally at war with each other. But according to Christianity, evil not only depends for its existence upon the permission of God, who tolerates it for awhile only because he can turn it to good, but God will also destroy *all* evil in the end and banish it from his creation forever. What this means should now be clear. Even the annihilation of the wicked would represent a permanent defeat for a loving God and would leave a permanent stain on his creation; and even if God could purge the bitter memories of that defeat from the minds of others, he could not purge the infinitely worse memories from his own mind. So nothing short of everyone being reconciled to God and to each other in an inclusive community of love could possibly qualify as a decisive victory over evil.

Towards a Christian Theology of Suffering

Now it is from the perspective of Love's final victory over evil, I believe, that a Christian should try to understand the sufferings of this life. From Love's point of view, anything less than total victory would be a disaster of unimaginable proportions; indeed, the permanent loss of a single person would probably outweigh— over an infinite stretch of time—all of the temporary evils, as horrendous as they might seem to us in the present, that the world has seen so far. So, for that reason alone, Love will endure a lot over the short term, and even ask others to endure a lot, in order to achieve its final victory over separation and estrangement.

This may explain in part the relatively casual attitude towards suffering that we sometimes find in the New Testament. Paul, for example, pretty much dismisses the sufferings of this life when he writes: "I consider that the sufferings of this present time are not worth comparing with the glory about to be revealed to us" (Romans 8:18). That future glory, he seems to suggest, will more than compensate for all of the travails experienced along the way. His point is not, of course, that the brutal rape and murder of a young girl is less evil than we might have thought; he would probably have condemned the vicious attitudes and the selfishness that make such atrocities possible even more harshly than we moderns do. Nor is it that we should not yearn for a time when all such suffering will be a thing of the past. But what seems to horrify Paul even more than the suffering of an innocent victim, whether it be the suffering of Jesus Christ or that of an innocent child, is the reckless disobedience, the *sin*, of the one whose *intention* it is to harm the victim. Confident that in the end God will somehow protect the victim from irreparable harm, Paul thus agrees with Plato that injustice, even in the case of a brutal rape and murder of a young girl, harms the one who acts unjustly far more, or at least in a far more direct way, than it does the victim.

Even more startling, perhaps, than Paul's off-handed dismissal of the sufferings of this life is the New Testament teaching that we should *expect* to suffer, that we should count it a *privilege* when we do suffer, and that we should *rejoice* in our sufferings. In the fourth chapter of I Peter, we read:

> Beloved, do not be surprised at the fiery ordeal which comes upon you to prove you, as though something strange were happening to you. But rejoice in so far as you share Christ's sufferings, that you may also rejoice and be glad when his glory is revealed (I Peter 4:12-13).

The idea that we should rejoice in our sufferings, like the New Testament idea that we should love our enemies and do good to those who do evil to us, is indeed startling. One is apt to wonder whether such a thing is humanly possible, which in a sense it clearly is not. For my own part, at least, I doubt that I could rejoice in the midst of even moderate suffering, not to mention severe and protracted suffering. But there nonetheless is, I believe, a perspective from which all of this begins to make sense, and even those of us who are not saints can perhaps catch a fleeting glimpse of why it makes sense.

When some of the rare saints, such as those facing martyrdom, do manage to rejoice in their sufferings, they presumably do so not because they are masochists, not because they desire suffering for its own sake, and not because they fail to appreciate how wonderful life can be when it is free from suffering; they do so because they have somehow come to see their suffering as a personal sacrifice in the present for the sake of a greater joy in the future. We see this most clearly, perhaps, in the suffering and death of Jesus Christ, and here I would emphasize a point that Christian theologians have sometimes neglected: the sense in which, according to the New Testament, Jesus' sufferings benefited *himself*. I have no doubt that, as depicted in the New Testament, Jesus' motives were entirely altruistic; he did not act with his own benefit principally in view. Neither do I doubt that the benefit he received from his own sufferings depends logically upon the benefit that others have received from them. Nonetheless, the letter to the Hebrews makes two points abundantly clear: first, that it was "for the sake of the joy that was set before him" that Jesus "endured the cross" (Hebrews 12:2); and second that, in addition to being "crowned with glory and honor because of the suffering of death," Jesus was actually made "perfect through sufferings" (Hebrews 2:9-10). Behind both of these remarkable claims, there seems to lie a more basic assumption of a mystical nature.

> But we see Jesus, who was made a little lower than the angels for the suffering of death, crowned with glory and honour; that he by the grace of God should taste death for every man. For it became him [God], for whom are all things, and by whom are all things, in bringing many sons unto glory, to make the captain [or the pioneer] of their salvation perfect through sufferings. For both he that sanctifieth and they who are sanctified *are all of one*: for which cause he [Jesus] is not ashamed to call them brethren (Hebrews 2:9-11, KJV—my emphasis).

Here we encounter the familiar theme that Jesus suffered and tasted "death for every man" (literally "for the sake of all"). But we also encounter an explanation of why *it was fitting* that this should be so. It was fitting, we read, because both Jesus and those for whose sake he suffered and died are "all of one." But how so? How should we interpret Jesus' oneness (or solidarity) with the rest of humanity? According to the author, Jesus both "partook of the same nature" as human beings (2:14—RSV) and was made "like his brothers and sisters in every respect" (2:17). Beyond that, we have the simple fact that he regarded those for whose sake he suffered and died as his *brothers and sisters*; that is, he drew no distinction in his own mind between their best interest and his own, or between the conditions of their future happiness and the conditions of his own future happiness, or between what was good for them and what was good for him. So when the author of Hebrews affirms that both Jesus and those for whom Jesus suffered and died are "all of one," he seems to have in mind the very kind of point upon which we have insisted repeatedly (in Chapter 8 above and elsewhere). Jesus was no more of an isolated monad than you and I are, and his future happiness was no less dependent upon the future happiness of others than yours and mine is.

And similarly for the Father himself. Theologians have sometimes depicted God, the Father, as if his own happiness were utterly independent of that of created persons. But as we have seen, such a picture is inconsistent with the New Testament proclamation that God *is* love, that it is God's very nature to love. Even as my knowing that my daughter had come to a bad end would undermine my own happiness, so much more would a loving God's knowing that a child of his had come to a bad end undermine *his* happiness. But the truth, I want to suggest, is even more astounding than that. God's oneness with us, even in our estrangement, is so intimate that, even as we experience the world through our bodies, so God experiences it as well: Every pain we experience is therefore a pain that God experiences, and every torment we endure is a torment that God endures as well. When I was an undergraduate, one of my classmates liked to proclaim: "Poetic justice: God damned to the hell of his own creation!" I doubt that he knew how close he had come to a profoundly religious vision of God, according to which God enters his own creation with every child that is born and literally experiences the world from the child's point of view. Such a God, so compassionate and so identified with those whom he loves into existence, could not possibly experience a creation such as ours as anything other than a kind of temporary damnation. But with this difference: Insofar as God sees clearly the end from the beginning and contemplates the glorious future in store for those who endure suffering in the present, he continues to rejoice even as he suffers along with his suffering children.

Now it is in this context, I suggest, that we should try to understand the claim that Jesus himself was made perfect through his suffering. How, one may ask, could someone who according to the New Testament knew no sin (see II Corinthians 5:21) and was thus utterly innocent have been perfected through his sufferings? An answer commonly given is that through suffering Jesus was perfected *in his role as savior*;[1] and though that seems right as far as it goes, one should not, I would argue, minimize the implication in the

---

[1] See F. F. Bruce, *The Book of Hebrews* (Grand Rapids: Eerdmans Publishing Co., 1990), p. 80.

text that Jesus' sufferings somehow made *him* more complete or whole. F. F. Bruce asks: "If the Son of God is the effulgence of his Father's glory and the very impress of his being, how can he be thought of as falling short of perfection?"[2] The answer depends upon the kind of perfection in question. If the essence of God is love, if God is now in the process of creating objects of his love, and if God himself suffers along with his suffering children, then there is a personal sense in which not even God, despite his metaphysical perfections, is now complete or whole or yet "all in all." For in no loving relationship can the one who loves be complete or whole until the one who is loved is also complete and whole; in that respect, the process whereby the children are reconciled and made whole is also a process whereby the Father is completed and made whole. The Father is not yet, but one day will be, "all in all."

Observe also the parallel in the text between God's "bringing many sons [and daughters] unto glory" and his making "the pioneer of their salvation perfect through sufferings." It is fitting, the text seems to suggest, that the pioneer should suffer, and it is fitting for just this reason: His suffering enabled God to bring many sons and daughters to glory, and the joy of seeing these sons and daughters brought to glory—of seeing them reconciled to each other and to God—is just what makes the pioneer himself complete and whole. For the very reason that he and they are "all of one," he cannot be complete and whole until they also are complete and whole. The reconciliation of the world, in other words, was both the object and the ground of the joy, set before Jesus, that enabled him to endure suffering and death; and to the extent that his sufferings were a benefit to others, they were a benefit to himself as well.

Completing the Sufferings of Christ

Consider next the context in which the New Testament places the suffering of Christians and other innocent persons. We observed in the previous section that, according to I Peter 4:12 and

---

[2]*Ibid.*

13, Christians should actually rejoice in their sufferings. But we did not there discuss the reason given for such rejoicing.

According to the text, we should rejoice in our sufferings, because in suffering innocently ourselves we thereby share in the sufferings of Christ. So now we must ask: What does it mean to share in the sufferings of Christ? It means, surely, that all who suffer innocently are, like Jesus Christ himself, instruments through whom God reconciles the world to himself. Paul thus declares: "I am now rejoicing in my sufferings for your sake, and in my flesh I am completing what is lacking [or *incomplete*] in Christ's afflictions for the sake of his body, that is, the church . . ." (Colossians 1:24). And though some commentators have found this text worrisome because they fear the apparent implication that the work of Christ is in some way incomplete, I see nothing worrisome here at all. No Christian would claim that Christ's work is already complete in the sense that *we* no longer have any work to do, any message to proclaim, any acts of charity to perform, or any suffering to endure. From an eschatological perspective, as some theologians like to call it, Christ's work, as depicted in Hebrews and elsewhere, is indeed complete: "For by a single offering he has perfected for all time those who are sanctified" (Hebrews 10:14). From the perspective of the here and now, however, Christ's work will not be complete until it is finally completed *in us*, until our perfection as sons and daughters of God is fully accomplished. So in that sense, everyone who suffers on behalf of others helps to complete what so far remains incomplete in the suffering of Christ.

At this point, some will no doubt observe, quite properly, that the sufferings of innocent children (and also those of lower animals) are different from those of Christ in at least one all-important respect: Whereas Jesus, given the Christian understanding of his life, *voluntarily* suffered and died on behalf of others, small children are often in no position even to understand their suffering; much less are they in a position to submit to it voluntarily. And if small children are in no position even to understand their suffering, then neither are they in a position to rejoice while in the midst of it.

All of this is unquestionably true. Nor should we, even in the interests of theodicy, lose sight of how genuinely tragic the sufferings of the most helpless among us can sometimes be. As a matter of faith, if you will, I am prepared to endorse two points: first, that all children who suffer in the present will at some future time rejoice in their past sufferings; and second, that such suffering also completes the suffering of Christ in a special way and in a way that nothing else could. Before elaborating further upon these matters, however, I must first clarify an important point. Christians have always believed that God brings good out of evil; they have also insisted that the sufferings of the innocent, like the sufferings of Christ, serve a redemptive purpose. Beyond that, the Christian faith, I have insisted, rests upon the assumption that the truth about the universe is ultimately glorious, not tragic. There are no *irreducible* tragedies and no instances of *irreparable* harm. But there are plenty of *temporary* tragedies—many human sins, for example—and plenty of things in the here and now that ought not to be. For though tragedy never has the final word, on the Christian view, it can be very real over the short run; and though God may have a justifying reason, grounded in a loving purpose, for permitting such temporary tragedies as sometimes occur in human history, *we* have an obligation to work against them and, in particular, to ameliorate human suffering wherever we can.

But how, one may ask, could this be? How could *we* have an obligation to work against the very thing that God has a justifying reason to permit? The answer, I want to suggest, lies in the philosophical perspective already set forth in Chapter 10. If the free choices of created persons are genuine obstacles that God must work around (and in some cases overcome), then it is quite possible that God cannot achieve his long range loving purposes without permitting a certain amount of tragedy over the short run; it is also possible that God faces obstacles that others, through whom he is trying to work, do not face. It is possible, for example, that our free choices have put God in the following position with respect to certain evils: Even though *others*, such as you and I, could prevent these evils without, at the same time, eliminating a greater good (and thereby making matters worse), *God* could not. It is even possible that, if God should try to eliminate all tragedy from human life in the present, he would succeed only in undermining the future happiness of everyone, including himself.

Consider, by way of illustration, the young daughter of a vicious child beater, an innocent child whose deepest yearning is that her daddy should love her. As many social workers have found to their chagrin, merely to separate such a child from her father sometimes does more harm than good because what the child wants, even more than to escape suffering, is reconciliation and love; additional separation is precisely what she does not want. Of course God himself would have many options to consider in a case such as this; he could, to begin with, have put the child in a different family altogether. But as we saw in Chapter 10, we have no way of knowing what the ultimate consequences of such an action would have been, whether it would have resulted in less tragedy or perhaps even more tragedy over the long run; and furthermore, whatever *God's* options may have been, the *father* is clearly in a position to achieve a specific good that God could not achieve alone. For it is at least possible that God could not *both* prevent the beatings *and* satisfy the daughter's yearning for reconciliation with her father. But the father obviously *could* do both; he could stop beating his daughter and, at the same time, satisfy her yearning for reconciliation. So the father clearly has an option that God does not have, and the daughter's sufferings are genuinely tragic because the father has failed, in a way he should not have, to meet his responsibilities as a father towards her.

Nor are natural evils, such as a child's suffering from leukemia, any different from moral evils in this regard. For what God can do by way of preventing a case of leukemia without, at the same time, eliminating a greater good, such as the victim's own future happiness, may also depend upon the free choices of others, that is, upon the path others have chosen to follow. It may depend, for example, upon how tenaciously those whom the victim loves cling to their own illusions, or upon how diligent others are in searching for a cure, or, more generally, upon how ready the rest of us are for a world in which real threats and dangers, and real possibilities for temporary harm, no longer exist. For as we have seen repeatedly, none of us are isolated monads whose future happiness can be guaranteed apart from the happiness of others; none of us can achieve supreme happiness until we have learned the lessons of love; and none of us can learn the lessons of love except in an environment in which genuine, albeit temporary, tragedies are possible.

Accordingly, my general claim, elaborated more fully in Chapter 10, is that we have no reason to believe that God could achieve his loving purposes for the world without permitting some temporary tragedies. But from the perspective of the Christian faith, we have every reason to believe that God is striving to overcome tragedy and to do so by reconciling the world to himself. And it is within this redemptive context, I believe, that we should place the New Testament teaching concerning the suffering of the innocent, including the suffering of innocent children. According to Paul in Colossians 1:24, those who suffer innocently thereby complete what so far remains incomplete in the sufferings of Christ. So let us consider, for a moment, the hardest case of all, the transforming effect that a child's suffering can sometimes have upon the arrogant and the powerful. Nothing, it seems, arouses compassion and melts the hearts of others in a comparable way. Pictures of white racists attacking innocent black children virtually guaranteed the end of segregation in the United States; pictures of mangled children in Vietnam and more recently in Bosnia brought home, in a way that nothing else could, the sheer horror of modern warfare; and pictures of starving children or of children buried in the rubble of an earthquake have sometimes brought the world together in ways that some might have thought impossible. The very weakness and helplessness and innocence of these children can sometimes pierce the hardest of hearts—which is why, perhaps, so many strive so mightily to insulate themselves from the reality of such suffering. In so insulating themselves, however, they merely betray their own vulnerability in the face of such suffering.

Mind you, I am not here claiming to have identified the specific goods that justify, apart from any other consideration, God's permitting the tragedies in question. I am not claiming, for example, that the end of racial segregation in this country is the specific good that justified God's permitting white racists to attack black children. We should be suspicious, perhaps, of any effort to justify *this* specific evil with reference to *that* specific good. But as I indicated above, I *am* making the following claim of a more general nature: God permits temporary tragedies because he cannot achieve his loving purpose, namely the reconciliation of the world, in any other way and because the alternative to his achieving that loving purpose would be a disaster of unimaginable proportions. I also want to endorse the New Testament idea that God *responds* to tragedy by employing it as a means of redemption. And all of this does suggest a general *kind* of good that, according to the Christian religion, will be an essential part of any compensation for the miseries of this life. The good in question is reconciliation and love, the overcoming of separation and estrangement; in the case of those who suffer innocently, it will also include, more specifically, the unique joy of knowing that one has not suffered in vain, of knowing that one's suffering has been a divinely sanctified instrument in the battle against separation (sin) and estrangement (death). Exactly how the sufferings of the innocent, whether they be the sufferings of Christ or those of other innocent persons, enable God to win the battle against sin and death is a mystery that the sources of the Christian faith never fully address. But we can, perhaps, catch glimpses of the mystical truth to which these sources point. In the case of our abused child, God might very well employ her suffering—in the next life, if not in this one—as a means of revelation to the father, perhaps even by forcing him to experience, both vividly and from the child's point of view, the very pain he inflicted; and if God should thereby get through to the father, bringing about the very reconciliation for which the child yearns, he might in fact satisfy her deepest yearnings in a way that he could not have done simply by protecting her from all *temporary* suffering.

Nor is there any question here of the child being a sacrifice for the benefit of someone else more fortunate than she. It is the child's *own* deepest yearnings that God must ultimately satisfy, and it is to her that he must ultimately impart blessedness and joy. Indeed, the whole point of the vision I have tried to articulate in this essay is that no conflicts of interest exist at the most fundamental level. Harm that befalls one person is, in the end and over a long enough stretch of time, harm that befalls all, and similarly, any benefit of a redemptive kind that one person's suffering has for others is again a benefit for the one who suffers as well. A friend of mine, Conrad Brown, likes to insist that sooner or later we all get burned by tragedy, and perhaps he is right about that. But God draws the line, I have argued, at irreparable harm. He confines the tragedy within definite temporal limits and then uses the tragedy, even as he does the sufferings of Christ, as one of the means by which he reconciles the world to himself.

The Christian Hope for the Future

The Christian reply to the problem of suffering finally comes down to the idea that creation costs something; that is, not even an omnipotent God could create free, independent persons and perfect them as Sons and Daughters without paying a heavy price, both in terms of creaturely suffering and in terms of his own suffering as well. In no other environment, except one in which innocent victims sometimes suffer temporarily, could God perfect his loved ones and secure supreme happiness for all of them in the future; in no other environment could he achieve his ultimate victory over sin and death and reconcile the world to himself. So God suffers himself and also permits others to suffer as the price he must pay for a worthwhile creation.[3] But though God does permit his loved ones to suffer, the final good he has in store for each of them, once he achieves his victory over sin and death, will more than compensate for any suffering endured along the way. In the words of John Hick, that future good "will not be a [mere] reward or a compensation proportioned to each individual's trials, but an infinite good

---

[3]Paul thus writes: "The creation waits in eager expectation for the sons [and daughters] of God to be revealed. . . . We know that the whole creation has been groaning as in the pains of childbirth right up to the present time. Not only so, but we ourselves, who have the first fruits of the Spirit, groan inwardly as we wait eagerly for our adoption as sons [and daughters], the redemption of our bodies. For in this hope we were saved" (Romans 8:19,22-24—NIV).

that would render worth while *any* finite suffering endured in the course of attaining it."[4]

Christianity, then, is a religion of consolation in the face of suffering and hope for the future. It consoles us with the idea that all suffering serves a redemptive purpose, and it offers the hope that one day all suffering will be a thing of the past. But just how reasonable is such a hope? I believe that the foundation for the Christian hope—namely, the belief in a supremely perfect God—is eminently reasonable,[5] though I have not tried to argue the point here. My purpose in this essay has been simply to work out the implications of Christian hope with as much consistency as possible. By way of a concluding reflection, however, let us consider, for a moment, the alternative to hope, namely despair, and let us ask which attitude, hope or despair, seems more reasonable, given a healthy skepticism about the world in which we live. If we view life as a kind of wager or bargain, even as Blaise Pascal did, which seems more reasonable: to view the world through eyes filled with hope?—or to view it through eyes filled with despair?

Of course the *experience* of despair, like that of hope, is typically a matter of degree, particularly over the short run; and even those whose philosophy implies a complete absence of hope can often stave off the feeling of despair for awhile. They can always live in denial, for example, or succumb to self-deception, or perhaps even resort to powerful anti-depressants—though the prospect of one's own death, or that of a loved one, will likely shatter the facade in the end. But even after the facade is shattered, some might choose simply to embrace despair, as Bertrand Russell does in the following passage, with a kind of heroic defiance. Writes Russell:

> That man is the product of causes which had no prevision
> of the end they were achieving; that his origin, his growth,

---

[4] John Hick, *Evil and the God of Love* (New York: Harper and Rowe, 1966), p. 377

[5] To argue the point would, of course, require another volume or two.

his hopes and fears, his loves and his beliefs, are but the outcome of accidental collocations of atoms; that no fire, no heroism, no intensity of thought and feeling, can preserve an individual life beyond the grave; that all the labors of the ages, all the devotion, all the inspiration, all the noonday brightness of human genius, are destined to extinction in the vast death of the solar system, and that the whole temple of man's achievement must inevitably be buried beneath the debris of a universe in ruins—all these things, if not quite beyond dispute, are yet so nearly certain that no philosophy which rejects them can hope to stand. Only within the scaffolding of these truths, *only on the firm foundation of unyielding despair* [my emphasis], can the soul's habitation henceforth be safely built.[6]

With characteristic honesty (and also characteristic dogmatism), Russell here embraces, without subterfuge, a philosophy of "scientific materialism" that excludes the very possibility of hope for the future. He sees clearly that such a philosophy can rest only upon "the firm foundation of unyielding despair."[7] Those of us who have not yet abandoned all hope for the future can only marvel, perhaps, at the many dubious propositions that Russell regards as "nearly certain"; he seems as far removed from a healthy

---

[6]Bertrand Russell, "A Free Man's Worship," reprinted in Paul Edwards, ed., *Bertrand Russell: Why I am Not a Christian and Other Essays on Religion and Related Subjects* (New York: Simon and Schuster, 1957), p. 107.

[7]When Russell speaks of "unyielding despair," he does not mean to deny, of course, that life has its satisfactions and even its joy. Even if death brings an end to all of our ambitions and aspirations, there are definite goods that at least some people achieve in this life. And just as, according to the platitude, it is better to have loved and lost than not to have loved at all, so it may be better to have lived and died than not to have lived at all. But the very goodness of life would also render, I suggest, its cessation, particularly in the case of our loved ones, a terrible evil. No conceivable good could compensate for the death of a loved one, if death is truly a form of annihilation. And even if death does not imply annihilation, nothing short of a final restoration and reconciliation of all persons could stave off despair forever.

skepticism as the most rigid orthodox believer. He presumes to know, for example, that nothing "can preserve an individual life beyond the grave," though he nowhere says how he came to know this; he even presumes to know that human beings are "the product of causes which had no prevision of the end they were achieving." He presumes to know many things, in other words, that in the very nature of the case he could never discover by empirical means. But he is at least clear sighted concerning the alternatives. Having rejected hope as a form of wishful thinking, he concludes that a hardheaded realist has no alternative but to embrace "unyielding despair."

In luminous contrast to such "unyielding despair" stands the Christian hope for the future. Unlike Russell, Christians believe that the real world consists of far more than trillions upon trillions of blind particles flying around without purpose or knowledge of the human lives they have created on one tiny globe; the real world is an expression of supreme love, supreme intelligence, and supreme power. Such an understanding provides, in fact, the only real alternative to ultimate despair, and few are even the Christians who have worked out this alternative with any degree of consistency. For contrary to the teaching of many Christian churches, the Christian hope, as we encounter it in the New Testament and in some of the early Christian theologians, is inclusive, not exclusive; it embraces not only all human beings, but the entire creation as well. It even embraces, I would argue, the animal kingdom, though that is another story. It satisfies our loftiest desires and deepest yearnings in a way that no lesser hope could.

So is the Christian hope a form of wishful thinking, as Russell seemed to believe? Here we should perhaps distinguish between *wishful* thinking, on the one hand, and *hopeful* or *optimistic* thinking, on the other—where the former, but not the latter, is pathological in the Freudian sense. That the Christian hope is indeed a form of hope and therefore a form of *hopeful* thinking is an obvious tautology. But it hardly follows that such thinking is pathological. To the contrary, *hopeful* thinking—insofar as it expresses our loftiest desires and deepest yearnings—is far more reasonable, given what we know (or do not know) about the universe, than Russell's "unyielding despair." For whereas hope is compatible with the absence of certitude, despair is not; whereas hope is compatible with a healthy skepticism concerning the nature of the world, despair is not. Despair requires that, like Russell, we regard a host of dubious propositions as "nearly certain." It emerges only when we know, or think we know, that our condition is hopeless. So even if there were no such thing as revelation, and even if we had no positive grounds for believing in God beyond a vague sense that the power responsible for bringing the universe and, more specifically, human life into existence must be wondrous indeed, we would still do well, I contend, to stake everything on hope rather than upon despair.

It is a point that Pascal saw clearly in his famous (but much misunderstood) wager.[8] When Pascal wagers, or decides to conduct his life on the hypothesis, that God exists; when he wagers that supreme power lies on the side of supreme love, he in effect stakes everything on hope rather than upon despair. And contrary to a widespread misinterpretation, Pascal's wager, as set forth in the eleventh of his *Pensees*, is entirely positive in its thrust. Nowhere in this discussion does he embrace anything like the following absurdity: If God should exist and I should fail to wager *here and now* that he does, I will suffer an infinite loss. How *could* he say anything like this? Even if I do not wager (or place my trust in God) today, perhaps I will tomorrow; and even if I never wager in this life, perhaps I will in some other. According to Pascal, however, I have everything to gain and nothing to lose by wagering *here and now*—by deciding here and now to conduct my life on the assumption—that God exists. It is as if I could enter a sweepstakes whenever I wanted, without risking a cent, simply by signing up; and the sooner I enter, the greater the chances for an early payoff. If that were true, it would always be rational to enter sooner rather than later; and if the payoff were desirable enough, it would be utterly irrational to put off entering forever.

But isn't wagering on the existence of God inconsistent with the psychology of belief? Insofar as believing something is essentially

---

[8]Blaise Pascal, *Pensees*, 11.

a matter of being persuaded of it, we can hardly manufacture beliefs by simple acts of will; I can no more manufacture a belief in Santa Claus, for example, than I can change lead into gold. So if, for whatever reason, I remain unpersuaded of God's existence, even as I am of the existence of Santa Claus, how is a relevant wager even possible?

The answer requires that we understand the wagering metaphor properly. To wager, as Pascal understands it, is not *essentially* a matter of manufacturing belief at all, though it sometimes can lead to belief; it is instead a matter of choosing to act *as if* a certain hypothesis is true, and it is, in that respect, perhaps closer to *hoping* than it is to *believing*. A good illustration might be a woman who continues to hope that her husband will one day return to her from the battlefield. Although she may have her fears and her doubts, she will not close off completely the possibility of his return; to the contrary, she will continue to think of herself (and to act) as a married woman, continue to plan for a joyous reunion, and continue to stake a good portion of her future happiness on the hope of such a reunion. And similarly for those who wager that God exists. Whatever doubts they may have on an intellectual level, they will nonetheless remain open to the *possibility* of God's existence and receptive to the transforming work of God within. They will also continue to think of themselves (or at least to act) as children of God, perhaps even as chosen vessels through whom God will eventually achieve his victory over injustice and separation; and they will begin preparing for the greatest joy possible—namely, union with God—by opening their hearts to him, by acknowledging their failures, and by cultivating a more loving attitude towards others.

Conceived in this way, wagering that God exists seems altogether reasonable; we have everything to gain and nothing to lose by embracing a consistent philosophy of hope rather than a consistent philosophy of despair. For no one truly thrives in the absence of hope; and if the most worthy object of awe and admiration, the most sublime being conceivable, does exist, then nothing could be more glorious than union with that being; nor could there be any greater consolation in the face of suffering than the belief that God will use our sufferings as a means of reconciling the entire world, including all of our own loved ones, to himself. So if such a being does exist, then the sooner we are united with him, the sooner we stand to gain a transformed life and greater possibilities for joy than we can now perhaps even imagine.

Nor need we have any fear, at this point, of the so-called "many gods objection," which so many have raised against Pascal's wager. Behind this traditional objection lies the idea that those who adhere to different religions, or even to different sects within the same religion, sometimes hold conflicting beliefs of the following kind: Whereas some Christians may believe that God will reject and punish eternally all Muslims, some Muslims may also believe that Allah will reject and punish eternally all Christians. So within the context of such exclusivism as this, the rewards and punishments, as conceived by Christians and Muslims, would in effect cancel each other out; hence, the imagined rewards and punishments alone could never provide grounds for wagering upon one of these gods rather than the other. But this objection has no relevance at all in the present context. It is hardly surprising that, between two spiteful and vindictive "gods," we would have no rational grounds for preferring (or wagering upon) one of them over the other—not when either one of them would undermine, as we have seen repeatedly in previous chapters, the very possibility of supreme happiness. Only a supremely perfect God—supremely loving as well as supremely powerful—could guarantee an infinitely glorious payoff; so if the greatest gift a Creator has to offer is himself, then no lesser god could even compete with a supremely perfect God when it comes to the payoff. To wager on hope rather than despair is, accordingly, to stake one's life and future on a supremely perfect (and therefore a supremely loving) God, not some narrow sectarian god.

Because such a wager is entirely positive in its thrust, its motivation has nothing to do with fear of eternal rejection or fear of an infinite loss. If supreme power lies on the side of supreme love, then none of us, whether Christian, Muslim, or even atheist, need fear that the One who loved us into existence in the first place might wantonly abandon us in the end. Nor need we worry that an honest mistake in theology will somehow jeopardize our future. For if a perfectly loving Creator does exist, then he knows us from the inside out far better than we know ourselves; he appreciates the ambiguities, the confusions, and the perplexities we face far better than we do; and he understands the historical and cultural factors that shape our beliefs far better than any historian does. Such a Creator—so loving, intimate, and wise—would know how to work with us in infinitely complex ways, how to shatter our illusions and transform our thinking when necessary, and how best to reveal himself to us in the end.

But however glorious and however secure our final destiny may be, there remains the matter of our *present* condition: our alienation from others, our dissatisfaction with life, the sickness in our soul. We must also contend with all of the miseries, all of the trials and tribulations, in this present "veil of tears," and herein lies the context in which we must *now* choose between hope and despair. If we succumb to despair in this context, then for as long as we remain mired in it, we lose our capacity to enjoy life and yet gain nothing immediately in return; as the psychoanalyst Eric Fromm once commented, "When hope has gone life has ended, actually or potentially."[9] If that is true, as I believe it is, then we cannot truly embrace life without embracing hope, and we cannot embrace hope consistently, I have argued, without embracing God as the only consistent foundation for hope.

In a very real sense, of course, we all gain, whether we now wager or not, if a supremely perfect God exists. How could it be otherwise when hope is inclusive?—when any worthwhile hope for Ted Bundy's mother must, of necessity, include hope for Ted Bundy as well? But that in no way detracts from the importance of our present choices. For though our present choices cannot alter our final destiny, they most assuredly can affect our chances for happiness in the present and in the near term future; and though our glorious inheritance cannot elude us forever, it most assuredly can

---

[9]Eric Fromm, *The Revolution of Hope* (New York: Harper and Rowe, 1968), p. 13

elude us for a lifetime, or perhaps even for several lifetimes. So our choices do have very real consequences in our lives; indeed, these consequences are one of the means by which God will transform us in the end and thereby secure our final destiny. When we finally weary of our own selfishness, petty jealousies, and lust for power; when we learn at last, perhaps through bitter experience, that these lead only to ruin and cannot bring enduring happiness, that nothing short of union with God and reconciliation with others will satisfy our own deepest yearnings; when we discover that the Hound of Heaven has finally closed off every alternative to such a union, we shall then, each of us, finally embrace the destiny that is ours.

Hi Fi,

I found this book
a real blessing,
see what you
think of it.

C.

INDEX

Printed in the United States
118128LV00012B/2/A

9 781581 128314